Archives in the Ancient World

καλόν, ὦ ἄνδρες Ἀθηναῖοι, καλὸν ἡ τῶν δημοσίων
γραμμάτων φυλακή. ἀκίνητον γάρ ἐστι.

Wonderful, you men of Athens, wonderful is the
custody of the public records, for unshakable is [the record].

Aeschines, *Against Ctesiphon* 75.

Archives in the Ancient World

Ernst Posner

Harvard University Press, Cambridge, Massachusetts, 1972

To Verner W. Clapp

Whose inquiring mind looks to the past
as well as to the future and whose understanding
encourages the exploration of both.

Preface

In a wry sense this book might be considered an act of atonement on the part of its author. During the more than twenty years when I taught courses in the history and administration of archives, I failed to pay due attention to the archives of the ancient world, and it was only in 1958, during a happy Fulbright year in Rome, that I became fully aware of the continuity of archival practices and problems that should make the history of ancient archives part of the archivist's professional experience.

Although this study is thus related to my teaching in a program of courses offered by American University in cooperation with the National Archives, it may have some value for the archival profession in general and also for orientalists and classicists who are concerned with preserving and interpreting the products of the archival process. Writing was invented to make past experience available for future reference; hence the techniques designed to achieve that end are an important aspect of man's experiment in living in society. Now essential source material for the re-creation of our early history, records are, in their genesis, the tools of administrative endeavor. They are not merely interesting documents; they are part and parcel of the culture from which they stem.

With that conviction in mind, this essay in archival history is not limited to the techniques required and used for the keeping of archives. Archives administration is so intimately connected with the governance of secular and religious affairs and with the individual's conduct of his business that it must be viewed within the context of the cultures in which the archives originated and which now they help to bring back to life. An effort has been made, therefore, to picture archival developments against the background of the societies of which they were a part. This approach has forced me, having been brought up as a student of medieval and modern history, to venture into unfamiliar territory. Because of this, I have often preferred to let the scholarly witnesses speak for themselves rather than attempt formulations of my own. For the same reason I have found it impossible to consult the many publications of clay tablet and papyrus records. In a few instances only, where hints in the literature seemed to invite examination of the records themselves, have the original sources been studied. The introductions to some of these publications, however, have been examined for information about the circumstances surrounding the discovery of clay tablet and papyrus records. Otherwise, I have relied on what specialists have taught me about the archives of the ancient Near East, and in that way I am indebted to many of them, especially to A. Leo Oppenheim's *Ancient Mesopotamia*. Professor Oppenheim's spelling of Mesopotamian names has been followed in the first chapter of the book.

Interrupted by academic duties and later by a survey of American state archives, work on this study was resumed in 1964. Its completion was facilitated by a grant, in 1967, from the Council on Library Resources, Inc., an organization that has become a generous sponsor of archival activities and has moved to fulfill many needs of the archival profession. The Council's past executive president, Verner W. Clapp, has read the manuscript of this volume and has made many helpful suggestions. It is with respect for his knowledge and with gratitude for his friendship that the study is dedicated to him.

I also wish to acknowledge the kindness and help of the staffs of the many institutions whose collections I was privileged to use, foremost among them the American Academy, the Deutsches Archäologisches Institut, and the Istituto Pontificio Biblico, all in Rome. Since 1964 the facilities of Dumbarton Oaks, Washington, D.C., and the advice of members of its faculty and library staff have been of inestimable help. Saddened by the loss of a dear friend, I wish to thank the late Elizabeth Hawthorn Buck, whose searching mind and literary taste have improved the text of this book. My deeply felt gratitude also goes to Elizabeth Suttell, who edited the manuscript. But for

her painstaking effort and keen understanding, numerous defects of the manuscript would have remained undetected. I am
further obliged to Pauline C. Gates for conscientiously com-
piling and typing the index.

Washington, D.C.   E.P.
January 1970

Contents

1 2 3 4 5 6 7 8 9 0 1 2 3 4 5 6 7 8 9 0 1 2 3 4 5 6 7 8 9 0

Illustrations

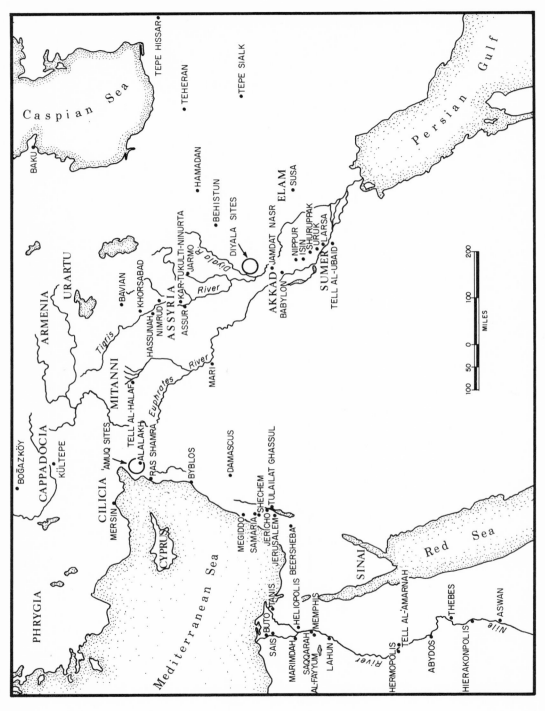

Outline map of the early Near East.

Archives in the Ancient World

Introduction

The History of Ancient Archives: Scope, Limitations, and Design

A book on the history of ancient archives—even a slim volume —must justify its existence. Popular works on the physical remains of the cultures of antiquity have followed each other in rapid succession and have had a wide appeal. The story of our oldest archives, however, lacks the aura of excitement and glamor that surrounds the great architectural and sculptural discoveries in ancient Mesopotamia, Anatolia, Egypt, Crete, and Mycenaean Greece. The keeping of archives, nevertheless, constitutes a significant aspect of mankind's experience in organized living; without these archives, in fact, the story of our past could not be told.

To those actively engaged in archival work the history of archives administration should be a serious concern, not merely a subject of curiosity. Beyond that, archivists must feel a need to explore the origins of their profession, to understand the circumstances and forces that have determined its evolution, and, with such understanding, to anticipate and prepare for the future.[1]

Apart from its professional relevance, however, the history of archives can claim a wider appeal. Since archival material is a primary source for the historian and the social scientist, those engaged in analyzing and reconstructing the story of our civilization should be thoroughly familiar with the genesis and character of the archives of successive ages, their significance as components of the various cultures, and the considerations that help account for their survival.

1. On the archivist's concern with the history of archives and on the spirit in which it should be treated, see Leopoldo Sandri's thoughtful article "La storia degli archivi," *Rassegna degli Archivi di Stato*, XVIII (1958), 109–134. Professor Sandri has dealt with the same subject in "La storia degli archivi," a paper read before the VIth International Archival Congress in Madrid, *Archivum*, XVIII (1968, published in late 1970), 101–113. See also the discussion of his paper on pp. 139–156, and the resolution adopted by the Congress: "The Congress expresses the wish that the International Council on Archives, by every means in its power, interest itself in the history of archives and encourage and support studies in this field" (*ibid.*, p. 217).

Finally, even those not actively engaged in historical research should know about the archival sources that constitute the basis of the histories they are reading and that will furnish the basis for future histories. Also, since we are living in an age in which our everyday life is affected by a multiplicity of recorded public and private relationships and in which our wallets are bulging with identification cards evidencing such relationships, we may derive wry satisfaction from the knowledge that to some degree those before us were made as record conscious as we are forced to be. In ancient Egypt, too, everybody was "catalogued and inventoried."[2]

Medieval and modern archives have been the subject of a wide variety of studies, and the story of the archives of these two periods has been thoroughly explored. We still lack, however, a synthesis that makes the development of the archives as an institution fully understandable and that also gives due attention to the growth of archival thought. Except for individual articles on archives-keeping in ancient Mesopotamia, Greece, and Rome, no effort has been made to provide an integrated picture of the archival institutions and practices of antiquity. As we all know, in the Middle Ages, a period of great experiment in governmental decentralization, record-making and record-keeping became a concern of local authorities, and it was only in the Byzantine Empire and in the Arab lands that the governing of great empires still demanded record-keeping on a large scale. In Western Europe, on the other hand, where the direct nexus between the state and the individual had ceased to exist, records were no longer created on a country-wide basis, as had been the case before the downfall of the Roman Empire. But ancient institutions and practices lingered on, and in time would directly and indirectly influence record-making and record-keeping in the cities and nation states that emerged out of feudal Europe.

When compared to the small volume of medieval archives, the archives of the ancient world seem to have much in common with those of our own times. The Greek and demotic records of

2. See Chap. 2 below.

Ptolemaic Egypt "constitute bodies of archives" and these bodies, "by virtue of their number and their nature, resemble those of the more recent ages."[3] A system of organization and administration that can truly be called bureaucratic, and the cheapness and availability of writing materials—both lacking during the Middle Ages—resulted in a mass production of records on clay and papyrus that created preservation problems similar to those confronting the archivist in the age of paper. These circumstances make the study of ancient archives particularly interesting and rewarding. In fact, in the great river cultures of the Nile and of the Euphrates and Tigris, where the control of material, men, and man-made installations became inevitable, we find already those basic types of records that may be called constants in record creation, whatever the nature of governmental, religious, and economic institutions. These include:

1. The laws of the land.

2. Records consciously created and retained as evidence of past administrative action. These records may be in the form of the "royal skins" of the Persian kings, the *commentarii* or daybooks of Roman officials, the registers of the Popes and the Patriarchs of Constantinople, or the chancery rolls of the English kings.

3. Financial and other accounting records originating from the need of a ruler or other authority to administer his domain and its resources, such as the records of the palace and temple economies of the ancient Near East.

4. Records of the ruler or other authority to assure his income from land and persons not belonging to his immediate domain, namely: land surveys, commonly called cadastres; land records that establish legal ownership of areas of the land and make possible their orderly transfer from owner to acquirer; records establishing tax obligations from real property.

5. Records facilitating control over persons for purposes of

3. Claire Préaux, *L'économie royale des Lagides* (Brussels, 1939), p. 10.

military service, forced labor, and the payment of a capitation or personal tax.

6. "Notarial" records of state agencies or state-authorized persons that safeguard private business transactions between individuals.

Although in one form or another these constants in record creation are encountered among the records that have survived from antiquity, are we justified in calling these records archives? There are two basically different definitions of the word archives. One of them limits the term to noncurrent records that, because of their long-range value, have been transferred to an ad hoc agency, called an archives, and it is in this sense that the term is used in German. American usage, as it has developed during the last decades, shows a somewhat similar approach in that it considers as archives only those records that have lasting value, regardless of whether they are still in the hands of their creators or have been turned over to the custody of an archival agency. In the majority of countries, however, and particularly in the Romance countries, the records of any agency or institution are designated as its archives. In other words, the terms records and archives are used interchangeably. In Italian, for instance, *archivio* stands for records in general. If the records have outlived their everyday usefulness but are still under the care of their creator, they are called an *archivio di deposito*. Records of demonstrated or demonstrable value become the concern of a general archives (*archivio generale*), in which archival materials of many origins are assembled.

Except for a few isolated cases, the general archives is a product of the last two hundred years. Although the Tabularium, the archives of Republican Rome, showed a tendency to absorb records of various administrative origins, the idea of concentrating in one place the archives of different creators was alien to ancient and medieval times. The ancient world did not even have the concept of an *archivio di deposito*, for nowhere are there to be found arrangements revealing an intention to differentiate administratively between current records and those no longer regularly needed for the dispatch of business. It was only in the Middle Ages that a discriminating attitude toward the value of records developed. This was expressed in the practice of copying important records in cartularies so as to have them available for frequent use, while the originals were carefully protected in an inner sanctum, as, for instance, the Byzantine *skeuophylakion*. By and large, however, it was the emerging recognition of the research value of records that led to the distinction between records of daily usefulness and others to be preserved because of their long-range importance.

In the ancient period, this distinction was not made; and this means that by archives we must understand all kinds of records. In fact, the term archives itself may be slightly inappropriate, for even in its broadest meaning the word suggests an intention to keep records in usable order and in premises suitable to that purpose. In the Near East, where great quantities of records have been found on excavation sites, only rarely could any part of the site be identified as an archives room. Most of the time we cannot tell whether we are dealing with an archival aggregate or with a collection of trash, the equivalent of a modern waste-paper basket. And yet we cannot exclude such *disjecta membra* from our consideration, because they may still reveal a pattern worth discovering. When Bernard P. Grenfell, Arthur S. Hunt, and J. Gilbart Smyly discovered the mummies of the "papyrus enriched" holy crocodiles in Egyptian Tebtunis, they sensibly decided to include in the first volume of their publication a "classification of papyri according to crocodiles," for papyri in the belly of the same animal might reveal relationships reflecting their administrative provenance and an original arrangement.[4]

Such insight of early papyrologists, of which more will be said later, compares favorably with the attitudes of the Assyriologists toward their clay tablets. Understandably, in the age of the early discoveries about the middle of the nineteenth century, the remains of the palaces and temples, monuments, sculptures,

4. *The Tebtunis Papyri*, I (London, 1902), xvi–xvii.

and artifacts captured the enthusiasm and guided the activities of the excavators, while the humble clay tablets ranked low in their scale of values. This attitude changed, of course, when the writing on the tablets could be deciphered and read and when their importance as historical sources was appreciated. Interest was focused, however, on what the individual document, called a text, had to say, on its content and on its significance as a literary or historical witness. The lowly *Wirtschaftstexte* (economic texts) and administrative documentation in general were slighted. What was worse, the interrelationships of the tablets were disregarded, and when they were published their character as elements of larger assemblages was neither taken into consideration nor made apparent.

Although it is easy to criticize the earlier Assyriologists for not recognizing the archival nature of much, if not most, of their source material, archivists should refrain from raising their voices in righteous indignation, for a good part of the blame must be laid at their doorsteps. Archivists have never been persuasive salesmen of their cause, nor have they always succeeded in convincing scholars of the contributions they can make to other disciplines. Nevertheless, the extent to which archivists for a century ignored the significance of the great clay tablet discoveries is simply amazing; and since they ignored them they could not and did not object to the dismembering of archival bodies by Assyriologists. It should be borne in mind, however, that archivists during this period were still dedicated to the subject approach to documents, and that they themselves disrupted bodies of archives in order to rearrange them into subject-oriented collections under headings such as *Biographica, Ecclesiastica*, and *Militaria*. True, *respect des fonds* and the principle of provenance began to guide the work of archivists during the second half of the nineteenth century, and should have enabled them to suggest their application to the records of ancient Mesopotamia. But until quite recently, archivists have turned their backs on the first great chapter in the history of their profession.

Besides the clay tablets, the papyri of Egypt are the other large body of original record material that has survived from the ancient world. In dealing with this material, papyrologists were in no better position than the Assyriologists. On the contrary, much of their material came from the refuse heaps of the Fayyûm, that is, from record dumps; and the native diggers sold piecemeal what they found there, so that papyri of the same provenance are now scattered in libraries and collections all over the world. More often than not, therefore, papyrologists had to work with isolated pieces and fragments rather than with bodies of records. And yet, even in the early stages of the discipline, the archival point of view was present in the papyrologists' thinking. In fact, when Josef Karabacek, head of the Imperial-Royal Library of Vienna, took charge of the vast body of papyri that Archduke Rainer of Austria had acquired from the Vienna antiquarian Theodor Graf in the 1880's, he thought that he had before him the holdings of a single large provincial archives.[5] This was, of course, not the case, but it shows that, in spite of the fragmentary nature of the papyrus material, its provenance was always borne in mind. In line with that early readiness to accept an archival approach to the papyri, the great work of Ludwig Mitteis and Ulrich Wilcken, *Grundzüge und Chrestomatie der Papyruskunde* (Leipzig-Berlin, 1912), definitely established the archival character of most of the papyrus material. In this great work of historical and legal scholarship, the administrative genesis of the papyri was clearly delineated. Papyri were considered in their relationship to governmental functions and activities, to financial administration, taxation, agriculture, the military, and so on. Throughout much of the literature on the papyri, their "precious quality of constituting dossiers"[6] is realized, and this realization is brought to bear on their publication. In Karl Preisendanz' *Papyrusfunde und Papyrusforschung*, there is constant reference to the archival character of the papyri discovered, and more recently Erwin

5. Karl Preisendanz, *Papyrusfunde und Papyrusforschung* (Leipzig, 1933), p. 112.
6. Préaux, *L'économie royale*, p. 12.

Seidl has attempted to identify the various kinds of Ptolemaic archives,[7] although most of them have been scattered. In view of the wide dispersion of papyrus archives, the plan of the late Fritz Heichelheim to compile a guide to the Greco-Roman archives of Egypt would have been a great and eminently useful achievement.[8] Regrettably this guide, which was to be organized by types of archives, has not been published.

Viewing the history of ancient archives as a whole, it is clear that our knowledge rests on uneven and incomplete foundations. In Section 20 of their well-known *Manual for the Arrangement and Description of Archives* (New York, 1968), S. Muller, J. A. Feith, and R. Fruin say this about the archivist's task: "The archivist deals with a body of archives just as the paleontologist deals with the bones of a prehistoric animal; he tries from these bones to put the skeleton of the animal together again." Similar but far more difficult is the task of the historian of ancient archives who—to retain the metaphor—sets out to bring to life a creature of the past with only the footprints and a few bones to go by. Although for some periods there is a wealth of pertinent data supporting a reconstruction; for others this is lacking. Where neither archival sites nor their contents are known, the archival historian, rather than giving an account of the archives that existed, must be satisfied with telling what archives should have existed. As a result, the history of the ancient archives must remain uneven and partly contestable. In the case of the countries of the Near East and the Aegean, it stems from our having unearthed numerous archival installations of one kind or another with their contents; and in the case of Egypt, where archival depositories have not been discovered, we have at least great quantities of records and excellent information about their genesis and the way they were kept. A totally different situation confronts us in ancient Greece and in Rome. True, the foundations of the Athenian Metroon have been laid bare, and

7. Erwin Seidl, *Ptolemäische Rechtsgeschichte*, 2d rev. ed. (Glückstadt, Hamburg, and New York, 1962).

8. Fritz Heichelheim, "Bericht über ein Papyrusverzeichnis nach Gauen, Archiven und Jahrhunderten geordnet," *Chronique d'Egypte*, VII (1932), 137–150.

Rome's Tabularium still looks down on the Forum Romanum. But unless reproduced on stone or bronze or referred to in the literature, we do not know the records themselves nor the conditions under which they were kept.

Other difficulties, too, stand in the way of a great design embracing all the archives of the ancient world. Records written on wood tablets or on leather have almost completely vanished. In addition, there are vast areas and peoples for which, in the absence of systematic efforts, information about archives is largely lacking, as for instance Urartu, north of Assyria. Information is also lacking for Carthage and Etruria, two lamentable gaps in our knowledge. Finally, we cannot tell what excavations now in progress in Mesopotamia and Asia Minor or undertaken in the future will add to our store of knowledge.

Although these considerations largely determine the degree of completeness of a history of ancient archives, there are certain phenomena that indicate important interconnections and, in fact, continuity in matters of archives-creation and archives-keeping. One of these interconnections, for instance, throws revealing light on the endurance of administrative and record-keeping practices in an area that saw a succession of regimes. When the Greeks under Alexander the Great conquered Persia and seized its archives, they called them the "royal skins" (*diphtherai basilikai*), for leather, in addition to the clay tablet taken over from Elam, served the Persians as a writing medium. The term *diphtherai* was inherited by the Arabs and the Turks, and in the form *deftar* it designates a key series in Turkish archival terminology. With the Arabs the term went to Sicily, where *defetarii*, the Italianized version of it, indicate the financial records of the Norman *doana regia*. To close the circle, the term returned from Turkish into modern Greek as *tefteri*, which means notebook.

Other instances of interconnection and possible transfer or exchange of administrative and archival experience seem plausible but are not yet confirmed. Did the beginning of a "royal notariat" in Syrian Ugarit⁹ influence developments in the Greek cities of Asia Minor and on the Greek mainland, where the notarial function became an integral part of the duties of the city archives? Was it Greek precedent that led to the establishment of the *kibotoi* (record chests) in Ptolemaic Egypt, and later to the institution of the property record office, or must we rather look for a connection between these institutions and those of Pharaonic Egypt? Was Greek practice with regard to the official recording of private transactions responsible for the institution of the *gesta municipalia* toward the end of the Roman Empire? Generally speaking, do these constitute instances of cultural transfer rather than cases of parallel development? And are we aware of similar instances of interconnection in the matter of record-making rather than record-keeping? The field seems to be wide open. Throughout this book, the relationships between the archives and the organizations that created them will be discussed, but the process of the creation itself and the various types of records created will be referred to only incidentally. Insofar as the Middle Ages are concerned, these two problems have been thoroughly explored. No such general study of the diplomatics of the ancient period has been made, although Harold Steinacker's *Die antiken Grundlagen der mittelalterlichen Privaturkunde* (Innsbruck, 1927) clearly showed the feasibility of such a study in regard to the private legal document.

In 1934 Ulrich Wilcken, addressing the Third International Congress of Papyrologists in Munich, and incidentally referring to Steinacker's pacemaking book, discussed the need for an ancient diplomatics, "a discipline that does not yet exist."¹⁰ Leopold Wenger, the great jurisprudent, had called for a history of ancient law that would deal with legal developments in the entire Mediterranean area. Ancient diplomatics, Wilcken felt, should parallel as well as support the realization of the

9. See Chap. 1 below.

10. Ulrich Wilcken, "Über antike Urkundenlehre," in Walter Otto and Leopold Wenger, eds., *Papyri und Altertumswissenschaft* (Munich, 1934), 42–61.

concept of ancient legal history. He also made it clear that ancient diplomatics should not limit itself to legal documents, as did medieval diplomatics, because the medievalists lacked the profusion of other documents available to the Assyriologist and the papyrologist. Ancient diplomatics was to work with a broader concept of diplomatics that was to include "ordinary" letters and records (*Akten*) of all kinds.

In discussing the objectives and uses of ancient diplomatics, Wilcken said: "Transfer of documents to and their preservation in archival establishments is also a problem of diplomatics. We already have a number of pertinent studies."[11] It is in accordance with Wilcken's ideas that this study of ancient archives has been undertaken. Such a study cannot be more than a first attempt to deal with a very complex problem. I hope, nevertheless, that the following pages will contribute toward recognizing the history of ancient archives as a worthwhile field. Its elaboration should assist area and era specialists in recognizing the care of archives as an important aspect of the cultures they are dealing with, and in correctly interpreting their written remains, while it extends the professional perspective of the archivist to a field hitherto neglected.

In its great design, the contours of Western archival development can already be discerned. There is good reason to believe that "the princely courts of the Occident owe their archival organization as well as their register techniques to a twofold inheritance: the ancient Roman institutions as continued in the tradition of the Roman curia and the chancery practices of the ancient Orient that reached [these courts] through the administration of the Fatimid Arabs of Egypt and Sicily, which, [in turn], had absorbed Persian influence."[12] In the East, on the other hand, Persian experience, and with it the art of record-keeping, determined the character of financial administration of all of the Near East down to the eighteenth century.[13]

11. *Ibid.*, p. 48.
12. Walther Hinz, "Das Rechnungswesen orientalischer Reichsfinanzämter im Mittelalter," *Islam*, XXIX (1949–1950), 119.
13. *Ibid.*, p. 4.

[1] *The Clay Tablet Archives*

1. *The Archival Approach to the Clay Tablets*

In his *West-Östlicher Diwan* (1819), Goethe defined the depth of historical awareness a wise man should have:

> He who'd know what life's about
> Three millennia must appraise;
> Else he'll go in fear and doubt,
> Unenlightened all his days.

It is one of the most momentous phenomena of the last 120 years—comparable in a way to the discovery of America—that a new dimension of almost two millennia has been added to the history of mankind as it was known in 1850. Before the clay tablets of the Near East had become available to us and could be deciphered and studied, we were unable to penetrate beyond the stories of the Bible. Now we can view with profound respect the cultural achievements of the countries surrounding the eastern Mediterranean, and we can begin to assess their interrelations with, and their possible influence on, the cultures of Greece and Rome and the Arab world. What has happened may be the finest example of the importance of the preservation and subsequent utilization of source material that had remained unknown for many centuries. It confirms emphatically the famous dictum by Fustel de Coulanges: "No sources—no history."

The overwhelming significance of the discovery of new sources suggests the appropriateness of studying the way in which these source materials were kept, a study, needless to say, that is dear to the heart of the archivist; for preservation is his first and unavoidable duty. Other disciplines have preceded the archivist in exploiting the vast store of data that the explorations of the last 120 years have furnished and in elucidating and analyzing them from the vantage point of the specialist's subject knowledge. Writings on the history of jurisprudence, of religion, of the arts and crafts, and many other subjects testify to the assistance and contributions that Assyriologists and Egyptologists owe to the cooperative interest of other disciplines.

Archivists, however, have failed until quite recently to take advantage of the work of the Assyriologists and thus to add further depth to the history of their field. Their reluctance to do so may be understandable; archivists, accustomed to dealing with material the originals of which they could handle, stayed away from the clay tablets they could neither decipher nor translate. They left a discussion of the tablets' nature to the Assyriologists who wanted to find out whether the accumulations of tablets they had found were library or archival holdings. In trying to arrive at a decision, the Assyriologists were handicapped by the fact that they did not have a clear conception of the difference between the two types.[1] As late as 1938, it was explained in the *Reallexikon der Assyriologie* that in order to be considered library material tablets must have been baked; "otherwise the designation as library is not justified but at best the term 'archives.'"[2]

A distinguished librarian, Fritz Milkau, was the first to differentiate in a practical fashion between clay tablets as library material and clay tablets as archives,[3] and thus to assist the Assyriologist-librarian A. A. Kampman in offering in 1940 a survey of *Archives and Libraries in the Ancient Near East*.[4]

1. On the ensuing controversy, see Johannes Papritz, "Archive in Altmesopotamien: Theorie und Tatsachen," *Archivalische Zeitschrift*, LV (1959), 12–13, and the literature referred to on p. 12, n. 4. This basic article is reviewed by A. Pohl, "Der Archivar und die Keilschriftforscher," *Orientalia*, XXIX (1960), 230–232.

2. Eckhard Unger, "Bibliothek," in Erich Ebeling and Bruno Meissner, eds., *Reallexikon der Assyriologie*, 2d ed., II (1938), 24.

3. Fritz Milkau, *Geschichte der Bibliotheken im alten Orient*, ed. Bruno Meissner (Leipzig, 1935). For the second edition of the *Handbuch der Bibliothekswissenschaft*, founded by Fritz Milkau, Georg Leyh, ed., III, 1 (Wiesbaden, 1955), Milkau's essay has been completely revised by the orientalist Josef Schawe (pp. 1–50); hereafter cited as Schawe, "Der alte Vorderorient."

4. A. A. Kampman, *Archieven en bibliotheken in het oude Nabije Oosten* (Schoten-Antwerp, 1942), a paper read in 1940 and first printed in the transactions of the Sixth Flemish Congress on Book and Library Problems. A summary in English is included.

In the same year, the Assyriologist Nikolaus Schneider published an article on the "archival systematics" of Sumer and Akkad under the Third Dynasty of Ur (ca. 2100 B.C.).[5] Archivists might consider this article a major breakthrough because its author succeeded in clearly stating the main characteristics of a clay tablet archives. His conclusions deserve to be quoted:

1. Documents and records written on clay were stored for future use in special archival premises.
2. This holds true of the so-called economic texts only. Library works are not represented.
3. Archival documents were stored in special clay containers that were manufactured and used exclusively for archival purposes.
4. To the clay tablet containers there were fastened clay bulls that gave three things: the identification of the container as a clay tablet container (*pisan-dub-ba*), an indication of the type of documents included, and the size of the document collection.
5. Documents were assigned to the different containers in accordance with a subject arrangement.
6. What was put into a container depended not on the number of documents but on the time period indicated [on the clay bull].[6]

In the writings of the late Godefroy Goossens, the usefulness of the archival approach to clay tablet accumulations was spelled out even more forcefully, especially in his article entitled "Introduction à l'archivéconomie de l'Asie Antérieure" (1952).[7] Goossens had been trained as an Assyriologist, but, for want of a position in his chosen field, served as archivist of his native city of Malines, Belgium, from 1945 to 1949. Although an archivist *malgré lui*, he developed a good grasp of the essentials of archives administration, thanks to the advice of his Belgian colleagues, among them Etienne Sabbe, and thanks to his careful study of the

5. Nikolaus Schneider, "Die Urkundenbehälter von Ur III und ihre archivalische Systematik," *Orientalia*, IX (1940), 1–16.

6. *Ibid.*, pp. 15–16. I understand that *pisan-dub-ba* is now read *šadubba*.

7. Godefroy Goossens, "Introduction à l'archivéconomie de l'Asie Antérieure," *Revue d'Assyriologie*, XLVI (1952), 98–107. Goossens is the author of the chapter on "Asie Occidentale Ancienne," in René Grousset and Emile G. Léonard, eds., *Histoire universelle*, I (Paris, 1956), 287–495. On Goossens, see G. Ryckmans, "Godefroy Goossens (15 avril 1912—22 février 1963)," *Syria*, XL (1963), 379–382.

famous Dutch *Manual for the Arrangement and Description of Archives*.[8] The *Manual*, Goossens felt, stated principles that could easily be applied to the field of Assyriology. Referring to paragraph 22 of that treatise, he stated: "For Assyriology this means that first of all the tablets must be studied according to their place of discovery." Goossens admitted one difficulty, however. Archives, he knew, are first classified—we would prefer to say arranged—then inventoried, and finally published. While ideal, this order of work could not be followed by the Assyriologist because the complexity of the questions raised made it necessary for publication to precede the other operations. Nevertheless, the "ensembles," that is, the original groupings, must be respected by publishing the texts by rooms or groups of rooms. Once that was done, the documents could be arranged, and an analytical inventory of them could be prepared. Goossens also called for a more thorough study of the diplomatics of Mesopotamia and the Hittite land in order to assist in reconstituting original record groups.

By 1956 Ernst Weidner could state with satisfaction that, while formerly with few exceptions archival aggregates had been disrupted, it had recently become the practice to publish clay tablets in their archival arrangement (*nach Archiven geordnet*). Such practice seemed to Weidner of vital importance, "for many studies in the fields of history, cultural history, and geography become possible only after it has been determined what documents belong to a certain body of archives."[9]

If one peruses the recent literature of the field, he would be unable to discover any direct influence of the writings just mentioned upon the thinking of Assyriologists. Their practices, however, show clearly that the views set forth by Schneider, Goossens, and Weidner have now prevailed. A cursory study of the more recent excavation reports—those on Mari, Ugarit,

8. S. Muller, J. A. Feith, and R. Fruin, *Manual for the Arrangement and Description of Archives*, trans. Arthur H. Leavitt, 2d ed. (New York, 1968).

9. Ernst Weidner, "Amts- und Privatarchive aus mittelassyrischer Zeit," in Kurt Schubert, ed., *Vorderasiatische Studien: Festschrift für Viktor Christian* . . . (Vienna, 1956), pp. 111–118.

Pylos, and Nimrud, for instance—reveals that the archival approach to the tablets has been accepted de facto: the exact spots where the tablets were found are entered on survey maps, and the tablets themselves are numbered as found so that the original relationships between them are on record, even if the texts are published in a different, possibly a subject arrangement. The arguments for the archival approach have been convincingly summed up by Johannes Papritz, a professional archivist, in his study of the archives of ancient Mesopotamia.[10]

Now that archivists have joined other subject specialists who have traced the history of their disciplines back to the days of Sumer, a history of archives administration must begin with archives-keeping in the ancient Near East. In surveying its development, our emphasis will be on the problems of physical preservation, storage, and use of archival materials. To understand them, much will have to be said about their genesis and the role of record-making as an aspect of the governance of secular and religious affairs. More studies, however, are needed of the ways of doing business, of the types of records created, and of the methods of organizing them, in short, of the diplomatics—in Goossens' sense—of the era before aspects of record administration other than storage and preservation can be dealt with.

Our aim, then, is to discuss the record-keeping techniques of all the areas that used the clay tablet (figure 1) as the principal medium for recording and imparting information. This broad approach appears not only expedient but also legitimate, first of all because methods of communication and consequently techniques of preserving the products of the communication process depend on the physical makeup of the medium used, as does its survival. That the clay tablet had an excellent chance of enduring appears from the mere fact that more than 400,000 tablets have been found.

Furthermore, if we speak of the area of the clay tablet as an object susceptible of historical treatment, because it derives

10. Papritz, "Archive in Altmesopotamien."

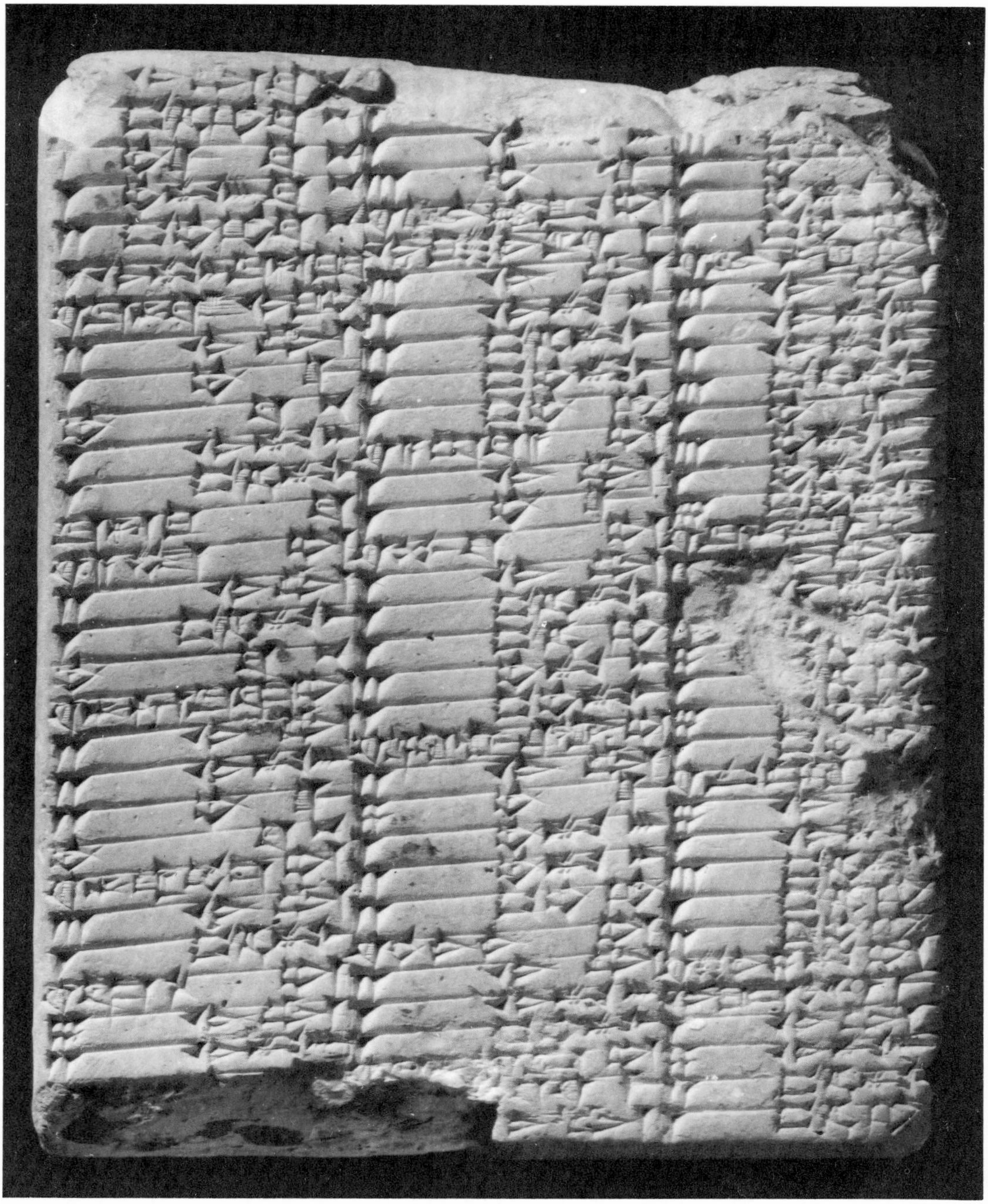

Figure 1. Example of a clay tablet in the form of a ledger from the Ur III period.

unity from the writing material used, we follow the thought of two great jurisprudents, Marian San Nicolò and Paul Koschaker.[11] They developed the concept of cuneiform law (*Keilschriftrecht*) to provide a common basis for understanding the legal institutions and practices of a vast area embracing Mesopotamia, Elam, Urartu (Armenia), Anatolia, and northern Syria. I intend, however, to disregard the kind of writing on the tablets in order to include in this discussion those countries that, while writing on clay, used noncuneiform script, such as Crete and Mycenean Greece. To the archivist, certainly, this concept of a clay tablet civilization, although broader and more diffused than that of cuneiform law, seems justified because the physical nature of the writing medium is the fundamental element that determines the genesis, the organization, and the preservation of archival material.

Before we begin to describe the archival institutions and techniques of the clay tablet countries, the reader ought to be cautioned against assuming that the clay tablet took care of all the record-making needs of these countries. First of all, we must realize that what A. Leo Oppenheim has called operational devices could be employed as recording and control media, making written records unnecessary.[12] In the archives of an administrative office in Nuzi (now Yorghan Tepe), a hollow tablet with forty-six little stones in it was found. By means of a number of such containers it would have been possible to keep the numerical distribution of animals and their movements between pasture, plucking places, fields, and their ultimate destinations clearly and constantly in evidence without a written record. One is reminded of the tally sticks of the early English Exchequer.

Secondly, we are realizing more and more that, in addition

---

11. See V. Korošec, "Keilschriftrecht," in Bertold Spuler, ed., *Handbuch der Orientalistik*, I, supplement 3 (Leiden and Cologne, 1964), 49–219, where the pertinent writings of Koschaker, San Nicolò, and other jurisprudents are listed on p. 49, n. 1. See also Koschaker's article on cuneiform law, *Encyclopedia of the Social Sciences*, XI, 211–219.

12. A. Leo Oppenheim, "On an Operational Device in Mesopotamian Bureaucracy," *Journal of Near Eastern Studies*, XVIII (1959), 121–128.

to clay tablets, ivory and wooden boards were also used for writing purposes. The latter could be written on directly or covered with a thin layer of wax upon which impressions were made with a stylus. How far back the use of writing tablets can be traced we are not certain. In the Hittite Empire there were wood tablet scribes, but no real tablets had come to light anywhere in the Near East until a number of ivory and wooden writing tablets were discovered in a well in the Northwest Palace of Nimrud.[13] This was indeed a sensation, because it warned us that the use of the writing board may have been more widespread than we had assumed before.

The sixteen ivory boards originally constituted a polyptych to which further leaves could be added and which was diagnosed as the "deluxe" copy of a compilation of omen texts ordered by Sargon II (721–705 B.C.) for his palace in Khorsabad (figure 2). But while ivory was rare and its use limited to very special purposes, wood, although more expensive than clay, was a convenient medium for ordinary administrative recording. Waxed tablets were handy for business transactions of many

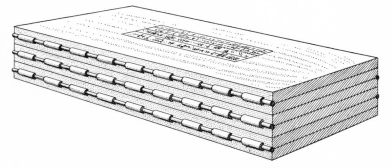

Figure 2. Reconstruction of the top three leaves of the Nimrud ivory writing-boards.

13. D. J. Wiseman, "Assyrian Writing-Boards," *Iraq*, XVII (1955), 3–13; Margaret Howard, "Technical Description of the Ivory Writing-Boards from Nimrud," *ibid.*, 14–20; M. E. L. Mallowan, *Nimrud and Its Remains*, I (London, 1966), 148–162. Mallowan (p. 162) considers "still most valuable and authoritative" the article by T. M. McKenney Hughes, "On Some Waxed Tablets Said to Have Been Found at Cambridge," *Archaeologia*, LV (1897), 257–282.

kinds, such as keeping up-to-date records of taxes received and owed, payrolls, inventories of stores, and the like, and we can be certain that the Mesopotamian administrator was quite aware of the advantages of this medium.[14] On a wax tablet he could add, subtract, and erase at will, and the same tablet could be reused after the surface had been smoothed out. On the battle-field, for instance, when there was no time to prepare clay tablets and let them dry, media other than such tablets were preferred, as we can see on a number of reliefs. A relief of Sennacherib (704–681 B.C.) shows two scribes in the process of recording the number of enemy prisoners and dead (figure 3). One of them keeps a score on a wax tablet, while his colleague uses a scroll that probably was of leather rather than of papyrus.[15]

Hitherto, the oldest wood tablets known (ca. 250 B.C.) were the accounts of an Egyptian schoolmaster who had taken his class on a trip to the Delta during the summer holidays.[16] Nimrud has now furnished us an example that confirms the use of the wood tablet almost five hundred years earlier. It has been surmised that the Assyrians inherited the wood tablet from the Hittite Empire,[17] where wood was quite plentiful and where the

14. Marian San Nicolò, "Haben die Babylonier Wachstafeln als Schriftträger gekannt?" *Orientalia*, XVII (1948), 59–70, a splendid article that suggests "the not infrequent use of wood for cuneiform writings . . . especially in areas of administration and accountancy of the state and the temple." As early as 1928, R. P. Dougherty, "Writing upon Parchment and Papyrus among the Babylonians and Assyrians," *Journal of the American Oriental Society*, XLVIII (1928), 109–135, showed convincingly that "writing on parchment was practiced extensively in Mesopotamia contemporaneously with writing upon clay from the eighth century B.C. to the second century B.C., i.e. during Assyrian, Neo-Babylonian, Persian, and Greek regimes." The extent to which papyrus was used cannot be ascertained. For Persia Richard T. Hallock reports on p. 4 of the introduction to *Persepolis Fortification Tablets* (Chicago, 1969) that twenty texts record the delivery of hides and that probably these hides were used as writing material, since other tablets speak of a "tablet on hide" and of "Babylonian scribes (writing) on hides."

15. Wiseman, "Assyrian Writing-Boards," p. 12.

16. M. E. L. Mallowan, "The Excavations at Nimrud (Kalḫu), 1953," *Iraq*, XVI (1954), 107.

17. Wiseman, "Assyrian Writing-Boards," p. 11, although the author thinks that the wax tablet may also have come to Assyria in the wake of "increased contact with the West resulting from the campaigns of Tiglath-Pileser I (ca. 1100 B.C.)," or as a result of the growing influence of Aramaic in the eighth century.

Figure 3. Scribes of Sennacherib of Assyria in the process of recording a head count of enemy dead, one using a hinged diptych and his colleague writing on a scroll.

wood tablet scribes were a class apart from the more highly regarded group of clay tablet scribes. That, in Nimrud at least, the wood tablet played an important role as an instrument of writing appears from an order for the issuance of writing boards that specified the number of leaves each board was to have:

(1) 2? writing boards . . .
(2) of 5 leaves . . .
(3) 2 *ditto* . . . of 4 (leaves) each
(4) 4 *ditto* . . . of 3 (leaves) each
(5) . . . *ditto* . . . of 4 *ditto* (leaves) each
(6) *ditto* of 3 *ditto* each
(7) . . . *ditto ditto* of 2 *ditto* each
(8) . . . of 3 *ditto* each.[18]

By hinging more leaves onto it, the record could be expanded at will, and information entered on the wax surface could be erased and supplemented whenever desired.

It is probable that the wood tablet as a writing device was known in Mesopotamia long before there could have been any Hittite influence and that, in fact, its use preceded that of the clay tablet. In an article pointedly entitled "Sie schrieben auf Holz" (They Wrote on Wood) and thus inviting comparison with the title of Chiera's well-known *They Wrote on Clay*, Helmuth T. Bossert has produced impressive evidence from which it appears that, "when writing was invented in Mesopotamia, tablets were not made of clay but of wood."[19] He rests his case on the ideogram for writing tablet of the Uruk IVb-period (about 3000 B.C.), which consists of a wood tablet with a knob for a handle at the upper end. If Bossert's theory is correct, it would tend to confirm that the Sumerians came to lower Mesopotamia from the mountains to the east, where wood was plentiful, and that they abandoned its use and turned to clay

18. Barbara Parker, "Administrative Tablets from the North-West Palace, Nimrud," *Iraq*, XXIII (1961), 41.

19. Helmuth T. Bossert, "Sie schrieben auf Holz," in Ernst Grumach, ed., *Minoica: Festschrift zum 80. Geburtstag von Johannes Sundwall* (Berlin, 1958), pp. 71, n. 13, and 72.

in the Euphrates–Tigris basin, where wood was hard to come by.

Although we cannot guess how much of Mesopotamia's record production has escaped us because of perishable writing materials, undoubtedly the clay tablet remained the standard medium for recording data of all kinds. It prevailed from the end of the fourth millennium B.C. until the days of the Achaemenids, when cuneiform was superseded by the simple Aramaic script and when with that script the clay tablet began to disappear.[20]

In terms of time and space, the extent of the clay tablet region was immense. It embraced the lands of the Euphrates and Tigris Rivers and nearby territories, such as Elam and Urartu, the Hittite Empire, Phoenicia, and the Aegean cultures of Knossos, Pylos, Mycenae, and Thebes.[21] It thus included most of the early civilized world, and it continued over a period of about three thousand years. For more than half the time mankind has communicated in writing, most of the writing has been on clay, and this record output far exceeded that of all of Europe during the Middle Ages.

For this output not only the geographical extension of the clay tablet area and its life span are responsible. Rather, we must seek its explanation in the cultural achievements and particularly in the needs of societies functioning on a high level of administrative technique, for—as we are likely to forget— writing was invented to serve the administrator rather than the man of learning. It did not originate "for the purpose of glorifying kings or praising the gods, but as a result of the economic everyday needs of an industrious and highly talented people, bent on gaining an existence in newly occupied territory."[22]

Writing owes its origin to the Sumerians, a gifted people endowed with a remarkable talent for organization and a sense

20. According to Wiseman, "Assyrian Writing-Boards," p. 13, n. 122, the latest dated tablet in the British Museum is A.D. 44/5 (B.M. 45982).

21. On the tablets recently discovered at Thebes, see William D. McDonald, *Progress into the Past: The Rediscovery of Mycenaean Civilization* (New York, 1969), pp. 351–352.

22. Hartmut Schmökel, *Ur, Assur und Babylon: Drei Jahrtausende im Zweistromland* (Stuttgart, 1955), p. 12.

of orderliness that approached a national characteristic.[23] Where the Sumerians came from when they entered southern Mesopotamia, we do not know. We do not even know whether they actually made the transition from using pictorial signs to a system of syllabic writing, because possibly they only applied to the Sumerian language a system of writing they found in their new seats. The large socioeconomic units they created, the temples and palaces, and particularly the building and maintenance of a network of canals necessitated making and keeping "long lists of rations given out to men, women, and sometimes children; contracts with seasonal workers; records of tax arrangements of all kinds; documents concerned with the renting of fields and gardens; records referring to the handling of staples within large organisations";[24] and the like. In a society depending on and dedicated to bureaucratic administration, careful administration of the record assumed its rightful place, once writing had been invented. From then on the care of archives evolved consistently as the great empires of the Babylonians, Assyrians, and Hittites came into existence. In fact, they could not have functioned, and are not thinkable, without the effective use of written communication in administration.

I do not intend to survey site by site[25] the archival repositories that have been discovered; this would be tantamount to retelling the thrilling story of excavations in the Near East.[26] Nor can I dwell in detail on the spread of the clay tablet from Sumer in

23. Tom B. Jones, "Bookkeeping in Ancient Sumer," *Archaeology*, IX (1956), 17; also in his *Paths to the Ancient Past* (New York, 1967), p. 137. See also Maurice Lambert, "La naissance de la bureaucratie," *Revue Historique*, CCXXIV (1960), 1–26, and "Le premier triomphe de la bureaucratie," *ibid.*, CCXXV (1961), 21–46.

24. A. Leo Oppenheim, *Letters from Mesopotamia* (Chicago and London, 1967), p. 4.

25. This approach has been used by Kampman and Schawe and by Mogens Weitemeyer in his *Babylonske og assyriske arkiver og biblioteker* (Copenhagen, 1955).

26. The story of the excavations to about 1945 is well told in André Parrot, *Archéologie Mésopotamienne: Les étapes* (Paris, 1946). The more recent work by Karl Heinz Bernhardt, *Die Umwelt des Alten Testaments*, I (Gütersloh, 1967) contains an up-to-date account of the Near East excavation sites, the discoveries made, the writings and languages used, and the pertinent literature.

southern Mesopotamia to the upper reaches of the Euphrates and Tigris Rivers and to Crete and the Peloponnesus. This development began early in the third millennium, when the Sumerians entered the light of history and founded such great cultural centers as Uruk, Ur, Kish, and Lagaš. Sumerian rule collapsed first when Semitic tribes from Akkad (about 2475 B.C.) under the leadership of Sargon I appeared on the scene, and it fell definitively—after a short period of Sumerian renaissance, the Neo-Sumerian era—when Hammurapi (ca. 1792–1750 B.C.), a political and military genius of the first order, established the hegemony of Babylon. This, the Old Babylonian period, was followed by the rule of the invading Kassites and by that of the Mitannis in the northwest, an era called the Dark Ages. Then, in the fourteenth century B.C. all of western Asia began to fall to the Assyrians, who advanced systematically from their original seats at Assur, Calah (now Nimrud), and Nineveh to the Mediterranean and under Assurbanipal (668–626 B.C.) to upper Egypt. But Assyrian rule, too, was not destined to last. In 612 B.C. Babylon once again carried the day, until finally the Achaemenids of Persia—Cyrus and his son Kambyses—conquered all of Asia Minor, Babylon, and Egypt, and Darius (521–485 B.C.) created his gigantic empire.

Meanwhile, at the outskirts of the core area of present-day Mesopotamia, other civilizations had emerged that also used the clay tablet as a means of communication. The Hittites, Indo-Europeans who had established themselves in Anatolia, founded a great empire whose history, including its expansion into Mesopotamia and Syria, has become known to us only as a result of excavations of the last fifty years. In Syria itself French excavations have revealed the importance of the later Phoenician center of Ugarit. Clay tablet archives have also been unearthed in Knossos on Crete, in the Palace of Pylos, and in Mycenae.

Tartaria in Transylvania, part of Rumania, can now be considered the farthest outpost of the clay tablet area. There excavations in 1942–1943 and in 1961 have produced a number of clay tablets with what seems to be some primitive kind of writing. The tablets have been compared to the early tablets of Mesopotamia of the Uruk and Jemdet-Nasr period.[27] Outside the area in which the clay tablet predominated, a very important clay tablet archives, part of the foreign correspondence of Amenophis III and IV, was found in El Amarna in Egypt, where otherwise papyrus was the normal writing material.

2. *Archival Institutions*

To attempt to deal with the archival practices of so vast an area over so long a time may well be considered an impossible task and may, in fact, lead to unwarranted generalizations. There are certain periods for which we lack specific information, and there are certain political centers, such as those of the Hurrians and the Mitanni and those of Elam and Urartu, that have not left us archival accumulations of considerable size. If, nevertheless, we try to derive from our present stock of knowledge a comprehensive picture of archival practices, we are doing so on the strength of the fact that the prevailing use of the clay tablet made fairly uniform techniques almost mandatory.

A study of the archives of ancient Greece and Rome must rely almost exclusively on information derived from inscriptions and literary sources. In the case of the archives of the ancient Orient, literary sources are lacking; but, on the other hand, thanks to the excavations we can study the archives, or what is left of them, *in situ*. This would seem to be a great advantage. Unfortunately, during the earlier excavations far too little attention was paid to the circumstances under which accumulations of clay tablets were discovered, and even after modern methods of archaeology had been developed and adopted, the attention of archaeologists was so sharply focused on the content of the tablets that for a long time their interrelationship was not appreciated. Is it not revealing that in speaking of tablets they

27. M. S. F. Hood, "The Tartaria Tablets," *Antiquity*, XLI (1967), 99–113, with a reproduction on plate XVI.

mostly used the terms literary and nonliterary documents (German, *Text*; French, *texte*) and seemed to avoid our terms "records" and "archives" where they would be applicable?

It has been estimated that nine-tenths or more of the tablets discovered are "economic texts—lists and accounts of the accounting office, [and] purchase, lease, and loan contracts,"[28]— that is, archival documents—, and so the institutional genesis of most of the accumulations found is no longer in question. In regard to their relationship to library material, it now seems commonly acknowledged that "in the ancient Orient no distinction was made, as a matter of principle, between record and literary product, between archival establishments and libraries. Every accumulation of clay tablets would start from archival holdings and possibly expand by taking in literary pieces."[29] It might be argued, for instance, that part of the so-called omen texts—it has been estimated that 50 per cent of the tablets we have from Assurbanipal's library belong to the omen literature—are intimately related to the process of Mesopotamian government and could be considered of record rather than literary character. Thus, in Assyria, where queries replaced the inspection reports of the diviners of the Middle Babylonian period, these "queries contain divine answers (affirmative as a rule) to questions that are quoted *in extenso* concerning the appointment of officials, the loyalty of generals, and the actions of the enemy,"[30] and played a role in the decision-making process. One might compare these queries to the position papers and the reports of experts of modern times;

28. Hartmut Schmökel, "Mesopotamien," in Schmökel, ed., *Kulturgeschichte des alten Orient* (Stuttgart, 1961), p. 46.

29. Carl Wendel, *Die griechisch-römische Buchbeschreibung verglichen mit der des vorderen Orients* (Halle, 1949), pp. 11–12.

30. A. Leo Oppenheim, *Ancient Mesopotamia: Portrait of a Dead Civilization* (Chicago, 1964), p. 217. "The Arts of the Diviner" are interestingly discussed on pp. 206–227 of this work. H. W. F. Saggs, *The Greatness That Was Babylon* (New York, 1968), p. 307 of the Mentor Books edition, says: "The prognostications in the omen-literature fall into two main classes—those which concern the king, high officials and the country, and those which concern private persons. Astrological omens and those concerned with liver-divination relate to public affairs, whilst the other types (dreams, casual meetings, movements and so on) relate to private affairs."

reference collections of them would be consulted in dealing with future cases.

This does not mean that libraries in our sense did not exist in the ancient Orient. We know of a good many temple libraries, frequently attached to temple schools. The famous library of the Nineveh Palace had all the characteristics of such an institution, and Mogens Weitemeyer has very convincingly demonstrated that special techniques were developed for the control of library material and that these techniques differed from those applied to archival holdings.[31] It is probably safe to state that in the ancient Orient archival establishments preceded and out-numbered libraries and that frequently archival and library materials were preserved in the same institution. In the case of the latter, however, the custodians were aware of the necessity of providing certain control devices that could be dispensed with where records were involved.

Provision for keeping records was made at the various centers of political, economic, and religious endeavor, and thus all types of archival organization known to us were already in operation in the ancient Near East, progressing from simple storage facilities to archival establishments of considerable size.[32] It should be borne in mind, however, that, since at the beginning these various spheres of activity coincided or were closely intertwined, the differentiation between state, religious, and business archives was slow in developing. Thus, in Sumer—

31. Mogens Weitemeyer, "Archive and Library Technique in Ancient Mesopotamia," *Libri*, VI (1956), 225–232.

32. To assist the reader in locating the archives referred to in the text, the most important ones in Mesopotamia are listed here by region:

(1) In Sumer: Lagaš-Girsu (Telloh), Šuruppak (Fara), Ur (Mugaiyar), Uruk (Warka).

(2) In Akkad (Babylonia): Dēr, Kish (Tell Akhimer), Nippur (Niffer), Sippar (Abu Habba).

(3) In Assyria: Dur Šarrukin (Khorsabad), Calah (Nimrud), Niniveh (Kuyundschik), Nuzi (Yorghan Tepe), Shemshara and, on the Middle Euphrates, Mari (Tell Hariri).

(4) In Asia Minor: Hattuša (Bogazkeui), Kaniš (Kültepe).

(5) In Syria: Ugarit (Ras Shamra), Alalakh (Tell ᶜAtchāna).

A breakdown by period and type of establishment is found in Weitemeyer, *Arkiver*, p. 88.

where the moon god Nanna was the king of Ur, had his ministers and his court, and owned most of the land, administering it through his "Directors of Livestock, Dairy Work, Fishing, and Donkey Transport,"—the god's abode was "at once temple and palace, government offices and stores and factories,"[33] and his archival establishment consequently combined the features of a state, an institutional, and a business archives. After the collapse of Sumerian rule, the political and religious spheres tended to separate and real state archival arrangements begin to be more sharply discernible. Those of the "government" of Babylonia, for example, constituted "a sizeable archival establishment (e-dubba) which contained careful lists of the population of the realm and of the receipts and expenditures of the state and many other important items," headed by a "director of archives (pisan dubba)."[34] It must have been and remained a functioning unit, for at a much later time a search was made "in the house of rolls where the treasures were laid up in Babylon" for a decree of Cyrus authorizing the Jews to rebuild the "house of God in Jerusalem."[35]

As a result of the excavations of recent decades, public archival agencies—or at least concentrations of public records—of astonishing magnitude have become known to us, and some of the most important ones will be discussed here in chronological order. We begin with the archives of Mari on the Euphrates River, where French Assyriologists, guided and inspired by André Parrot in a long series of campaigns, have discovered the ruins of a royal palace of vast proportions.[36] An important political center during the early second millennium, although

33. Sir Charles L. Woolley, *Excavations at Ur: A Record of Twelve Years' Work* (London, 1954), p. 144.

34. Bruno Meissner, *Babylon und Assyrien*, I (Heidelberg, 1920), 120.

35. See Chap. 4 below.

36. On the results of the Mari excavations, see Kampman, *Archieven en biblioteken*, pp. 35–37; Schawe, "Der alte Vorderorient," pp. 35–36; Weitemeyer, *Arkiver*, pp. 40–43; Papritz, "Archive in Altmesopotamien," pp. 26–28; and André Parrot, *Mission archéologique de Mari*, II, *Le palais: Architecture* (Paris, 1958), pp. 80–81, 102, 162–163, 217–219, 288–292. See also Parrot's earlier *Mari, une ville perdue . . . et retrouvée par l'archéologie française* (Paris, 1936).

subject to invasion and domination by its powerful neighbors to the east, Mari has bequeathed us some 20,000 tablets of the period of its Assyrian ruler Šamši-Adad I (1813–1781 B.C.) and of Zimrilim, who ended Assyrian rule only to succumb to the onslaught of the great Hammurapi in the thirty-second year of that ruler. The significance of the record material found is enhanced by the fact that the various archival depositories or accumulations are clearly related to the main functions of the Mari government, that is, that in the palace the offices in charge of "housekeeping" activities were separated from those dealing with foreign relations and other important activities of the rulers and that archival offices reflected this separation of functions.[37] Room 115, for instance, held the diplomatic records of the last two rulers of Mari. One can easily visualize the king in his nearby conference room (Room 132) "perusing some letters arriving at the palace and then having them taken to a place sufficiently near at hand so that he could have them brought out again when he needed them."[38] As will be seen later, the most important series found were surveyed and reclassified by archivists of Hammurapi when Mari was occupied by the Babylonians.

Records dealing with the economic affairs of the palace—contracts, accounting records, lists of laborers and their compensation, and other documents reflecting the administration of the royal household—were found in various parts of the building: in Room 5 with its several hundred tablets originally kept in jars; in Room 108 (almost a thousand tablets); in Room 110, which produced "an abundant assemblage of tablets of an economic character"; and finally in Rooms 215–218, where metallurgical workshops seem to have been located. Included in this large body of records were census lists of men subject to

---

37. Goossens, "Introduction," *Revue d'Assyriologie*, XLVI (1952), 98–107.

38. Parrot, *Le palais*, p. 80. See also Godefroy Goossens, "Classement des archives royales de Mari," I, *Revue d'Assyriologie*, XLVI (1952), 137–154 (Goossens has distinguished twenty-two sequences or dossiers among the 364 tablets published at that time), and J. M. Rankin, "Diplomacy in Western Asia in the Early Second Millennium," *Iraq*, XVIII (1956), 68–110.

military service[39] and a roster of more than two hundred women (slaves, widows, and sacred prostitutes), who may have been needed for manual labor.[40] Under Zimrilim a man by the name of Iasîm-Sumû, who had been trained in the school for scribes, appears in the role of head of the accounting office and in charge of the tablets of the palace.[41]

The fourteenth and fifteenth campaigns of the Mari mission in 1964 and 1965 have revealed the remnants of an earlier palace, from about 2400 B.C., and of an even earlier structure preceding it. Some three hundred tablets were found in the level under the Zimrilim Palace, mostly of the time of King Iahdun-Lim and pertaining to the palace administration. André Parrot regretfully admits of that period of the history of the palace: "One thing we still miss if we want to have a complete picture of life in a palace of the third millennium: the archives. They existed certainly."[42] Parrot believes that Lugalzagesi, king of Umma and Uruk, was "the great culprit" responsible for the destruction of the earlier palace.[43]

If Mari shows an interesting effort to decentralize administrative responsibilities and the corresponding archival storage facilities, Ugarit (Ras Shamra) reveals further progress in that direction. Excavated since 1929 by F.-A. Claude Schaeffer[44] and his French colleagues, the remains of this Syrian palace—

39. J. R. Kupper, "Le recensement dans les textes de Mari," in André Parrot, ed., *Studia Mariana* (Leiden, 1950), pp. 99–110.

40. Maurice Birot, "Un recensement de femmes au royaume de Mari," *Syria*, XXXV (1958), 9–26.

41. Birot, "Les lettres de Iasîm-Sumû," *Syria*, XLI (1964), 25–65.

42. André Parrot, "Les fouilles de Mari: Seizième campagne (Printemps, 1966)," *Syria*, XLIV (1967), 25–26.

43. Parrot, "Les fouilles de Mari: Quatorzième campagne," *Syria*, XLII (1965), 24.

44. Claude F. A. Schaeffer, "La première tablette," *Syria*, XXXIII (1956), 161–168. The discussion of the results of the Ugarit excavations is principally based on Schaeffer's "Exposé préliminaire," in *Le palais royal d'Ugarit III*, published under Schaeffer's direction, Mission de Ras Shamra, VI (Paris, 1955), pp. ix–xxx, and on his "Fouilles et découvertes des XVIIIe et XIXe campagnes, 1954–1955," in Schaeffer and others, *Ugaritica IV*, Mission de Ras Shamra, XV (Paris, 1962), 1–150. See also Kampman, *Archieven en bibliotheken*, pp. 45–48; Schawe, "Der alte Vorderorient," pp. 40–44; A. Pohl, "Bibliotheken und Archive im alten Orient," *Orientalia*, XXV (1956), 105–109; Papritz, "Archive in Altmesopotamien," pp. 32–33.

Ugarit is located a few kilometers north of the seaport of Latakia, the ancient Laodicea—have acquainted us with a local system of alphabetic cuneiform writing that was used for internal purposes. In their intercourse with other powers of the Near East, however, the scribes of Ugarit, obviously well prepared by their training in the local school for scribes, used Akkadian, the language of diplomacy and of foreign trade, and also Egyptian and Hittite hieroglyphic writing, as the situation seemed to require. The results of the Ugarit excavations have been particularly gratifying because they have revealed the organization of offices with their record units exactly where they were when Ugarit was conquered. Functional delegation becomes reasonably clear from the location of the record units, which, one is inclined to think, reflects the planning of some official in charge of "buildings and grounds." Schaeffer has pointed up the importance of the Ugarit results:

At Ras Shamra we have the advantage of being able to determine the classification that was applied by the very creators of the cuneiform documents found in the palace, the one that was adopted by the royal administration of Ugarit. This classification reveals not only a surprisingly perfect administrative organization. It also contributes to an understanding of the documents.[45]

The following administrative and record-keeping installations have been identified so far:

1. *The Archives West.* The office of receipt of the treasurer in charge of the provinces exclusive of the capital was located in Rooms 2–5 to the left of the main entrance of the palace so that taxpayers could make their payments without entering the building. A narrow chamber with particularly massive walls must have housed the archives of this office, obviously a major operation, because what seems to be its payroll specifies as many as ten clerks assigned to the archives and the treasury.[46]

2. *The Archives East* was housed at the very opposite end of the

45. Schaeffer, ed., *Ugarit III*, p. xi.
46. *Ibid.*, pp. xi–xv.

palace, some 80 meters from the Archives West, in Rooms 54–56 and in the room above Staircase 33. Its premises were easily accessible for persons coming from the interior of the city and understandably so because here, it appears, were centralized records pertaining to matters financial and legal of the capital and the countryside immediately surrounding it. Its situation thus corresponded to that of the Archives West, which was to serve persons coming from outside the capital or from the seaport.[47]

3. *The Central Archives*, in eight rooms around Court IV, was "the legal archives *par excellence* of the palace, in which there were preserved the property records of an entire kingdom and in which were recorded (*enregistrés*) the changes resulting from purchases, exchanges, wills, and gifts that occurred in the real and movable property holdings (*les possessions foncières et mobilières*) of the entirety of the citizens of Ugarit." Schaeffer has not hesitated to call the Central Archives "this vast royal notariat." To enhance their durability, tablets in this archives were found to be of exceptionally strong and wellrounded format, and they were written on and baked with great care. In terms of the number and size of its premises and of the quantity of documents found, the Central Archives appears to have been the most important of the services housed in the Palace of Ugarit.[48]

4. *The Archives South*, also located in rooms off Court V, had records in Akkadian cuneiform script that had to do with relations with the Hittite lands to the north. The scribes attached to this office did not draft any documents, but had "essentially the function of archivists classifying documents received at the palace of Ugarit that came from the Hittite countries to the north."[49]

---

47. *Ibid.*, pp. xvii–xviii, xxii.

48. *Ibid.*, pp. xxiii–xxx. See also G. Boyer, "La place des textes d'Ugarit dans l'histoire de l'ancient droit oriental," in Schaeffer, ed., *Ugarit III*, pp. 284–287.

49. Schaeffer and others, *Ugaritica IV*, p. 29. See Jean Nougayrol, "Les archives internationales d'Ugarit (Ras Shamra—17e campagne)," in Académie des Inscriptions et Belles Lettres, *Comptes rendus* (1954), pp. 30–41, 239–248. Nougayrol succeeds in

5. In the *Archives Southwest*, in Room 81 off Court V and in one of two rooms on the second floor, records in the alphabetical script of Ugarit prevailed. Among the different archival installations of the palace, the Archives Southwest seems to have had a special task that distinguished it from the other archival offices in the palace and gave it some of the functions of a central expediting unit.[50] In the first place, it appears to have been charged with operating the oven for firing tablets, about 1 meter high and 1.20 meters in diameter at the base. The oven was found in the southwest corner of Court V, unfortunately smashed when an adjacent wall collapsed. Capable of holding about a hundred tablets, the oven had been stocked just before catastrophe overtook the palace; of the tablets in it, thirty were found intact. Since only the Archives Southwest had an oven of this kind, it seems safe to assume that the installation served all the offices of the palace. In fact, the Archives Southwest may have been "some kind of appraisal office (*bureau de triage*) where the documents that had just been written by the clerks in the offices were centralized to have them fired and whence they were redistributed to the archival units that were to take care of their classification and preservation."[51] Archives Southwest may also have been in charge of dispatching the documents that were to be sent to the provinces or to foreign countries. Finally, since there were found copies or translations into Ugaritic alphabetical cuneiform of documents the originals of which must have been in Babylonian, the clerks of Archives Southwest may have been assigned the duty of translating messages from abroad that the royal government wanted to have available in the native language.

6. *The Archives of the Little Palace* was a surprise discovery during the nineteenth campaign in 1955.[52] Found in Rooms 203

---

reconstituting a number of relatively intact dossiers that throw much light on Ugarit's precarious position in the shadow of the Hittite Empire.

50. Schaeffer and others, *Ugaritica IV*, pp. 31–37, 47–51, 91.

51. *Ibid.*, p. 91.

52. *Ibid.*, pp. 121–127, 145–146.

and 204 on two levels of this palace, the tablets in Babylonian cuneiform appear to stem from an administration that had to do with the import and export of goods in bulk, activities "based on the ports to the south of Ugarit, the economic outlook of which was principally directed to the south, that is, toward Palestine and Egypt as well as toward Cyprus and the Mycenean countries in the west." The special charge of this archival office once again confirms the rational organization of Ugarit's administrative arrangements.

7. Accumulations of tablets were found in the palace workshops that produced luxury goods to be used as gifts to the kings of Ugarit's neighbor countries or as tributes to its foreign overlords.[53] The weapons that were found on the same premises may have belonged to guards posted near the workshops and archives for their protection.

Seen from the vantage point of the archivist, the results of the excavations at Hattuša (Boghazkeui) have been somewhat disappointing, or at least inconclusive; for, while they have revealed the existence and part of the history of the Hittite Empire as an important center of power and culture that flourished from about 1700 to 1200 B.C., the situation with regard to the state's archives is by no means so clear as that found in Mari and in Ugarit. Earlier enthusiasm that extolled the discovery of the Hittite state archives has now given way to a more sober appraisal based on the conviction that, notwithstanding the significance of the documentation discovered, the true state archives of Boghazkeui has not been found[54] and may never be found.

On the hill crowned by the palace and subsidiary buildings,

53. *Ibid.*, pp. 93–103.

54. For the history and results of the German excavations in Boghazkeui, see the publications and reports of the Deutsche Orient-Gesellschaft and especially Heinrich Otten, "Bibliotheken im alten Orient," *Das Altertum*, I (1955), 67–81; Kurt Bittel and others, "Vorläufiger Bericht über die Ausgrabungen in Boğazkoy im Jahre 1957," *Mitteilungen der Deutschen Orient-Gesellschaft*, CXI (1958), 1–84. I have not been able to avail myself of Kurt Bittel, *Hattusha* (London, 1970). See also Kampman, *Archieven en biblioteken*, pp. 42–45; Schawe, "Der alte Vorderorient," pp. 37–40; Papritz, "Archive in Altmesopotamien," pp. 28–31.

a number of storage installations have been identified. The first one to be found and excavated from 1907 to 1912 was located in Building E in Rooms 4 and 5. Here treaties with foreign powers—among them the famous treaty of 1269 B.C. with Ramses II of Egypt—and correspondence with these powers were intermingled with tablets that must have been part of a library; and, according to Heinrich Otten, the treaties were not the originals but possibly reference copies, for they lacked the seals the originals would have carried.[55] But how did the correspondence become intermingled with library holdings? Since no precise records were kept during the early excavations and since the pertinent publications do not indicate the spots where the tablets were found (which would make it possible to reconstitute the former groupings), the nature of the installation in Building E has remained undetermined and will probably remain so.

Building A, discovered in 1931, has furnished us some 3,600 tablets, almost two-thirds of them in Room V, where the unusually large and carefully inscribed and burnt tablets had been stored vertically on shelves along the walls. The tablets clearly represent library rather than archival material. The same holds true of the tablets recently discovered (1957) in the nearby Building K. Two of the walls of this depository and possibly a third one were equipped with low benches supporting wooden shelves on which the tablets were stored. Kurt Bittel suggests that the place was a branch installation of that in Building A or else that it served as an overflow repository.[56]

The only site in which tablets preponderantly of a record nature were located is Building D,[57] which had an audience room and hence may have been an important seat of government activity. It yielded 450 fragments of tablets, including

55. Papritz, "Archive in Altmesopotamien," p. 27, n. 57.
56. Kurt Bittel, "Untersuchungen auf Büyükkale," *Mitteilungen der Deutschen Orient-Gesellschaft*, CXI (1958), 57–61.
57. Heinrich Otten, "Inschriftliche Funde . . . 1953," *Mitteilungen der Deutschen Orient-Gesellschaft*, LXXXVII (1955), 13–25; Papritz, "Archive in Altmesopotamien," p. 31; Otten, "Das Hethiter Reich," in Hartmut Schmökel and others, eds., *Kulturgeschichte des alten Orient* (Stuttgart, 1961), p. 411.

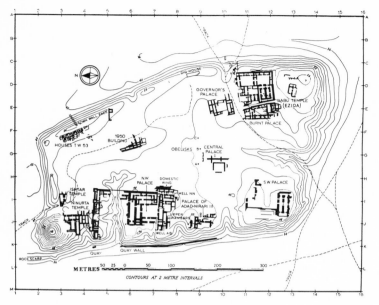

Figure 4. The Acropolis of Nimrud.

correspondence with Egypt, and, in the same building, some royal land grants and about two hundred clay bulls that may have been attached to similar land grants of Mursïli II. The grants may have been revoked by Hattušili and the documents themselves, because written on wood tablets, perished while the clay seals survived. The use by the Hittites of the wood tablet as a writing medium is well documented and may have been standard for internal administrative purposes. This would help to explain that vast holdings of records pertaining to the economy of the palace, such as we have encountered in other places, have not been found in Boghazkeui.

Calah (Nimrud) is the youngest of the great metropolises of the ancient Near East. Once the capital city of Shalmaneser I (1274–1245 B.C.), it was rebuilt by Aššurnaṣirpal, and the excavation conducted by M. E. L. Mallowan and so admirably described in his *Nimrud and Its Remains*[58] has acquainted us with

58. Mallowan, *Nimrud and Its Remains*, 3 vols. (London, 1966).

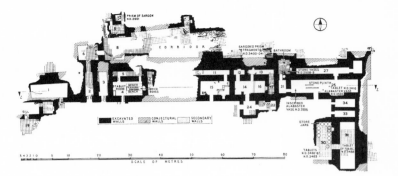

Figure 5. Northern wing of the Northwest Palace of Nimrud, showing location of tablet rooms.

the wonders of the site that provided space for a number of palaces, for the temple district of Ezida, and for the houses of well-to-do citizens (figure 4). As a result, records of various levels of government, archives of the temple, and business papers of individuals were discovered in this one location.

We begin with the records of the imperial chancery,[59] which occupied Rooms 4 and 5 in the northern extension of the Northwest Palace (figure 5). Room 4 was equipped with burnt-brick benches for the chancery clerks and with two rows of brick boxes that were open at the top (figure 6) and must have "served as file cabinets for the different classes of documents which had to be immediately available for reference, while Room 5 behind may have been used as a permanent store."[60] The more than 350 tablets found of the period of Tiglath-Pileser III (744–727 B.C.) and Sargon II (721–705 B.C.) have to do with the central direction of the affairs of the state. Among them was a clay cylinder that Sargon had seized in distant Uruk (the biblical Erech, now Warka) and for which he had substituted a version designed to correct a derogatory report of victories over Assyria.[61]

59. *Ibid.*, I, 165–175.
60. *Ibid.*, I, 172.
61. *Ibid.*, I, 175. For the full story, see below.

Figure 6. Brick bench and "filing cabinets" in Tablet Room 4 in the northern wing of the Northwest Palace of Nimrud.

Records concerning the management of the palace economy were kept separate from these politically important records. Housed in Rooms 11–17, rooms adapted to serve both as places of business and as magazines, the tablets deal with loans of silver and grain, with the sale of slaves and land, and with court judgments.[62]

Records of lower levels of government were found in the Governor's Palace situated about 200 meters southeast of the Northwest Palace and housing the offices of the governors of the district and the city as well as that of the chief land registrar. Their records were found in the Tablet Room K. Most of the records of the chief land registrar were concerned with "agriculture, the tithe, the harvest and the collection of wheat and barley; there were also numerous loans, credit notes, dockets and memoranda in which occur lists of cattle, gold, silver, copper, bronze, and lead."[63] Documents submitted by the county and town commissioners were stored separately in Rooms 404 and 459.

Another administrative center was outside the acropolis area in Fort Shalmaneser, founded by Shalmaneser III (859–824 B.C.) and meant to serve as fortress, arsenal, and palace. Here the *rab ekalli*, the master of the household, had his quarters, and the records of six occupants of this office were contained in the debris in Rooms SE 1, 2, 10 and 11 of the fort.[64] Records were also found in SW 6, the wine cellar. That this room actually was the wine cellar is confirmed by records of the issue of wine and beer by the storekeeper, who at one time had more than four thousand gallons of wine in his custody. According to the receipts, governors from the provinces, possibly convened for a conference, enjoyed the contents of the wine cellar. Rooms NE 48 and 49 of the fort contained what is left of an important set of administrative and economic records that, although found in the debris, might have been kept in these rooms originally.[65]

62. *Ibid.*, I, 176–178.
63. *Ibid.*, I, 46.
64. *Ibid.*, II, 379, 408.
65. *Ibid.*, II, 397, 400.

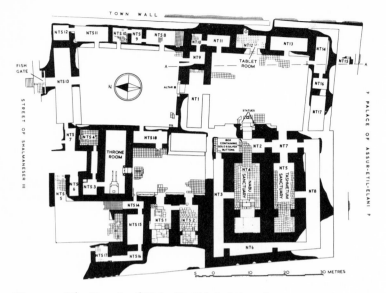

Figure 7. The Temple of Nabu (Ezida) in Nimrud.

Nimrud's acropolis also accommodated the Ezida, a complex of buildings including the temple of the god Nabu (figure 7). Opposite the sanctuary, the excavators discovered the Tablet Rooms NT 12 and 14–16. Adjacent to Room 12 was a deep well, obviously meant to provide water for the scribes, who had to moisten and soften the tablet clay. Tablets found included "incantations, prayers, hymns, liturgies, medical and astrological texts, menologies, and hemerologies, that is to say calendars of favorable and unfavorable days and the like"—in other words, the reference files of the temple's staff.[66] Business records found in NT 14 and 16 tend to show the temple in the role of an agricultural bank, making loans of silver and grain to temple employees and to people living in various places.[67]

In the Ezida district the king had a separate establishment built around a court corresponding to that in front of the temple. Rooms NTS 9–10, opposite the throne room, appear

66. *Ibid.*, I, 274.
67. *Ibid.*, I, 277.

to have been used for clerical purposes, and tablets found there belong to the period of seven Assyrian monarchs, among them Tiglath-Pileser III (744–727 B.C.). Mallowan comments on the location of these tablet rooms as follows:

> It is interesting that the situation of NTS 9–10 across the court, opposite the throne-room and the sanctuaries, is exactly in keeping with the contemporary arrangement at Khorsabad where the archive rooms bore a similar relationship to official and religious apartments across the court. With this we may also compare the situation of NT 12, the tablet room, which likewise was placed on the other side of the courtyard opposite the sanctuary of Nabu.[68]

Wealthy members of the Nimrud community were allowed to live on the acropolis, whence they had a splendid view over the outlying parts of the city. One of the houses there belonged to Shamash-shar-usur, who for almost fifty years advanced silver or grain to harvesters and "took security on land, houses and personal services. His constant preoccupatioñ seems to have been with the supply of birds," which probably he furnished to the temple of Ištar for divination purposes.[69] A wealthy and shrewd operator and the head of a large family, he could afford a spacious building, both residence and office, in which, off the inner court, a number of small rooms were set aside for storing goods and business records. Room 19 served as his archives room (figure 8).

While naturally more modest in size, the administrative and record-keeping facilities in Nestor's Palace on the acropolis of Pylos show the characteristics of similar accommodations in Mesopotamia (figure 9). As luck would have it, the first trench Carl W. Blegen had dug laid bare the archives installation of the palace.[70] Room 7, in all probability the office of the tax collector, was located at the left of the palace entrance, its use for administrative purposes being suggested by the fact that it had a floor of

68. *Ibid.*, I, 237.
69. *Ibid.*, I, 188.
70. Carl W. Blegen and Marion Rawson, *The Palace of Nestor at Pylos in Western Messenia.* I. *The Buildings and Their Contents*, pt. 1 (Princeton, 1966), 92–99.

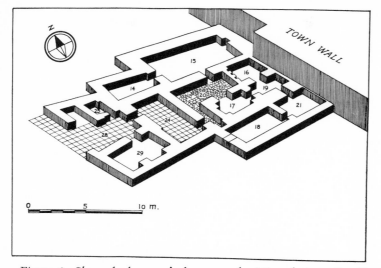

Figure 8. Shamash-shar-usur's house on the Nimrud Acropolis. He kept his archives in Room 19. Room 18 was the family burial vault.

Figure 9. Nestor's Palace on the Acropolis of Pylos. Plan of site, 1960 (surveyed, measured and drawn by J. Travlos). Rooms 7 and 8 are to the left of the main entrance.

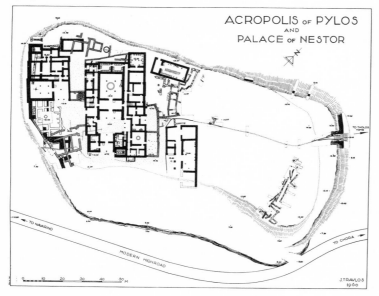

tramped clay while the rooms in the palace had stucco floors. Although three hundred tablets and fragments of tablets were recovered in this room, the adjacent Room 8, narrower than the tax collector's office, must have been the archival storeroom proper (figure 10). Around three of its sides, it was equipped with clay benches, from 0.30 to 0.40 meters in height and from 0.45 to 0.75 meters wide at the top. About 150 tablets and fragments of others were found lying in groups on these benches. Considerably more were found in groups on the floor. Different storage systems appear to have been used, for some of the tablets must have been tied in bundles with string or ribbon[71]— presumably a case of horizontal filing. Others were kept in wicker baskets. Hinge-like pieces of bronze indicate wooden boxes may also have been used.

The temple archives were no less important than the state or palace archives. Because the temples were major centers of economic activity, they had to use an elaborate system of record-making and bookkeeping if they were to function effectively; hence they produced voluminous records. From the considerable literature on the subject, Edward Chiera's description of the procedures of the counting-room of one of the large temples of ancient Babylonia may be selected as especially graphic:

The men who brought their offerings were given a receipt, and merely a memorandum of the affair was written down by the temple scribe and placed in a basket. At the end of the week these memos were taken out, the various offerings noted on them classified, and a ledger tablet made to incorporate the totals. At the end of the month, the weekly reports, in turn, were incorporated in a monthly report, and at the end of the fiscal year ledgers were written which summarized the total obtained from the monthly reports.[72]

This was done on a large tablet with many columns of writing. The tablets were ultimately removed to the archives and stored

71. *Ibid.*, p. 97.
72. Edward Chiera, *They Wrote on Clay*, ed. George C. Cameron (Chicago, 1956), pp. 85–87.

Figure 10. General view of the Pylos site. In the foreground, the tax collector's office (Room 7) and next to it the archives room with its clay benches (Room 8).

there.[73] Equally careful records were prepared for expenditures. For example, even in a relatively small organization like the temple's mill in Sagdana near Telloh, daily loan records were kept, noting with painstaking exactitude the name of the worker, the type of his work, and his output. In addition to full-time personnel, there were some half-time laborers on the payroll. A few women and children were also employed.[74]

Archival repositories of a good many temples have been discovered.[75] Clay tablets of Uruk go back to the period from 2600 to 2400 B.C., but also include economic material of the Neo-Babylonian and Persian periods. A few other important accumulations of temple records might be mentioned. As we have seen, the temple of Ur had an advanced organization for the control of its business records;[76] Sippar (early second millennium), the home of the sun god Šamaš, produced, in addition to about 60,000 items of its temple archives, a collection of teaching material of the temple school; in Nuzi, a center of the Hurrians, the temple's records were kept next to the cella in a room that could be entered by means of a ladder only; and in Assyria the archives rooms of the contemporary temples at Khorsabad and Nimrud, dedicated to Nabu, the patron saint of scribes, show "a similar relationship to official and religious apartments across the court."[77]

As one might expect, throughout the archives of private individuals and families, business records prevail. Among the earliest business archives are those of Assyrian businessmen trading in Kaniš in faraway Cappadocia. Having organized them-

73. For further information on the subject of bookkeeping, see also Tom B. Jones, "Bookkeeping in Ancient Sumer," *Archaeology*, IX (1956), 16–21, with seven figures, reprinted in his *Paths to the Ancient Past* (New York, 1967), pp. 136–147; and Anton Deimel, S.J., *Sumerische Tempelwirtschaft zur Zeit Urukaginas und seiner Vorgänger* (Rome, 1931).

74. Nikolaus Schneider, "Die Lohnbücher der Mühle von Sagdana," *Archiv für Orientforschung*, III (1926), 121.

75. For the following see the listing of temple archives in Weitemeyer, *Arkiver*, p. 88, and the respective comments in Schawe, "Der alte Vorderorient," Kampman, *Archieven en biblioteken*, and Weitemeyer, *Arkiver*.

76. See p. 14 above.

77. See p. 42 above.

selves as a community or chamber of commerce called *kārum*,[78] the merchants apparently decided to establish a joint repository for the records of the *kārum* members.[79] Not all of them, however, made use of this facility, for one is almost tempted to say that an archives room was "standard equipment" of a merchant's house. Houses of Level II of the Kaniš site, a level representing the period when Kaniš was a fully developed trading center, show the following typical layout: one part of the house was used as office space, a second provided the living quarters, and a third served as archives and storeroom.[80] Archives rooms were sometimes located in a corner of the house, separated from the living quarters like an office so that business could be conducted there in private. Of the 105 houses brought to light in Level II 70 had archives rooms, and scattered tablets were discovered in the other 35.[81] Pots, boxes, and shelves were used for storing records, and some records were found in the fireplaces where they had been placed to be baked; evidently there had not been time to remove them when a fire destroyed Level II. In fact, the conflagration occurred so suddenly that the traders were unable to open their "incoming mail," some of which was found in unopened envelopes.

The excavations in Nuzi (now Yorghan Tepe), a provincial center of the Hurrians in Assyria, have produced records that illustrate economic activities of the palace, of the temple, and of private citizens.[82] Those of the palace stem from the early Akkad period; that is, the last quarter of the third millennium.

---

78. The word, originally meaning harbor, later assumed the meaning of colony. On the *kārum* see Paul Garelli, *Les Assyriens en Cappadoce* (Paris, 1963), pp. 174–175, 204–205.

79. Kampman, *Archiven en biblioteken*, p. 37; Schawe, "Der alte Vorderorient," pp. 36–37; Papritz, "Archive in Altmesopotamien," p. 36. Of a similar nature was an establishment at Dēr (Sippar-Iahrurum), where Sir E. A. Wallis Budge discovered the combined archives of various families of merchants, consisting of vats, each of which contained the archives of one family. See Weitemeyer, *Arkiver*, p. 39, and the sources referred to there.

80. For the following, see Garelli, *Les Assyriens*, p. 22, and TahsinÖzgüç, "The Art and Architecture of Ancient Kanish," *Anatolia*, VIII (1964), 27–48.

81. Özgüç, "Ancient Kanish," p. 34.

82. Chiera, *They Wrote on Clay*, pp. 176–191; Weitemeyer, *Arkiver*, pp. 22–24.

Those of the temple and of the private citizens fall into the second half of the second millennium. The private archives discovered are among the most interesting of the kind because of their origin and their contents.[83] They belonged to a group of well-to-do individuals who, outside the city proper, lived in pretentious homes that reflect the living standards of an Assyrian suburbia. Outstanding among the archives are those of the three generations of the Tehiptilla family, almost a thousand tablets found in a former well-equipped bathroom that had been converted to use as an archives room.[84] The records document the clever but perfectly legal means by which the well-to-do succeeded in depriving the little fellows of their property.[85]

In the same community, Šilwi-Tešub, son of the king, had his lavish home, surpassed in size only by the palace itself. "Its stores of inscribed tablets show its owner to have been a man whose wide commercial and public interests were in keeping with his high rank."[86] Copper nails found among the records indicate that the prince used wooden boxes as containers, while his neighbor Zigi may have stored his tablets in the large jars that were set in niches in the wall. These jars were empty but a large collection of tablets was found on the floor.

The sharp business practices of ancient Near East merchants are also illustrated by the records of a family group centering around a certain Ninurta-Uballit of the last quarter of the seventh century.[87] Besides lending money and deftly handling real estate, the group specialized in buying small children from families in distress and selling them at a profit, a business that flourished at the time when Nippur was being beleaguered

83. R. F. S. Starr, *Nuzi*, I (Cambridge, Mass., 1939), 333–347.

84. *Ibid.*, pp. 333–334.

85. Chiera, *They Wrote on Clay*, pp. 176–186. By analyzing the archives of a Babylonian family, Tom B. Jones, *Paths to the Ancient Past* (New York, 1967), pp. 148–164, has neatly shown how a farmer's family in the Babylonian town of Dilbat (Dēlem) succeeded in building up its real estate holdings.

86. Starr, *Nuzi*, I, 337.

87. A. Leo Oppenheim, "'Siege-documents' from Nippur," *Iraq*, XVII (1955), 69–89.

by Nabopolassar. When the siege had to be lifted, the dealers hid their archives in the rear of Ninurta-Uballit's property, apparently afraid of being killed or run out of town by the enraged citizens. Reluctance to have his dealings exposed after his death may have contributed to one businessman's wish to have his records buried with him.[88]

Outstanding among the later business archives are those of the Egibi and Murašû families of Babylon. Those of the Egibi family (690–480 B.C.) document the business activities of six generations of a family[89] that, from humble beginnings, reached its greatest prosperity under Itti-Marduk-balatu (ca. 575–520 B.C.). Dealing in real estate and slaves and also engaging in banking operations, the Egibis, capitalists and businessmen, amassed a considerable fortune so that Itti-Marduk-balatu's sons inherited thirteen houses, three building lots, more than a hundred slaves, and numerous fields and cattle.

The archives of the Murašû firm at Nippur,[90] consisting of 730 baked tablets and dating from 455 to 403 B.C., were discovered in 1893. With its sixty-odd agents, the firm concentrated on managing the fiefs of the Persian landlords who did not want to administer them themselves. The Murašûs thus served as "intermediaries between the owners of the estates and the cultivators, that is, between the capitalists and the producers."[91]

3. Archival Techniques

If then on all levels and in all spheres of human activity the care and preservation of records played a significant role, need as well as experience was bound to result in providing appropriate storage facilities for records and developing techniques suitable to their administration. To understand them, the

88. Stephen Langdon, *Ausgrabungen in Babylon seit 1918* (Leipzig, 1928), p. 52.

89. Raymond D. Bogaert, *Les origines de la banque de dépôt* (Leiden, 1966), pp. 105–118.

90. Guillaume Cardascia, *Les archives des Murašû: Une famille d'hommes d'affaires babyloniens à l'époque perse (455–403 av. J.C.)* (Paris, 1951); Bogaert, *Les origines*, pp. 118–121.

91. Bogaert, *Les origines*, p. 119.

physical makeup and other characteristics of these records must be explained briefly. Though we know of the use of wooden and ivory writing-boards, examples of which have been unearthed recently, clay tablets constituted the usual writing material. Clay was available in abundance. To make it malleable enough to receive impressions, scribes had to have a source of water at hand, and so in Nimrud, for instance, in Tablet Room NT 12, there was a deep well of small diameter, intended for the use of the scribes who prepared the tablet clay.[92] Even if only sun-dried, tablets had a certain durability, while baked tablets were practically as indestructible as stone. More often than not, this baking process was later supplied by fire at the time when the storage accommodations were destroyed.

We are not in a position to state what types of tablets were considered worthy or in need of being baked for better preservation. In fact, the process as such is not mentioned in any of the documents we have. It has now become of particular interest because in Court V of the Palace of Ugarit in Syria Schaeffer and his collaborators found the remains of an oven for the firing of clay tablets.[93] Individuals might also decide to bake tablets for better preservation, using their fireplaces for the purpose, as did some of the Assyrian merchants in Kaniš in Anatolia.[94]

The format of the tablets varied greatly from about 1 × 1 to 30 × 40 centimeters. At first tablets were usually square with

92. Mallowan, *Nimrud*, I, 271.

93. See p. 34 above.

94. On the posthumous baking of tablets, see André Parrot, *Archéologie Mésopotamienne*, II (Paris, 1953), 72–73, 88. R. M. Organ, "The Conservation of Cuneiform Tablets," *British Museum Quarterly*, XXIII (1961), 52–58, deals with the entire preservation process. In an article in Russian on the making of the Babylonian cuneiform tablets, *Vestnik Drevney Istorii*, no. 1 (1956), 134–142, N. N. Semenovič reports on his experimental reconstruction of the tablet-making process. Verner W. Clapp has kindly called my attention to the following pertinent story in Sir Austin Henry Layard, *Discoveries Among the Ruins of Nineveh and Babylon* (New York, 1856), p. 298: "According to a tradition, Seth wrote the history and wisdom of the ages preceding the Deluge on burnt and unburnt bricks, or tablets, that they might never perish; for if water destroyed the unburnt, the burnt would remain; and if fire destroyed the baked tablets, those which had not been exposed to heat would only become hardened."

rounded corners. As time went on, there developed a practice of making the front of the tablet flat and the back convex, either to provide for circulation of heat during the baking process, or "in order to store the tablets conveniently on wooden shelves in the archives, so that every one of them could be taken out without special effort."[95] Also, the edges of the tablets were made wider, which made it possible to write on them and use them for purposes of "docketing."[96]

Needless to say, the tablets could be written on only as long as the clay was still moist and susceptible to receiving impressions. This was a drawback, for it was impossible to use the same tablet over a period of time to make entries as the needs of business required. In bookkeeping operations, for instance, it called for the preparation of summary records, as has been shown above.[97] Writing was done with a wedge-shaped stylus that the scribe wore in a leather container attached to his belt. The nature of the tablet material, which made it difficult to produce curved lines, necessitated the transformation of the original pictorial signs into cuneiform characters, which, in turn, was part of the general process of transforming pictorial signs into characters representing syllables. This cuneiform system of writing, one of the greatest inventions in the history of mankind, was taken over by the Semitic tribes of Mesopotamia. From there it made its way into many other countries of the Near East.

Although the impressions on a clay tablet would normally be safe from tampering, it seemed important, particularly in the case of business documents, to provide for additional protection of the text. This was done by inclosing the tablet in a clay envelope (figure 11) on which the text of the transaction was entered again in identical terms.[98] The technique is referred to

95. Kurt Bittel and Rudolf Naumann, *Boğazköy-Ḫattusa* (Stuttgart, 1952), p. 55.

96. Sir Arthur Evans, *Palace of Minos*, IV, pt. 2 (London, 1935), 696.

97. Jones, "Bookkeeping in Ancient Sumer," 21, reports "that blank tablets were made in molds in advance of the day's business and that there were standard sizes for the different types of records."

98. See the excellent explanation of the process in Chiera's *They Wrote on Clay*, pp. 69–73.

Figure 11. A clay tablet in its envelope, found at Alishar Huyuk, Turkey.

in Jeremiah 32, where, in the presence of witnesses, Jeremiah gives the purchase document to Baruch, asking that "he take these evidences, this evidence of the purchase, both that which is sealed, and this evidence which is open; and put it in an earthen vessel, that it may continue many days."

The record material the clay tablet archivist had to deal with, had peculiarities that were bound to affect its handling: it was durable, but it was heavy and bulky. If these characteristics are borne in mind, it will be found that our early predecessors coped rather effectively with the problems of physical preservation. They understood, in the first place, that separate accommodations had to be provided for the storage of their records, for practically everywhere excavators found the clay tablets heavily concentrated in one or more rooms. Unfortunately the excavators could not always state with certainty whether they had discovered true archival installations or mere dumps, because the buildings had been destroyed by fire or enemy action. In a good many instances, nevertheless, the problem of providing storage facilities was thoughtfully approached and successfully solved. This could be achieved by adapting an existing structure to archival use, as was done in Ur, where kings of the Larsa dynasty converted the "Great Gate" into the "House of Tablets."[99] Generally speaking, there seems to have been a tendency to locate the archives rooms near or in the gates, which were centers of economic activities of all kinds.[100] A number of separate installations were provided for the Mari and Ugarit archives, obviously with a view to administrative needs and convenience and possibly in accordance with a preconceived plan.

The layout of an archival installation can best be studied in Lagaš (formerly identified with modern Telloh).[101] Here French excavators discovered the archives in "two distinct

99. Woolley, *Excavations at Ur*, pp. 142–144.

100. Weitemeyer, *Arkiver*, p. 62.

101. According to Thorkild Jacobsen, *Orientalia*, XXIII (1954), 450, and Albrecht Goetze, *Sumer*, XI (1955), 127, Telloh is to be identified with the city of Girsu and not with Lagaš.

groups of narrow galleries," designed "to furnish, within the smallest possible compass," a maximum of storage space, as shown in figures 12 and 13.[102] They were equipped with clay benches along the walls. Since the excavations were not carried through to completion, we do not know whether the two structures were interconnected,[103] nor can we tell whether they were above ground or in cellars under a building or courtyard. Weitemeyer is inclined to think that they were independent buildings situated around a courtyard.[104] At any rate, they had no doors and therefore must have been entered from above. This seems to have been a protective arrangement frequently used. It is also found in Nuzi, to mention one of the smaller installations, where the records were housed in a separate room adjacent to the temple cella. Similarly, in the consolidated business archives of Dēr (now Sippar-Iahrurum), the jars containing the clay tablets were stored in a separate room that had been partitioned off in a corner of a larger one and was accessible only from the roof of the building.[105]

Clay tablet archivists must have been well aware that tablets not hardened by baking were likely to crumble in the hot Mesopotamian climate unless stored in rooms with the proper humidity; and so, to provide the desirable atmospheric conditions, the custodians in charge of the archives of the Eanna temple in Uruk had their storage area equipped with a grooved floor. It consisted of a system of very low brick walls, running parallel to each other, so that in the furrows between them water could flow and evaporate. The archives building, erected in the Neo-Babylonian era and rebuilt under the Achaemenids, yielded economic records of the period from Sargon II of Assyria to Darius II of Persia. It is possible, therefore, that this "air con-

102. They are described by Léon Heuzey in Léon Heuzey, ed., *Découvertes en Chaldée par Erneste de Sarzec*, I (Paris, 1884), 437–438, and also by Kampman, *Archieven en biblioteken*, pp. 29–31, Schawe, "Der alte Vorderorient," pp. 26–27, and Weitemeyer, *Arkiver*, pp. 25–27, and "Technique," p. 220.

103. Heuzey, ed., *Découvertes*, I, 439.

104. Weitemeyer, *Arkiver*, p. 62.

105. See n. 79 above.

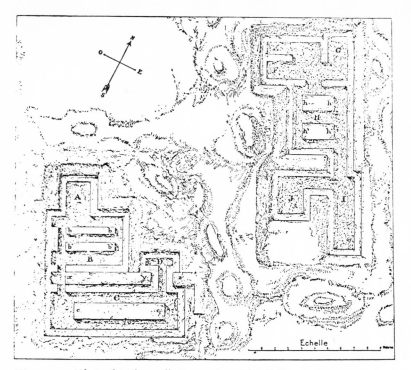

Figure 12. *The archival installations at Lagaš (Telloh).*
Figure 13. *General view of the excavations at Lagaš (Telloh).*

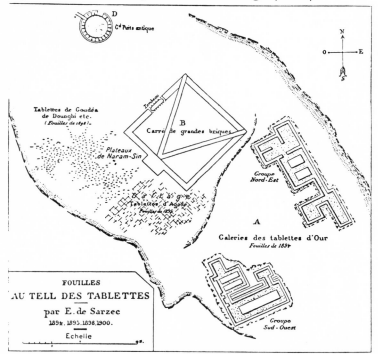

ditioning equipment" stems from the Persian period and hence represents a late development.[106] Before that time other devices may have been used to keep archives rooms properly humidified.

Though our information about archival structures and vaults of this period is certainly not plentiful, we have more satisfactory data on storage equipment and storage methods. If we may use modern terminology, it appears that three systems were available to the clay tablet archivist, all of them familiar to us. They were the pigeonhole system, the open-shelf system, and the container system, and they will be discussed here in that order.

We know of one case only where the pigeonhole system was used. In Room 5 of the Nabu temple in Khorsabad a group of niches arranged in three horizontal tiers was discovered. "The individual niches are 0.25–0.30m. square and 0.40–0.50m. deep, separated from one another by 10-cm. partitions." The fact that a few fragments of inscribed prisms and tablets were found within the niches tends to show that they were used for the storage of documentary material.[107] Related to the pigeonhole arrangement was the system used for intermediary storage in Room 4 of the administrative wing of the Nimrud Palace, where the chancery concerned with the imperial administration of Assyria was housed.

The open-shelf system enjoyed much greater popularity among the archivists of the period. It could be installed simply by providing brick or clay banquettes (figure 14), normally 50 centimeters high and 50 centimeters wide, possibly covering them with asphalt for greater protection, and arranging the tablets on them standing "on their edges, reclining against each other like a shelf of leaning books in an ill-kept library of

106. Heinrich Lenzen, *Vorläufiger Bericht über die . . . Ausgrabungen in Uruk-Warka, 1953–1955* (Berlin, 1956), p. 18; R. North, "Status of the Warka Excavation," *Orientalia*, XXVI (1957), 225.

107. Gordon Loud and Charles B. Altman, *Khorsabad*, pt. 2, *The Citadel and the Town* (Chicago, 1938), p. 46. The niche arrangement is shown there on plate 9C, also in Weitemeyer, *Arkiver*, fig. 13, and "Technique," fig. 5.

Figure 14. A typical archives room: the archives room of Shemshara.

today."[108] As an alternative, if the archivist was addicted to "horizontal filing," he could store his tablets in that fashion, tying them up in bundles; this system, needless to say, was possible only if the tablets were flat on both sides. Thus in Ugarit, where the excavators found a body of archives in "good order," tablets were discovered in piles or packages of sometimes more than ten.[109] The same system seems to have been in use in Pylos in Greece.

More frequently, archives rooms were equipped with wooden shelving as it is known to us, erected either on the floor or on the clay banquettes. While this shelving has not survived the vicissitudes of time, it must have existed, for wood ashes have been discovered in various archives rooms of the area.

The container system, finally, seems to have been the preferred system of storage, probably because it solved best the different problems of arrangement, control, and protection of the records. Baskets, jars, and boxes were used as containers. Baskets must have been relatively unsatisfactory; they afforded no real protection from unauthorized handling. They were used, however, possibly coated with bitumen. About 40 to 50 centimeters in height and width, they fitted the clay benches that seem to have been standard equipment of archival depositories.[110]

Boxes were made of wood or clay. Wood seems to have been popular with, and easily available to, the archivists of Knossos on Crete and of Pylos,[111] for bronze hinges and handles found there must have been used on these boxes. Wood probably seemed ideal from the standpoint of physical preservation, because in such receptacles the clay tablets could not rub

108. Albert T. Clay, ed., *Documents from the Temple Archives of Nippur* (Philadelphia, 1906), p. 1, quoting from the report of John H. Haynes, Director of the Third Expedition, 1893–1894. On Nippur, see the recent publication by Donald E. McCown and others, *Nippur.* I. *Temple of Enlil, Scribal Quarter and Surroundings* (Chicago, 1967).

109. Schawe, "Der alte Vorderorient," p. 44.

110. Weitemeyer, "Technique," p. 222.

111. Evans, *Palace of Minos*, IV, pt. 2, pp. 668, 694–695; Blegen and Rawson, *Palace of Nestor*, p. 99. Copper nails found in Nuzi also indicate the use of wooden boxes. See Weitemeyer, *Arkiver*, p. 24.

against material of the same kind, to the possible detriment of the writing on them. Furthermore, the boxes could easily be "labelled with ink-written inscriptions," as Sir Arthur Evans has pointed out.[112] For the most part, however, storage boxes were made of clay, and many of them have been excavated. Those found in Ur were exclusively made and used for archival purposes,[113] each of them bearing a clay label that indicated its contents. A box of the square type is shown in Weitemeyer's *Babylonske og Assyriske Arkiver og Biblioteker*.[114] It has a lid that can be lifted by a handle.

Equally widespread was the use of jars or vats for archival storage. In Kish, for instance, tablets were invariably "mixed up with fragments of large coarse jars," and whenever the excavators "came upon clusters of these thick sherds imbedded in the terribly adhesive clay, it was a certain sign that tablets would be found immediately. These broken jars were arranged about the sides of the rooms and contained the tablets."[115] Jars were also used in Mari, as well as baskets, and in the combined business archives of Sippar-Iahrurum, where a separate container was provided for the documents of each of the customers.

Still another and apparently unusual method of storage should be mentioned. In Nimrud late Assyrian tablets were found that had been provided with holes. Since remnants of string were still in the holes, it appears that these tablets were suspended on poles—an unusual case of vertical filing.[116]

Considering the magnitude of a good many installations, serious thought had to be given to ways and means of controlling the holdings and finding individual records. This must have been a relatively simple matter where the edges of the tablets

---

112. Evans, *Palace of Minos*, IV, pt. 2, p. 695.

113. Schneider, "Die Urkundenbehälter von Ur III," p. 15.

114. Figure 10.

115. Stephen Langdon, *Excavations at Kish*, I (1923–1924), 90; Schawe, "Der alte Vorderorient," pp. 31–32.

116. Barbara Parker, "Nimrud Tablets, 1956—Economic and Legal Texts from the Nabu Temple," *Iraq*, XIX (1957), 125.

were wide enough to receive a summary of the document, a sign that probably the documents had been packed together like books on a shelf.[117] Where documents not thus "docketed" were stored on open shelves, as in Bogazkeui, labels in the form of tablets, 6–7 centimeters long and 4–5 centimeters wide, could be placed in front of the aggregates of records they were to identify.[118] For the various kinds of container storage, too, clay labels served as guideposts. In Pylos these were made from "thinnish lumps of clay which, in most instances, were pressed deeply into the wicker fabric of the container, smoothed on top, and then inscribed."[119] Thanks to Schneider[120] we are particularly well informed about the labeling of the archives baskets and boxes of the Ur III period of Sumer. Labels consisted of three elements: (1) an identification of the receptacle as a document container, to distinguish it from other boxes; (2) an indication of the type of document found in the respective container or group of containers, together with information on the official responsible for the creation of the records; and (3) the inclusive dates. To illustrate the system, Schneider gives several examples taken from the class of court decisions, two of which may be quoted here:

1) pisan dub-ba . . . document container, court decision[s] [President was] Ur-ᵈkal, Prefect of the City, year Š 44.

6) pisan dub-ba . . . document container, court decisions are found herein, [President] Arad-ᵈNannar, Sukkal-maḫ and City Prefect, Commissioner Šu-ì-lí, Judges Lú-dingir-ra and Lu-ᵈNimgír-zu. Year ŠS 8.[121]

Normally each box contains the production of one year, in which case the label may explicitly state: "From the first to the twelfth month, 12 months." Where the documents of a longer period are housed in one container, this is indicated in a very

117. Evans, *Palace of Minos*, IV, pt. 2, p. 696.
118. Bittel and Naumann, *Boğazköy-Ḫattusa*, p. 56.
119. Emmett L. Bennett, Jr., ed., *The Pylos Tablets* (Princeton, 1955), p. ix; Blegen and Rawson, *Palace of Nestor*, pp. 97–98.
120. Schneider, "Die Urkundenbehälter von Ur III," pp. 1–16.
121. *Ibid.*, p. 5.

precise fashion thus: "From the first month of the year ŠS 5 to the eleventh month [and] the 26th day of the year ŠS 9, that is 59 months and 26 days including one intercalary month." Schneider aptly concludes that even "nowadays there cannot be a librarian or archivist who classifies and organizes his manuscripts and records with more painstaking accuracy and with the help of a more suitable system than was used in the realm of Sumer and Akkad at the time of the third dynasty of Ur."[122]

Scribes may have been instructed to facilitate the work of the archivists by preclassifying the records they prepared—that is, indicating in some prominent place on the tablet the subject class to which it was to be assigned. According to Anton Deimel, "one must watch for the main word of the signature because it indicates the type of the text."[123] It may, for instance, refer to a list of sacrifices, to the digging of canals or ditches, to the surveying of fields, to payrolls, and so on.

Where the "series"—Schneider enumerates some twenty of them—were so carefully identified, the archivist could probably service his records without the help of a checklist or inventory. As a matter of fact, the rare lists and other finding aids that have been preserved were designed to give access to "library material," that is, to individual items that were more difficult to control than accumulations of records, arranged in series or otherwise coherent sequences. To the best of my knowledge, we have only one primitive example of a checklist of archival tablets. It was found in Nuzi and simply gives for each tablet the name of the person or persons to which it refers.[124]

Efforts to provide an easily workable arrangement can be detected; and once again Ugarit, where the *classement* in general has not been disturbed, furnishes us with pertinent information. In the first place, the total accumulation has been broken up into major groups possibly reflecting the

122. *Ibid.*, p. 2.

123. Deimel, *Sumerische Tempelwirtschaft*, p. 79.

124. Weitemeyer, *Arkiver*, p. 23. For the library technique of cataloguing as applied to nonarchival material, see *ibid.*, pp. 74–76, and Weitemeyer's "Technique," p. 223.

administrative origin of the records. Within one of these groups
—the diplomatic or international archives—Jean Nougayrol
has demonstrated the "close coherence" of certain aggregates
by reconstituting "a relatively large number of political or
politico-economic 'dossiers,' such as the 'dossier' Suppiluliuma,
the 'dossier' Mursil II, the 'dossier' concerning the intrigues of
the daughters of Amurru around Ammistamru II, the 'dossier'
Initešub (King of Carkemis), etc.," [125] the first of which, for
instance, consists of eight documents. A comprehensive plan
of a similar kind has become apparent in Mari. Even where we
have not yet succeeded completely in deciphering the materials
discovered, as with the Knossos and Pylos tablets, the "picto-
graphic designs on their margins" and the "special formulas"
that accompany them show that they had a careful arrangement.[126]

Thanks to a lucky find, we can in at least one case observe
an early archivist in the process of arranging, or rather rearrang-
ing, and describing a small record group, one that, although
"noncurrent," must have been deemed of enduring value. In the
thirty-second year of his reign, Hammurapi of Babylonia
conquered the city of Mari. The city's last Assyrian king,
Šamši-Adad, had been succeeded by Zimrilim, whose rule, in
turn, was overthrown by Hammurapi when he conquered the
city. At that time, the most important series, those in Rooms
108 and 115, were reclassified by basket (*par panier*) by the
Babylonians.[127] We have a few basket labels with holes,
designed to be attached to the containers, which identify them
as basket "with letters of the servants of Šamši-Adad" and
baskets "with letters of the servants of Zimri-lim" and which,
on the back, give the dates according to years of Hammurapi.
It is the earliest example of a conqueror taking over and having

125. Nougayrol, "Les archives internationales d'Ugarit," p. 33.
126. Evans, *Palace of Minos*, IV, pt. 2, p. 694.
127. Schawe, "Der alte Vorderorient," pp. 35–36, and Weitemeyer, "Technique,"
p. 223, on the basis of F. Thureau-Dangin, "Sur des etiquettes de paniers à tablettes
provenant de Mari," in *Symbolae . . . Paulo Koschaker dedicatae* (Leiden, 1939), pp.
119–120. See also Wendel, *Die griechisch-römische Buchbeschreibung*, p. 103.

arranged for his use the records of a former enemy regime, and it testifies to the "record-mindedness" of the great Hammurapi as well as to the skill of his archivists.

That the latter as well as their rulers realized how important records are to administration, seems confirmed indirectly by the fact that few of them were found in Dur-Šarrukin (Khorsabad), seat of Sargon II (721–705 B.C.), who had wanted to shift the Assyrian capital from Nineveh to a city of his own. Since the quantity of records created during Sargon's regime must have been rather large, we are forced to assume that, upon his death, most of them were returned to Nineveh to serve the administrative needs of his successors.[128]

4. The Role of Archives

How much did the rulers value their archives, what measures did they take to protect them, and to what possible use did they put them? The isolated data we have do not enable us to answer these questions satisfactorily. Adopting the unfortunate distinction between administrative and historical archives, Goossens has stated that, "in Babylonia, in Assyria, in Anatolia, in Phoenicia, in Persia the administrative archives were well kept; the historical archives were ignored."[129] It may be rash thus to generalize on the basis of findings that are far from complete and conclusive, for there is no way of telling what archives are still hidden in the tells of Mesopotamia. Also it can be argued that the creators of records and their archivists showed themselves well aware of the value of their records, that they tried to protect them, that they realized their intelligence potential, and that they used them for historical narratives.

In quite a few instances excavators found archival materials not in the rooms equipped for their storage but scattered throughout the building; this may have been the result of hasty attempts to salvage them in the event of disaster or emergency. The excavations at Alalakh have furnished us with a

128. Loud and Altman, *Khorsabad*, p. 9.
129. Goossens, "Introduction," p. 100.

telling example. There, in the archives room, "the shelves had been swept bare"[130] when the Level IV Palace was burned, while almost 250 tablets were found in the nearby rooms and in the outer courtyard "as if dropped during a hurried evacuation."[131]

Not only the owner of the archives but also the conqueror of a city might show through measures he took that he considered the archives of the enemy a valuable part of the booty. We have referred already to the inventorying of the records of preceding regimes that Hammurapi had done by his archivists after he had taken Mari. Probably the earliest example of the seizure and identification of enemy records, it must have been intended to obtain information about Mari's dealings with the Hittites and with Egypt. Intelligence motives rather than historical interest were responsible for this exploitation of captured records.

There are, however, cases in which bona fide research use of older records must be assumed. Summaries of events in building inscriptions "show that they are but abstracts made for a specific purpose from longer written records."[132] An Assyrian ruler of the thirteenth century, for instance, was able to give some of the essential dates, undoubtedly on the basis of archival records, concerning the history of a temple at Assur that had been built some 580 years before.[133] That archivists were called upon to furnish information for commemorative inscriptions we can also gather from the story of the restoration of a boundary ditch between two cities. It gave an archivist of Entemena of the Lagaš dynasty in lower Mesopotamia an opportunity to discuss the background of the boundary conflict, using for the purpose records in his custody that reached back to the days of Mesilim, the suzerain of Sumer and Akkad about

130. Sir Charles L. Woolley, "Excavations at Atchana-Alalakh, 1938," *Antiquaries Journal*, XIX (1939), 8.

131. D. J. Wiseman, *The Alalakh Tablets* (London, 1953), p. 1.

132. D. J. Wiseman, *The Expansion of Assyrian Studies* (London, 1962), p. 20.

133. E. A. Speiser, "Ancient Mesopotamia," in Robert C. Dentan, ed., *The Idea of History in the Ancient Near East* (New Haven, 1955), p. 46.

2600 B.C.[134] Use of archival sources may have been a practice in Lagaš, for one of Entemena's successors had his archivists do background research which he used in an inscription glorifying the dedication of a new canal.[135] It showed good historical sense on the part of a ruler when Nabonidus (555–539 B.C.), the last king of the Neo-Babylonian dynasty, established a veritable museum of inscriptions and antiquities at Ur.[136]

Nothing, however, proves more strikingly that rulers could appreciate the role of the record as historical evidence than the story of the text of a clay cylinder, an "improved" version of which was substituted for the original, considered detrimental to the fame of Sargon II (figure 15). This cylinder, found in the chancery of the Northwest Palace of Nimrud, was that of:

Marduk-apal-iddina II, Merodach-Baladan of the Old Testament, a dissident Chaldaean Chieftain who had collided with three kings of Assyria and for a time usurped the throne of Babylon. The cylinder made an exultant reference to a victory over Sargon in 720 B.C. and to the consequent termination of Assyrian rule over Babylon. Sargon, however, had had the last word; not content with driving this dangerous enemy into the marshes and, as we have seen, rebuilding Babylon, he abstracted this unfriendly account from its place in a temple within the distant city of Erech and substituted a new and "improved" version in its stead. The execution of this counter-propaganda must have been entrusted to the scribes of Calah who, after they had completed this work, retained the adverse record in the city's archives, and unwittingly thereby evinced a true sense of history.[137]

134. Samuel Noah Kramer, *History Begins at Sumer* (Garden City, N.Y., 1959), p. 38; his "Sumerian Historiography," *Israel Exploration Journal* (1953), 220, 227; and his "Vox Populi and the Sumerian Literary Documents," *Revue d'Assyriologie*, LVIII (1964), 150. See also Oppenheim, *Letters from Mesopotamia*, p. 25.

135. Kramer, *History Begins*, p. 45. On the care with which rulers of Elam of the twelfth century B.C. preserved the brick inscriptions of their predecessors when restoring a temple, see Walther Hinz, *Das Reich Elam* (Stuttgart, 1964), pp. 106–107. One of them used the inscriptions to compile a list of the rulers of Elam and had it incised on a stele. Hinz refers to him as "the crowned archivist and historian."

136. Jørgen Læssøe, *People of Ancient Assyria: Their Inscriptions and Correspondence* (New York, 1963), p. 161.

137. Mallowan, *Nimrud*, II, 605. For details, see C. J. Gadd, "Inscribed Barrel Cylinder of Marduk-apla-iddina II," *Iraq*, XV (1953), 123–134.

Figure 15. Clay cylinder (with the victory message of Marduk-apal-iddina II) which Sargon II seized at Erech and for which he substituted an "improved" version.

Where business considerations had an influence on the mind of the record creator, he could be expected to provide for the long-term preservation of his documents. In an oblique sense, such consideration would prompt the temple priests to build and keep collections of omen tablets, just as the priests of the Apollo temple at Delphi later maintained their oracle archives.[138] Businessmen would naturally see to it that their records were kept for future use, and they did so quite effectively. The records of the Egibi banking family in Babylon, to give but one example, document the activities of six generations of that family from 690 to 480 B.C.

Having become accustomed to the bureaucratic way of life, the Mesopotamians naturally took it for granted that it also prevailed in the precincts of heaven and that, accordingly, the rule of the gods was based on creating and keeping the records

138. See Chapter 3.

that manifested their guidance. And these records were, indeed, of the highest importance, because they were the tables of destiny on which, each year, the fate of all mankind was laid down. Originally kept by the great god Enlil, the master of the lands and the winds, the tablets appear to have fallen into the hands of the evil deity Tiamat. They were wrested from her by Marduk, and it was he who from then on, on New Year's Day, entered on the tablets what was to happen on earth and in heaven. In doing so, he was assisted by his son Nabu, who, acting as his clerk with the stylus as his symbol, became the divine protector of the scribal profession.[139] In his temple, the Ezida, scribes deposited "as votive offerings, beautifully written tablets."[140] Record-keeping was practiced also in the nether world, for according to certain texts the ruler of the dead had the services of a scribe who kept the lists of those destined to die each day.[141]

Our discussion of the earliest period of archival work would certainly be incomplete without a word on the men who so wisely cared for what frequently were record accumulations of considerable size. It stands to reason that a man, before he could become useful as an archivist, had to master fully the difficult art of writing. It was taught in regular schools, mostly attached to the temples, and since it was said of well-trained scribes that they would shine brightly like the sun, many must have been anxious to obtain the training necessary for positions of such glory.

Scribes came from the upper strata of Mesopotamian society. Their fathers were "governors, 'city fathers,' ambassadors, temple administrators, military officers, sea captains, high tax officials, priests of various sorts, managers, supervisors, foremen, scribes, archivists and accountants."[142] Scribes were highly regarded, and to be an "egghead" was considered

139. Meissner, *Babylonien*, II, 125; Oppenheim, *Ancient Mesopotamia*, pp. 195, 197.
140. Oppenheim, *Ancient Mesopotamia*, p. 242.
141. *Ibid.*, p. 231.
142. Kramer, *History Begins*, p. 3.

respectable.[143] They played an overwhelmingly important role in the creation and transmission of Mesopotamian culture:

> What, then, . . . was the driving force that brought into existence and preserved the artistic and intellectual coherence that held Mesopotamia together, gave it its existential individuality, maintained and revitalized again and again the vast body of traditions and attitudes that constituted the backbone of this civilization? My answer is: the scribe—the scribe who wrote and copied signs on soft clay, the scribe who left us all these records through which we are able to follow, however inadequately, this millennial development.[144]

The preparation of legal and administrative documents naturally had its place in the rigorous training that future scribes underwent in the school called the tablet-house. An examination text includes as number 11 of sixteen questions the question: "How to draw, cover, and seal a document."[145]

While much has been written about the training of the Mesopotamian scribe, his later career in the service of the palace and the temple has been little explored. Benno Landsberger has guessed "that perhaps seventy percent of the scribes had administrative positions, twenty percent were privately employed, and the remainder became specialists in the diagnosis of illness, charms, magic, and other activities calling for some knowledge of writing."[146] The scribe's role has been compared to that of the clergy in medieval Europe, and his influence on the management of public affairs was certainly very great, for it was he who read the incoming mail to the king and prepared the replies.[147]

Inasmuch as it is known that the work of the scribe called

143. E. A. Speiser in the discussion of Benno Landsberger, "Scribal Concepts of Education," in Carl H. Kraeling and Robert M. Adams, eds., *City Invincible* (Chicago, 1960), p. 107.

144. Oppenheim, *Letters from Mesopotamia*, p. 8.

145. Kraeling and Adams, eds., *City Invincible*, pp. 99–101.

146. *Ibid.*, p. 119.

147. A. Leo Oppenheim, "A Note on the Scribes in Mesopotamia," in *Studies in Honor of Benno Landsberger* . . . (Chicago, 1965), pp. 253–256.

for "specialization" and that "there were temple scribes, army scribes, medical scribes, and priest scribes," [148] it is only reasonable to assume that wherever greater quantities of records had to be serviced certain scribes were detailed to the archives function. Thus, we know that in Ugarit ten scribes were specifically attached to the Archives West. If then a mere scribe was considered a person of high social standing—in the Hittite Empire the clay tablet scribe belonged to the dignitaries of the court and was called upon, as the king's substitute, to deliver his daily prayers before the god Telipinu [149]—the trust placed in him as a custodian of archives must have conferred upon him a special mark of distinction, manifest also in terms of his salary. In fact, in a list dating from the second year of King Bur-Sin of Ur (ca. 2253–2245 B.C.), which specifies the salaries of the priests and officials of ten different temples, the director of archives appears in the same class with the inspector of canals, the administrator of store houses, and the superintendent of laborers, receiving half the salary of the high priest's substitute, while, for example, the inspector of gardens and the inspector of police had to manage with only one-tenth of it. [150] Unfortunately, such archival prosperity was not an omen of future well-being for the profession.

Custody and control of the records could lead to administrative responsibility and power, as it often did in later civilizations. An archivist in charge of the accounting records of the temple was likely to have an overview of the entire economy of the institution and, if he was a man of initiative, he could assume the administration of its business. This could also happen in the palace administration, and so Iasîm-Sumû, in charge of the Mari tablets, succeeded in raising himself to a position of

---

148. Georges Contenau, *La vie quotidienne à Babylone et en Assyrie* (Paris, 1950), pp. 182–183.

149. The "wooden board scribe," on the other hand, is mentioned in the company of the blacksmith and other low-level personnel. See A. Pohl, "Bibliotheken und Archive im alten Orient," *Orientalia*, XXV (1956), 108, and Albrecht Goetze, "Kleinasien," in *Kulturgeschichte des alten Orients*, 2d ed., III, pt. 1 (Munich, 1957), 172.

150. Meissner, *Babylonien*, II, 56–57.

authority over the business administration of the principality and over the palace personnel.[151]

Even where the archivist did not move up into the executive group and remained confined to his custodial functions, he was certainly an indispensable part of the administrative machinery. In a society whose institutions depended on the central direction of men and materials toward the attainment of definite goals, use and preservation of the records ranked high, for rational administration of the record has always been bureaucracy's favorite child. That the evolution of archives administration furnishes the contrapuntal accompaniment to the main melody —the growth of bureaucratic administration—appears as true of the clay tablet era as it is of modern bureaucracies.

151. Birot, "Les lettres de Iasîm-Sumû," pp. 25, 27, 35.

It has been said of Egypt that, from the Ptolemies to the Byzantines and possibly even from the Pharaohs to the Caliphs, "the essential principles of [her] administration remained unchanged and constantly manifested their identity by producing the same consequences" because the different regimes adhered to the same philosophy of government, that of considering the country "a domain to be exploited rather than a fatherland to be ruled."[1] Obviously such exploitation could not be carried out except through the services of a powerful and well-organized bureaucracy, which in turn depended on the intelligent preparation and use of records, the bureaucrat's "tools of production," as Max Weber once called them. Rarely, indeed, has there been a bureaucracy as record-conscious as that of ancient Egypt. It not only used records as a tool of management but also contributed toward making record-consciousness integral and important in the life of the people. Had the Egyptians seen fit to write on clay, they might have left behind a wealth of documents easily exceeding that of the Mesopotamian countries. Except for potsherds, however, they used perishable materials, such as papyrus, leather, and wooden writing boards, with the result that only an infinitesimal part of the country's record production has been preserved.

Papyrus was the material most commonly used for public and private purposes. An Egyptian invention later appropriated by the Greeks, it was made by placing thin slices of the stem of the papyrus plant side by side on a plank or table and then superimposing on this layer another consisting of "slices running at right angles to those of the first layer. By pressing and beating the two layers became welded together; the tissue thus made was dried under pressure; lastly the surface was pol-

---

1. Victor Martin, "Les papyrus et l'histoire administrative de l'Egypte gréco-romaine," in Walter Otto and Leopold Wenger, *Papyri und Altertumswissenschaft* (Munich, 1934), p. 164.

ished with some rounded object possibly of stone, until it became perfectly smooth."² Normally twenty sheets produced in this fashion were pasted together in the factory, and these long strips were then rolled up with the horizontal fibers inside, ready to be written on with black carbon ink and a brush made out of a rush that grows in the Egyptian salt marshes. Although the durability of papyrus should not be underestimated, the product was bound to disintegrate in territory affected by the annual inundations of the Nile River. Thus, practically no papyri have survived in the Nile Delta, although thousands have been found elsewhere, especially on the fringes of the desert south of Cairo.

The other writing materials known to have been used in Egypt had a somewhat greater life expectancy. As can be seen on the representation of a session of the Supreme Court, the laws of the country were codified on forty rolls of leather spread out on four mats before the vizier, the president of the court.³ Similarly the official diary of the campaigns of Thutmosis III was "recorded upon a roll of leather" to be deposited in the temple of Amon.⁴ For ephemeral purposes, shards of vessels of all kinds offered themselves as a cheap and handy

2. Jaroslav Černý, *Paper and Books in Ancient Egypt* (London, 1952), p. 6. For details of the fabrication process, which has often been described, see N. Lewis, *L'industrie du papyrus dans l'Egypte gréco-romaine* (Paris, 1934), pp. 46–58; Karl Preisendanz, "Papyruskunde," in Fritz Milkau, ed., *Handbuch der Bibliothekswissenschaft*, rev. ed. by Georg Leyh, I, (Wiesbaden, 1952), 192–196; Leo Santifaller, *Beiträge zur Geschichte der Beschreibstoffe im Mittelalter*, I (Vienna, 1953), pp. 25–32; Leopold Wenger, *Die Quellen des römischen Rechts* (Vienna, 1953), pp. 78–88; Jan-Olof Tjäder, *Die nichtliterarischen lateinischen Papyri Italiens aus der Zeit 445–700*, I (Lund, 1955), 81–85; F. N. Hepper and T. Reynolds, "Papyrus and the Adhesive Properties of Its Cell Sap in Relation to Paper-Making," *Journal of Egyptian Archaeology*, LIII (1967), 156–157; Eric G. Turner, *Greek Papyri: An Introduction* (Princeton, N.J., 1968), pp. 1–16. In Europe the papyrus plant still grows at the so-called Fountain of Arethusa in Siracusa (Sicily) and along the Ciane River near that city. It is also found along the Upper (White) Nile, but no longer in Egypt.

3. Adolf Erman, *Ägypten und ägyptisches Leben im Altertum*, rev. ed. by Hermann Ranke (Tübingen, 1923), pp. 158, 172–174. Since the laws had to be consulted often, it is rather unlikely that they were written on papyrus. Norman de Garis Davies, *The Tomb of Rekh-mi-rēᶜ at Thebes*, I (New York, 1943), 31, thinks that rods or batons rather than leather rolls are represented.

4. James H. Breasted, trans. and ed., *Ancient Records of Egypt*, II (Chicago, 1906), 164.

substitute for expensive papyrus.[5] Furthermore, the excavations at El Amarna have shown that the Egyptians were not un-acquainted with the clay tablet as a carrier of messages, for, in addition to the many "letters received," there are also clay tablet copies of letters sent to various foreign potentates. It appears that at the time of Amenophis III (1408–1372 B.C.) and IV (1372–1354 B.C.) the clay tablet, cuneiform characters, and the Babylonian language constituted the generally accepted instruments of international intercourse in the entire area.

Compared to the stormy history of the Mesopotamian countries, that of Egypt, from its beginnings down to the Persian conquest, was relatively peaceful. This might lead one to believe that a great number of archival repositories have been discovered and that from them much can be learned about the archival practices of the country. Unfortunately, such is not the case. True, in El Amarna the diplomatic correspondence of two kings, the record office, and even the living quarters of the clerks have been found *in situ*. The famous tablets, however, "were said to have been found in the pit below the level of the floor in the main room to the east" of the record office. These tablets constitute, not an organized archives, but an assemblage of noncurrent material discarded and left behind when El Amarna was evacuated by the successors of Amenophis IV.[6] Furthermore, the great bulk of the El Amarna tablets were not obtained from systematic excavation. They stem from the clandestine diggings of the fellahin, who became amateur Egyptologists once they discovered that the century-old debris hills (*kôm*), their source of much-needed fertilizer (*sebakh*), also contained papyrus documents that could be sold

5. The writer of a letter might keep a draft or copy of it on an ostracon, as did a scribe complaining to the vizier under Ramses III. See Edward F. Wente, "A Letter of Complaint to the Vizier To," *Journal of Near Eastern Studies*, XX (1961), 252–257.

6. John D. S. Pendlebury and others, *The City of Akhenaten*. Part III. *The Central City and the Official Quarters*, I (London, 1951), 113–114. With regard to two ovens discovered in one of the record offices, the author raises the question: "Can there have been a hot drink corresponding to the perpetual coffee of modern government offices in the Near East?"

at a neat profit, particularly if cut up and marketed in small fragments.[7]

Even during the era of scientific excavation, which began with the pioneer work of Sir Flinders Petrie in the 1880's, only a few accumulations of temple and private archives but no major archival establishments with their holdings comparable to those of Ugarit, Mari, and Nimrud have been found.[8] As a result we lack much of the concrete evidence concerning storage installations and archival practices that we have for the countries of the clay tablet area. From individual documents, narrative sources, inscriptions, and tomb reliefs, however, we have learned a great deal about the outstanding role of records in Egyptian society and the resulting thoroughness of archival arrangements.

Neither in the administration of the country nor in the application of law was anything done without the compilation and presentation of records. In this economy based on the exchange of goods, whether it was a matter of measuring a quantity of grain or inspecting cattle, the clerks—scribes—were always present. In Egyptian art a scribe is represented crouched in front of his record chest[9] (figure 16) and his supply of papyrus rolls, a substitute rush behind the ear and a papyrus roll or wooden writing board in his hands. One of the models of the estate of Chancellor Meket-Rēᶜ charmingly illustrates the process of inspecting and counting the cattle for tax purposes, with four scribes sitting next to their master on a shaded platform as the cattle are driven past (figure 17). Two of the cattlemen and a third man, who may represent the tax collector, are keeping their own count on their fingers.[10] Even the smallest transaction

7. Karl Preisendanz, *Papyrusfunde und Papyrusforschung* (Leipzig, 1933), pp. 79–80, 110–117.

8. The same holds true of Egyptian libraries; see Josef Schawe, "Der alte Vorderorient" in Milkau-Leyh, *Handbuch der Bibliothekswissenschaft*, III, 3.

9. Figure 16 shows the scribe Nebmerutef of the House of Amon, doing his work under the protection of the god Thot who is represented as a baboon (see note 39 below). The statue is in the Louvre in Paris.

10. Herbert E. Winlock, *Models of Daily Life in Ancient Egypt from the Tomb of Meket-Rēᶜ at Thebes* (Cambridge, Mass., 1955), pp. 20–21.

Figure 16. Statue of the scribe Nebmerutef of the house of Amon, doing his work under the protection of the god Thot.

had to be recorded: if a working man received his share of grain or a government official his fuel, it was first necessary to issue a voucher and then to prepare a memorandum.

"According to Egyptian ideas, administering and preparing records are one and the same thing";[11] scribe stands for government official, and the terms for record depository and government agency are identical. Very appropriately, therefore, two of the main divisions of what we would call the Ministry of Agriculture were named the House of Measuring the Grain and the House of Counting the Cattle. Even in the army the scribe of the troops was one of the highest ranking officers, and princes of the royal house were not averse to having themselves represented in the role of a clerk. The insistence on putting every detail into writing caused a progressive subdivision of offices

Figure 17. Wooden model of inspection of cattle. From Tomb of Meket-Rēᶜ at Thebes.

11. Erman, *Ägypten*, p. 126.

and their staffing with numerous assistant chiefs, section chiefs, and other officials. In this bureaucratic state, the significance of written evidence was fully understood, as appears from annotations on documents, such as "to be copied" or "stays in the archives." And the writer of a letter might admonish the recipient: "Preserve my letter so that in the future you can use it as evidence!"[12]

Appreciation of the records was forced upon the entire people and penetrated into their thinking. According to Egyptian law, written complaints and defense had to be filed in lawsuits, and all business matters, such as purchases, leases, loans, and matrimonial agreements, had to be settled in writing if they were to be valid.[13] Even the dead, on the day of his final judgment, had to vindicate himself by means of a written statement,[14] and when dog-headed Anubis, the god of the dead, weighed the dead man's heart on a scale against a feather—considered the symbol of justice—ibis-headed Thot, patron

Figure 18. On the day of judgment, Thot, divine colleague of the scribes, records the result of the "weighing of the heart" of Hunifer.

12. *Ibid.* p. 127.

13. Hermann Kees, *Ägypten*, in Alt and others, *Kulturgeschichte des Alten Orients*, sec. I, pt. I, vol. III, 1 (Munich, 1933), 222.

14. *Ibid.*

saint of the scribes and secretary of the gods, stood ready with his writing board to record the result. In our picture (figure 18) the result is favorable to the late Hunifer; Am-mit—a monster part crocodile, part lion, and part hippopotamus, who has been expecting to devour the dead man's heart—is deprived of his prey, and Hunifer is presented by Horus to the great Osiris.[15]

The inevitable cumbersome effects of excessive writing and recording were aggravated by the fact that under the Pharaohs most of the time the country's administration was strictly centralized, although legally its two historic halves, upper and lower Egypt, were presumed to continue their separate existence. From all parts of the tightly controlled country records reached the royal court, and "whoever knows how much the Egyptian officials enjoyed preparing records, can imagine how many reports the Pharaoh had to read and how many royal decrees he had to issue."[16] As will be seen, however, he had in the person of the visier a powerful prime minister.

Another important reason for the accumulation of records may be found in the theory that all of the soil belonged to the king and that private property was "derived only from the exceptional transfer of royal prerogatives, as is every right and every rank." Therefore, although property might be sold or willed, the respective transactions called for royal certification, and consequently "every law suit involving real estate is to be conducted on the basis of the royal archives and the documents it preserves in its capacity of a land office."[17] Indeed, in the last analysis, the overwhelming significance of record-keeping in Egypt may be traced to the fact that the functioning of its economy and its government depended on creating, preserving, and having available two sets of records: the land records and the tax rolls. In his study of *Oriental Despotism*, or what he prefers to call "hydraulic society," Karl Wittfogel says that "the need

15. Sir E. A. Wallis Budge, *Osiris and the Egyptian Resurrection*, 2 vols. (London and New York, 1911), frontispiece to vol. II. See also Hermann Kees, *Totenglauben und Jenseitsvorstellungen der alten Ägypter*, 2d ed. (Berlin, 1956).

16. Erman, *Ägypten*, p. 74.

17. Kees, *Ägypten*, pp. 42, 44.

for reallocating the periodically flooded fields and determining the dimension and bulk of hydraulic and other structures provide continuous stimulation for developments in geometry and arithmetic,"[18] and he might have added in record-making and record-keeping. Wittfogel emphasizes that those who hold power in a hydraulic society must have at hand complete information on the labor force available, on the distribution of the land, and on the tax revenue to be expected; and, referring to Egypt, Mesopotamia, and other river cultures, he continues:

It is no accident that among all sedentary peoples the pioneers of hydraulic agriculture and statecraft were the first to develop rational systems of counting and writing. It is no accident either that the records of hydraulic society covered not only the limited areas of single cities and city states, of royal domains or feudal manors, but the towns and villages of entire nations and empires. The masters of hydraulic society were great builders because they were great organizers; and they were great organizers because they were great record keepers.[19]

In Egypt the annual inundations of the Nile River, mainspring of the country's agricultural riches, obliterated all boundary lines, and thus created conflicts between property owners that could not be decided without reliable cadastre and related records. Furthermore, because land records had to be used in determining a property owner's tax obligation, provision had to be made for keeping track of any changes that might affect the tax rolls. Strict control of the land, of its population, and of an individual's tax obligations (figure 19) was thus of the essence, and for this purpose all of Egypt was catalogued and inventoried.[20]

The place where every Egyptian was catalogued and inven-

18. Karl A. Wittfogel, *Oriental Despotism: A Comparative Study of Total Power* (New Haven, 1957), p. 29.

19. *Ibid.*, p. 50.

20. Jacques Pirenne, "L'administration civile et l'organisation judiciaire en Egypte sous la Ve dynastie," Institut de Philologie et d'Histoire Orientales, Université Libre de Bruxelles, *Annuaire*, III (1935), 371.

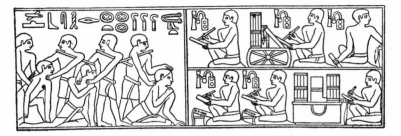

Figure 19. *"Collecting" taxes and recording receipts.*

toried was the office of the vizier.[21] Cast in the role of a prime minister of modern times, he was also charged with record-keeping duties that prompted James H. Breasted to call him the chief archivist of the kingdom.[22] During the first dynasties princes of the royal house served as viziers, but under the Fifth Dynasty the vizier's office became a career post. Although its prerogatives certainly dwindled in periods of upheaval and feudal disintegration of the state, on the whole it survived as the most important and powerful instrumentality of the central government. Thanks to the studies of Jacques Pirenne, we are particularly well informed about the viziers under the Fifth Dynasty (2750–2625 B.C.) and their functions. For the periods of the Middle and Late Kingdoms (2052–1778 B.C. and 1567–1087 B.C.), inscriptions in the tomb of Vizier Rekhmirēᶜ in the necropolis at El Gurna have bequeathed us the texts of two important documents, the "Installation of the Vizier" and the "Duties of the Vizier," which throw much light on the

21. All major works on Egyptian government and history deal with the office of the vizier. In addition to A. Weil, *Die Veziere des Pharaonenreichs* (Strassbourg, 1908), and other earlier studies, the pertinent sections in Jacques Pirenne, *Histoire des institutions et du droit privé de l'ancienne Egypte*, II (Brussels, 1934), 172–210, in his *Histoire de l'Egypte ancienne*, I (Neuchâtel, 1961), 153–173, and in Wolfgang Helck, *Zur Verwaltung des Mittleren und Neuen Reichs* (Leiden and Cologne, 1958), pp. 17–28, should be consulted. See also the literature on the vizier's installation and duties, cited in note 23.

22. James H. Breasted, *A History of Egypt from the Earliest Times to the Persian Conquest*, 2d ed. (New York, 1912), p. 82.

importance of this all-powerful office.[23] Because these instruments were formulated under the Middle Kingdom but were found inscribed in a tomb of the Eighteenth Dynasty (ca. 1568–1543 B.C.), one can assume that over the centuries they did not lose their validity entirely.

Tracing its beginnings back to the reign of Cheops of the Fourth Dynasty (ca. 2627–2513 B.C.), the office of the vizier was the key office of a highly centralized government. Its incumbent had the additional titles of director of the royal writings, director of all the works of the king, and president of the Great Court of the Six, the supreme court of Pharaonic Egypt. Other titles that occur in decrees and inscriptions indicate the vizier's supervisory control over all other departments of the government except the military. So extensive were his duties that at times under the Middle and New Kingdoms they were divided by appointing a vizier for upper and one for lower Egypt.

The archival responsibilities[24] of the vizier have been explored in detail for the period of the Fifth Dynasty, when he headed the House of the King. This was organized into four departments: (1) the House of the Royal Writings, that is the Chancery; (2) the House of the Sealed Writings, which was the registration department; (3) the House of the Writings or Archives, which provided archival service; and (4) the House of the Chief of Taxation. Field offices were established in the forty-odd nomes into which the realm was divided.

While the Chancery was in charge of expediting the orders of the king, the House of the Sealed Writings received all

---

23. The texts of these documents with comments are found in Georg Steindorff, *Urkunden des ägyptischen Altertums*, IV (Leipzig, 1909), 1103–1117; Breasted, *Ancient Records*, II, 270–281; Giulio Farina, "Le funzioni del visir faraonico," Accademia dei Lincei, *Rendiconti*, 5th ser., XXV (1916), 923–974; Davies, *Tomb of Rekh-mi-rēᶜ*, I, 88–94; Helck, *Zur Verwaltung*, pp. 17–64; R. O. Faulkner, "The Installation of the Vizier," *Journal of Egyptian Archaeology*, XLI (1955), 18–29. The documents are often referred to in the literature, as for instance in Breasted, *A History of Egypt*, pp. 82, 165–166, 233–245; Alexandre Moret, *Le Nil et la civilisation égyptienne* (Paris, 1926), pp. 323–327; and Kees, *Ägypten*, pp. 42, 183.

24. Pirenne, *Histoire des institutions*, II, 172–210.

"documents of exchange [of property], contracts, and testaments and gave them an authentic character by issuing them in the form of a 'royal charter' adorned with the seal of the state." This was done on the basis of formal declarations by the parties concerned and served the purpose of keeping the cadastre up-to-date and establishing the tax rolls.[25] The same purpose was served by the population census, which was taken regularly after the days of the First Dynasty, first in the north and later also in the nomes of the south. Pirenne thinks it improbable that the cadastre could have been useful unless the vital statistics were kept current.

Registered deeds and declarations were preserved in the cadastres and registers of vital statistics of the House of Archives (*per a*), administered by the director of archives under the supervision of the vizier. There these documents were entered "under the rubric," which "undoubtedly means that they [were] transcribed in different registers in accordance with the nature of the documents." The House of Archives had its own functionaries, called scribes of the House of Archives.[26]

We lack equally specific information on the archival procedures of the vizier's office for the Middle and Late Kingdoms. The Instructions for the Vizier, the remarkable document referred to earlier, tell us, however, that the scope of his archival responsibilities remained unimpaired. His office had charge of the cadastres and related records, the records of the population census, and the tax rolls compiled on the basis of the census. Testaments, too, were recorded in the vizier's office, for it was he who sealed them and who, when they went into effect, issued revised property titles to the heirs. Rightly, therefore, the vizier could call himself "one confirming the boundary records separating a landowner from his neighbor."[27] Also it was he who was "to fix the boundaries of any nome, any additional marshland, any temple fief, and any entry on possession." To

25. *Ibid.*, pp. 173–181.
26. *Ibid.*, pp. 181–182, 205–206.
27. Breasted, *A History of Egypt*, pp. 165–166.

cope with his considerable archival duties, the vizier and his staff must have had a system of arrangement that enabled them to retrieve information without delay. In cases of litigation involving property, for instance, decisions had to be rendered within three days if the property was located near the capital city, while for property in more distant parts of the country the time limit was two months. Procedures for consulting the records of other agencies were also spelled out in the Instructions for the Vizier: documents that belonged to any court, insofar as they were not confidential, could be sent to him under the seal of the magistrates and scribes concerned, and after the vizier has used them they were to be returned under his seal. Confidential documents were not to be released to him unless he sent an apparitor to obtain them in the interest of a petitioner.[28]

The Instructions for the Vizier state that the records of the nome, that is, the district, shall be "in his hall" so that he will be able to decide any question involving land. This has been interpreted to mean that all local archives were centralized and coordinated in the vizier's office.[29] If in the beginning there was complete physical concentration of local records, it must have been abandoned or relaxed in the course of time, for under the New Kingdom the nome agencies became preponderantly offices of record to which the vizier would delegate some of his functions, as, for instance, the recording of marriage contracts.[30] One would assume, however, that copies of such documents had to be filed in the vizier's office and that at any rate it continued to control archival activities on all levels of government.[31]

The vizier was not only the chief of the country's administrative apparatus. He also headed the judiciary, and in that capacity,

28. Davies, *Tomb of Rekh-mi-rēᶜ*, p. 93.

29. Breasted, *A History of Egypt*, p. 82.

30. Kees, *Ägypten*, pp. 220–221.

31. Other record-related duties of the vizier were (Davies, *Tomb of Rekh-mi-rēᶜ*, pp. 92–93; Helck, *Zur Verwaltung*, pp. 36–39): to receive certain officials of upper and lower Egypt and of Abydos, whom he appointed and who reported to him at the beginning of every fourth month, bringing their records and staffs with them; to keep an inventory of all oxen; and to receive a monthly report of all expenses and revenue.

too, he was concerned with record-keeping. As pointed out before, judicial procedure was in writing, so provision had to be made for the organization and maintenance of legal records. The Supreme Court and the lower courts of the nomes had their archival units in charge of the documents filed and generated, including the registers in which, in all probability, judgments were recorded. The archival office of the Supreme Court must have had custody of the laws of the land, for whenever the court was in session these laws on papyrus or leather rolls were spread out before it.[32]

Archival establishments existed in agencies throughout the government. The Department of the Granary, for instance, had its "superior archivists," and so did the House of the Treasury, the "White House." There was also an "archives of royal descendants" in the capital,[33] and surely the temples as centers of religious, cultural, and business activities created great quantities of record material. Occasionally they may have served as depositories for important state documents. This is suggested by the fact that, as mentioned before, Thutmosis III gave the records of his campaigns to the Amon temple at Karnak.[34]

How effective were the archival arrangements that we have tried to sketch? Although it would be rash to gauge them on the basis of a single case, we might refer to the experience of a widow who had been deprived of her fields.[35] She instituted proceedings against the intruder; since the parties involved produced conflicting evidence, the vizier, who had to decide in all lawsuits involving land, gave orders to check "the registers preserved in the Treasury and in the Department of the Granary for the purpose of taxation." The pertinent registers were obtained by the defendant accompanied by a priest, and since they

32. Pirenne, *Histoire des institutions*, II, 149, 182; see also n. 3 above.
33. Erman, *Ägypten*, p. 122.
34. Kees, *Ägypten*, p. 286.
35. Sir Alan Gardiner, *The Inscription of Mes* (Leipzig, 1905), pp. 26–28; see also Pirenne, *Egypte ancienne*, II, 191; Walther Wolf, *Kulturgeschichte des alten Ägypten* (Stuttgart, 1962), pp. 352–354.

supported his claim, the widow lost the lawsuit. Fifty years later, however, her son reinstituted proceedings in the course of which he was able to prove that the registers had been tampered with by eliminating the name of his mother, and his claim to the property was recognized. It appears from this story that although there was ample provision for preserving records their integrity was not necessarily safeguarded.

If records could be tampered with to change the evidence, it was even easier to destroy them in order to suppress their testimony completely—a likely event in a country in which the role of records as an instrument of social control was as fully understood by the people as it was in ancient Egypt. At any rate, it is there that we find the first example of a revolutionary upheaval directed not only against the "power structure," but also against the records on which its rule is based. About 2200 B.C., toward the end of the Sixth Dynasty, when the existing regime was overthrown and when the capital Memphis and the monuments of the Pharaohs were destroyed, the mob also turned against the record offices as the custodians of hated property rights. And so a document published under the title "The Admonitions of an Egyptian Sage" complains:

Indeed, the private council-chamber, its writings are taken away and the mysteries which were in it (?) are laid bare . . . Indeed, public offices are opened and their inventories are taken away; the serf is become an owner of serfs(?). Indeed, [scribes(?)] are killed and their writings are taken away. Woe is me because of the misery of this time! Indeed, the writings of the scribes of the cadaster(?) are destroyed, and the corn of Egypt is common property. Indeed, the laws of the council-chamber are thrown out; indeed, men walk on them in the public places and poor men break them up in the streets. Indeed, the poor man has attained to the state of the Nine Gods, and the erstwhile procedure of the House of the Thirty is divulged. Indeed, the great council-chamber is a popular resort, and poor men come and go in the Great Mansions.[36]

Not being favored by the results of excavations, we know

---

36. R. O. Faulkner, "The Admonitions of an Egyptian Sage," *Journal of Egyptian Archaeology*, LI (1965), 56.

very little about the nature of Egyptian record repositories and about methods of storage and arrangement. In the libraries of the Edfu and Philae temples—they were restored in Ptolemaic and Roman times—niches were used to accommodate papyrus rolls, and such niches may have been provided in Egyptian offices and repositories. As a rule, however, papyrus documents and rolls were stored in wooden chests or in jars. Scribes are often represented with their chests lying in front of them, and sometimes wooden boxes containing papyri were found in the tombs.[37] With administration and records looming so large in the life of ancient Egypt, it would be strange if the extant wall paintings and reliefs did not furnish us with a picture of an Egyptian office in operation. Indeed, we have one of the vizier's chancery under the Nineteenth Dynasty,[38] which has been discovered in the grave of Teji, private secretary of Meneptah, son and successor of Ramses II (about 1232 B.C.) (figures 20 and 21). The office consists of three parts. In the middle the chief of the office is pictured sacrificing to the god Thot with the assistance of a priest. To the left, the office proper is divided by two rows of columns into three small rooms. Of these, in the two end rooms scribes are busy preparing documents, and in the center room a document is being submitted to the minister for his signature. At the right side of the picture, a colonnade leads to the office chapel with the statue of the god Thot represented as a baboon.[39] The chapel is flanked by two rooms in which chests made of dark and light wood have been arranged in good order. Both of these rooms are identified as "Records Depository."[40]

37. Černý, *Paper and Books*, p. 30. Chests and jars have been found in the tomb of Tutankhamen and in other graves.

38. L. Borchardt, "Das Dienstgebäude des Auswärtigen Amts unter den Ramessiden," *Zeitschrift für ägyptische Sprache und Altertumskunde*, XLIV (1907–1908), 59–61. Hermann Kees, *Das Priestertum im ägyptischen Staat vom Neuen Reich bis zur Spätzeit* (Leiden and Cologne, 1958), has shown that not the Foreign Office but the Chancery of the vizier is represented.

39. According to Georges Posener, *Dictionary of Egyptian Civilization* (New York, 1962), p. 173, "Thot, a god of the Delta, assumed also the body of a great white baboon," when his cult came to Hermopolis, where the baboon had been a local deity.

40. In the translation of Borchardt: *Stätte der Schriften*.

Figure 20. The Office of the Vizier under Ramses II.

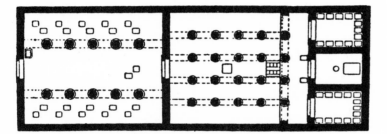

Figure 21. Reconstruction of the plan of figure 20.

Whether stored in chests or jars, papyrus rolls had to be identified so that it was unnecessary to unroll them in order to determine their contents. This could be done by placing at the beginning of the verso a docket that could be seen when the papyrus was rolled,[41] or, even better, by pasting on the roll a small piece of papyrus or parchment that carried a description of its content.[42] It is undoubtedly on the basis of dockets of either type that an industrious archivist of the Twentieth Dynasty prepared an interesting check list of the contents of two jars, one of which contained the records of the investigation of the robberies committed in the Thebes necropolis and

41. Černý, *Paper and Books*, p. 29.
42. Milkau-Leyh, *Handbuch der Bibliotekswissenschaft*, I, 194, n. 4.

the prosecution of the thieves.[43] Entries on this check list read as follows: "Receipt of the gold, silver and copper that, as was discovered, was stolen by the cemetery workers" and "Records of the copper and [other] things the thieves have stolen at the Place of the Beauties." Another example is the docket of a testament which is marked as "Declaratory deed w[hich the citoyenne Nau]makhte [made] of (?) their (sic!) property."[44]

If we realize the role of records in Egyptian life and the quantities of records that must have come into existence, we may be inclined to ask if procedures for the elimination of useless records might have been devised and applied. Undoubtedly such measures were not even contemplated as an administrative technique, but negligence, indifference, and the desire of officials to make a profit may have had a similar effect. In El Amarna, as we have seen, the diplomatic correspondence was simply left behind when the residence was abandoned; nobody, it seems, had any use for old tablets. Costly papyrus sheets, on the other hand, could be reused for official or private purposes when the information on them had become obsolete. Thus, the accounting clerk Khaemwose appropriated from the archives of his office two old rolls containing accounts of grain and timber and on their backs copied for his edification "the teaching of the King Merikerē and the prophesies of Neferrehu."[45] The main outlet for the steadily increasing quantity of records on hand, however, was provided by the needs of the embalmers, who used strips of papyrus for stuffing and wrapping the corpses during the process of mummification. Especially large quantities of material were needed for the processing of the holy crocodiles, and their cemetery in Tebtunis in the southern Fayyûm has furnished a good many records then considered as disposable. Without malice toward our Egyptian predecessors, may we assume that they sold useless papers to the undertakers

43. Erman, *Ägypten*, pp. 127–128. The records of the trial are found in Breasted, *Ancient Records*, IV, 208–221.

44. Černý, *Paper and Books*, p. 29.

45. *Ibid.*, p. 22.

without recording the transaction and paying the proceeds into the treasury?

Archivists may well have needed additional sources of income. In spite of meticulous record-making and record-keeping, the state was slow in paying salaries, that is, in delivering victuals such as geese and bread, to its officials.[46] As time went on, all the disadvantages of excessive centralization made themselves felt, administration became increasingly formalistic, and morale deteriorated. In fact, the records of the prosecution of the Necropolis thieves offer us a "picture of great depredation characterized by cheating, corruption, and embezzlement."[47] In the midst of such practices, archivists could not be expected to maintain their ethical standards unimpaired. Belonging to the upper crust of the bureaucracy, they were certainly exposed to temptations of all kinds. This assumption is confirmed by the tragic fate of Mai, a "scribe of the archives," that is an archivist, of King Ramses III (1198–1167 B.C.). His case is known to us from the records of the so-called Harem Conspiracy, a clever plot of Queen Tiji to dispose of her husband and elevate her son to the throne.[48] When it appeared that a great many persons inside as well as outside the harem had participated in the conspiracy, a special court was commissioned to deal with the accused. That two archivists, Mai and Peremhab, were appointed members of this court undoubtedly testifies to the high regard they and their colleagues enjoyed. While the trial was in progress, some of the harem women apparently bribed an infantry officer and a police captain charged with their custody, visited two of the judges "at their place of abode," and "caroused with them."[49] The incident became known. The persons involved were haled before the special court, "their crime seized them,"

46. Erman, *Ägypten*, p. 140.

47. Kees, *Ägypten*, p. 214.

48. The following is based on Breasted, *Ancient Records*, IV, 208–221. According to Wolfgang Helck, *Geschichte des alten Ägypten* (Leiden and Cologne, 1968), p. 198, Tiji was just one of the women in the harem, because Ramses had not decided to elevate one of the inmates to the rank of the "Great Royal Spouse"; this led to intrigues among the harem women.

49. Breasted, *Ancient Records*, IV, 219. The literal translation is: "made a beer-hall."

and their "punishment was executed by cutting off their noses and their ears." "The great criminal Mai, formerly scribe of the archives" and now deprived of his rank, was one of them, and although his fellow defendant, the former butler Pebes, took his life, Mai apparently survived the humiliation and disgrace.[50]

The records of the Harem Conspiracy trials have come down to us in two copies, the Judicial Papyrus of Turin, a "magnificent document," which, however, is "merely an abstract of the proceedings, evidently for filing in the royal archives," and the Papyrus Lee and Rollin, which "may have been part of the original scribal records of the prosecution."[51] In addition to the valuable information these documents contain, they furnish tangible evidence of the excellence of Egyptian record administration. It was to undergo further spectacular improvements when the successors of Alexander the Great brought to Egypt Greece's administrative know-how and when later the Romans instituted archival arrangements of a particularly significant character.

50. *Ibid.*

51. *Ibid.*, pp. 208a, 212. Subscribing to the idea expressed by A. de Buck, *Journal of Egyptian Archaeology*, XXIII (1937), 152–164, Hans Goedicke, "Was Magic Used in the Harem Conspiracy against Ramesses III?" *ibid.*, XLIX (1963), 92, believes that the entire group of texts "were meant as a record of the activity of Ramesses III as King to be presented in that final judgment in the netherworld." This to Goedicke seems "the only plausible explanation. Thus the group of papyri are to be understood as the notes for the King in his confession before Osiris."

[3] Greece

During the second millennium B.C. important centers on the Greek peninsula, such as Mycenae and Pylos, had been related to the Minoan civilization and had shared with it the art of writing and the use of the clay tablet for record purposes. About 1200 B.C. this civilization collapsed under the onslaught of barbarian tribes, and its ancient seats on Crete and on the Peloponnesus were destroyed. The following period of decline, during which even the art of writing may have been forgotten, came to a close, and the foundations of a great new culture were laid when the Dorians and subsequently tribes of Greeks from the northwest penetrated into the peninsula. Under the impact of this movement great numbers of the former inhabitants emigrated to the Aegean Islands and to the coastal regions of Asia Minor. The most energetic and successful of them, the Ionians, in the course of time extended their rule and gave their name to the entire area.

Thus in the tenth century the new nation of Hellenes began to emerge. It had its center in the Aegean Sea, which was surrounded by its settlements; and, because its outposts were situated on the Asian continent, its history was bound up closely with that of the great empires to the east. In contradistinction to the Orient, however, Greece achieved its magnificent civilization in the city-state, the polis. Confined to a small area because of geographical conditions and imbued with a strong sense of independence and particularism, the polis gave rise to a novel type of political life and government that could not fail to have a decisive bearing on archival organization and service.[1]

The historical significance of Greek archival developments found its most obvious expression in the fact that it was the Greek language that gave to the Western world the internationally accepted terms for the designation of official docu-

1. This discussion of Greek archival development has benefited from the advice and suggestions of Professor Homer A. Thompson.

ments, for the depositories in which they are kept, and indirectly for the persons who administer them. Moreover, the effectiveness of Greek archival institutions was later recognized outside the country itself. Cicero in one of his speeches contrasted it with the negligence of arrangements in Rome, where, he said, it was left to the archival janitors to decide what the laws of the commonwealth were.[2] And no less a witness than Aristotle testified to the role of archives in Greek public life when he identified the archives office as one of the indispensable institutions of his model state.

The fifth office deals with the registration of private contracts and court decisions; indictments have also to be deposited with it, and preliminary proceedings begun before it. In a number of states this office (like that of the city superintendent) is divided into departments, though a single officer (or board of officers) remains in general control of the whole. The holders of the office go by the name of public recorders, masters, plain recorders, or other similar titles.[3]

In the light of so weighty a statement, our knowledge of Greek archival arrangements is but scanty. In addition to wooden writing boards or tablets, perishable papyrus furnished the preferred writing material, and in Greece proper no remnants of an archival establishment have come down to our time nor has one been excavated, except for the Metroon, the city archives of Athens. What we know we owe chiefly to literary sources and in less degree to what we can infer from later developments during the Hellenistic period and in Hellenized Egypt, developments that are considered elsewhere in this book.[4]

That, as Aristotle stated, an archives office constituted an integral part of the government of the Greek city-state is amply confirmed. According to R. Dareste it was called *archeion* in twenty cities, while in others terms such as *dêmosion, dêmosia*

2. *De legibus* iii. 46 (*legum custodiam nullam habemus itaque eae leges sunt, quas apparitores volunt*).

3. Sir Ernest Barker, ed. and trans., *The Politics of Aristotle* (Oxford, 1952), p. 274.

4. See Chaps. 4 and 5.

grammata, chreophylakion, grammateion, grammatophylakion, and *syngraphophylakion* were used.[5] Characteristically these depositories served for the safekeeping of private as well as public material, and in this respect the role of the Greek archives seems to have differed from that of archival repositories in the Near East. True, we know that temple archives and the royal archives of Nineveh preserved private as well as official documents. Probably, however, except in Ugarit, deposition of private records in official custody was a voluntary act,[6] while in Greece it developed into a requirement: the compulsory registration of business transactions or what Egon Weiss has called a "general trend in the development of Greek archives administration to transform semipublic and private writings into public records."[7]

The peculiar development of Greek archival institutions may be understood as resulting from several causes. Historically speaking, it may have had its roots in the membership lists maintained by the phratries, phylae, and other associations of a public nature and in the lists of citizens.[8] At a more advanced stage, personal records were kept in the city archives, for in Cos a citizen's date of birth could be ascertained there, and in Ephesus the city chancery issued birth certificates upon payment of one drachma or a hundred drachmas for a certificate of illegal birth.[9]

While in these cases the documents preserved could be considered of general public interest, Greek cities at an early

5. R. Dareste, "Le χρεωφυλάκιον dans les villes grecques," *Bulletin de Correspondance Hellénique,* VI (1882), 242–243.

6. Marian San Nicolò, *Beiträge zur Rechtsgeschichte im Bereiche der keilschriftlichen Rechtsquellen* (Oslo, 1931), p. 145. According to Harold Steinacker, *Die antiken Grundlagen der frühmittelalterlichen Privaturkunde* (Leipzig and Berlin, 1927), p. 64, the system of public registration, forerunner of the public registration of private transactions, "is attested to for the Persian Empire and may be traced back to Assyrian times."

7. Egon Weiss, *Griechisches Privatrecht auf rechtsvergleichender Grundlage,* I (Vienna, 1923), 384. Weiss (p. 391, n. 112) disagrees with Bruno Keil, ed., *Anonymus Argentinensis: Fragmente zur Geschichte des Perikleischen Athen aus einem Strassburger Papyrus* (Strassbourg, 1902), who considers "the office records of the various officials the forerunner of archives administration."

8. Weiss, *Griechisches Privatrecht,* pp. 369–370.

9. *Ibid.,* p. 385.

date provided their citizens with facilities for the safe deposit of private records pertaining to property and other rights [10] and even for completing business transactions before archives officials acting in a notarial capacity. This second root of "compulsory registration" seems to have had its origin in the Greek institution of the *mnêmôn* or "memory man," who in primitive times functioned as an exclusively mental recorder of business affairs transacted in his presence, sometimes acting in conjunction with the judges. When the use of writing became more common, the *mnêmôn* began to record transactions, and thus the "office of the *mnêmôn* was transformed into an archival function." [11] Closely related to such an arrangement, although certainly later, was the Greek institution of the *syngraphophylax* or cosigner custodian, who witnessed legal transactions together with others and who assumed the custody of the documents thus signed. [12] Presumably, the *grammateus*, the secretary of the city government, was particularly well qualified to serve as *syngraphophylax* and would then keep the documents he had signed together with the official records. Thus the same person or office would become responsible for private as well as official documents.

This development reached its final phase when the validity of a transaction became dependent on its being entered in the *dêmosia grammata*, that is, the public records. This was the process of official registration or *anagraphê*. When such *anagraphê* of property took place, then, according to Theophrastus (ca. 372–287 B.C.), "registration tells whether a piece of property is free and unencumbered and the legitimate property of the seller." [13] Similarly, though at a much later time, Dio Chrysostomus testified that a contract received maximum validity if made

10. Ludwig Mitteis, *Reichsrecht und Volksrecht in den östlichen Provinzen des römischen Kaiserreichs mit Beiträgen zur Kenntnis des griechischen Rechts und der spätrömischen Rechtsentwicklung* (Leipzig, 1891), pp. 95–99, 170–173; Steinacker, *Die antiken Grundlagen*, p. 50.

11. Steinacker, *Die antiken Grundlagen*, p. 47, quoting Mitteis, *Reichrecht und Volksrecht*, p. 172; see also Weiss, *Griechisches Privatrecht*, p. 360.

12. Weiss, *Griechisches Privatrecht*, pp. 363, 369.

13. Steinacker, *Die antiken Grundlagen*, p. 47.

by means of entry into the *dêmosia grammata*.[14] The archives of the city-state thus became an institution that raised private documents to the rank of public records and imparted to the transactions recorded the benefits of state endorsement. The scope of transactions to be validated was considerable. It encompassed, in addition to indictments and court decisions, private contracts of all kinds, such as the sale of real property, ships, and slaves, loans, gifts, and the liberation of slaves; of these transactions those involving real estate and loans may have been the first to be registered.[15]

This combination of archival and notarial responsibilities became characteristic of Greek city government and seems to have followed it to the Greek colonies in southern Italy, Sicily, and Africa, where the Romans became acquainted with it and whence it may have influenced the genesis of the *jus gestorum* of Roman municipal magistrates and the institution of the *gesta municipalia*.[16] While it is possible to discover the roots of this combination of duties, its rationale is not altogether clear.[17] Leading authors have been inclined to think that it was prompted by fiscal reasons; they find this explanation particularly valid where the proceeds of *anagraphê* were farmed out. In the face of economic decline the Greek city-states had to look for new sources of income and discovered them in the fees to be paid for the mandatory deposit, registration, and eventually the preparation of business documents. Against this theory, it has been pointed out that *anagraphê* might have served as a practical and more lasting substitute for the publication of business transactions on the wooden bulletin boards of the community, the so-called *leukômata*,[18] and that financial motives played a secondary role only.

14. *Ibid.*, p. 49.

15. Weiss, *Griechisches Privatrecht*, pp. 400, 415.

16. Mitteis, *Reichsrecht und Volksrecht*, pp. 173–174; Steinacker, *Die antiken Grundlagen*, p. 51. See also Chap. 7 below.

17. The following is based on Steinacker's convincing discussion, *Die antiken Grundlagen*, pp. 50–51.

18. On *anagraphê* and the publication of documents on wooden boards and on stone, see the basic essay by Adolf Wilhelm, "Über die öffentliche Aufzeichnung von Urkun-

Intrinsically, the dual role of the Greek city archives may have found its justification in the very nature of the Greek city-state. Inasmuch as the state, the polis, was identical with, and the sum total of, its citizens (*politai*), many seemingly private aspects of their lives were of concern to the state. Characteristically "actions detrimental to parents, orphans, and heiresses—in Athens even idleness or prodigality"—were subject to public prosecution, presumably because each such case seemed to involve "a menace to the stability and property of the family, that is, an institution of vital interest to the state, politically as well as ritually." [19] *Anagraphê*, one of the foremost authorities in the field has said, "was practiced because of its public importance for everybody, not because of the private interest of individuals" or to enable them "to determine a legal situation." [20]

Morally as well as financially, the use of the city archives for the completion of business transactions and for the preservation of the pertinent documents must have strengthened their position as repositories of official records. Our understanding of how they functioned in this capacity has been hampered by another Greek peculiarity, namely the "pleasure derived from perpetuating on stone even rather extensive documents." [21] Greece was enormously rich in marble, which lends itself magnificently to being inscribed and to realizing a "democratic tendency toward plentiful publication of documents" [22] at government expense, a tendency so evident in the United States. As a result there have been preserved a great number of stone slabs or steles carrying the texts of official records, such as laws, decrees of the city community (*psephismata*) or other corpora-

---

den," a supplement to his *Beiträge zur griechischen Inschriftenkunde* (Vienna, 1909); Günther Klaffenbach, "Bemerkungen zum griechischen Urkundenwesen," in Deutsche Akademie der Wissenschaften zu Berlin, Klasse für Sprachen, Literatur und Kunst, *Sitzungsberichte*, no. 6 (1960), 5–42; Klaffenbach, *Griechische Epigraphik*, 2d rev. ed. (Göttingen, 1966), pp. 52–92.

19. Victor Ehrenberg, *Der Staat der Griechen*, I (Leipzig, 1957), 60.

20. Steinacker, *Die antiken Grundlagen*, p. 169.

21. Albert Rehm, "Die Inschriften," in Walter Otto, ed., *Handbuch der Archäologie im Rahmen der Altertumswissenschaft*, I (Munich, 1939), 215.

22. *Ibid.*, p. 229.

tions, conferrals of special honors upon deserving citizens, inventories of temples, accounts of authorities charged with building temples, and the like.[23] The multitude of official documents that have come down to us in this form gave rise to the now abandoned theory that these inscriptions were the official records of Greek agencies, and there was even talk of the "stone archives" of the Greeks. As Adolf Wilhelm has pointed out, however, "an administrative issuance, no matter how important and incisive, is never carved on stone."[24]

We now know that we must sharply distinguish between the archival preservation of records and their publication on wooden bulletin boards or stone.[25] Wooden boards or tablets, covered with white plaster or paint, were used to bring official issuances to the attention of the citizens and were roughly equivalent to the official gazette of modern times. In Athens they were displayed on the base of the statues of the Eponymous Heroes, who gave their names to the ten tribes (figure 22), and a fence surrounding the base or pedestal protected the writing on the *leukômata* from possible tampering.[26]

23. Erich Pernice, "Die literarischen Zeugnisse," *ibid.*, pp. 307–313.

24. Wilhelm, "Über die öffentliche Aufzeichnung," p. 249.

25. *Ibid.*, passim; Weiss, *Griechisches Privatrecht*, p. 357. Weiss says: "Deposition of the original in the archives and its recording on stone become clearly separate acts; it would be erroneous to assume that the latter embodied the legal content and constituted the text governing the legal relationships of the parties." Louis Robert, "Epigraphie," in *L'histoire et ses méthodes* (Paris, 1961), p. 459, wishes to correct "a rather widespread confusion" by pointing out: "The documents on stone are not the archives: they may be copies of the archives but not the originals."

26. American School of Classical Studies at Athens, *The Athenian Agora: A Guide to the Excavation and Museum*, 2d. rev. ed. (Athens, 1962), pp. 54–55. In his report on "The Athenian Agora: Excavations of 1968," *Hesperia*, XXXVIII (1969), 382–417, T. Leslie Shear, Jr., has shown that probably the monument of the Eponymous Heroes was originally located at the southwest corner of the Agora where the road from the Pnyx and the Areopagus opened into the square, and that it was transferred to its later location about the middle of the fourth century. This may have been done because the monument had partially blocked access to the Agora. There may have been another reason for the move, however. By the middle of the fourth century the Metroon was in full operation, and, as we now know, it accepted *leukômata* into its custody after they had served their purpose. Obviously they could be accessioned more conveniently from the new location of the monument opposite the archives building. One might even surmise that, although the monument was surrounded by a fence, the *leukômata* displayed were taken down at night and stored in the Metroon for better protection.

*Figure 22. The Eponymous Heroes, restored. On the base of the
monument a number of* leukomata *are seen.*

Incision on stone served a more permanent purpose. It was
intended to honor the person or persons mentioned in the
document reproduced and to bring it to the attention of as
many people as possible, or to facilitate access to the text of a
document that had to be consulted often and "had to be on the
books." The most magnificent example of this kind of publication is the famous code of laws of Gortyn on Crete, about 450
B.C. Inscription on stone was costly and hence was reserved for
the publication of important documents. It had to be especially
authorized, and if it involved decrees in honor of individuals,

these persons frequently had to bear the considerable expense. According to data we have for the temple administration of Delos,[27] seat of the Delian League, where papyrus, wooden boards, and stone were used discriminatingly, depending on the nature of the document, it cost 165 drachmas to incise a document on stone, while the same document could be reproduced on a *leukôma* for 6 drachmas. Hence marble was used only for the publication of "laws, decrees, and regulations discussed and voted upon by the assemblies, agreements on contracts to which the people were a party, accounts rendered by the magistrates, and, generally speaking, all acts of particular gravity or those that were to have permanent authority."[28]

The thousands of steles that we possess, therefore, are not archival documents; they are rather copies, frequently abbreviated, of original records deposited in the city archives. This relationship becomes quite clear in those cases where the texts inscribed include certain remarks "that were appropriate on the original documents only, such as the signatures of archons, secretaries, witnesses . . ., statements concerning accessioning into the archival depository and the furnishing of copies, as, for instance, on steles from Amorgos."[29] All available evidence seems to confirm that "the perpetuation of documents in a public or sacred place has nothing to do with the administration of archives (*Archivwesen*) in the proper sense of the word."[30]

Nevertheless, we must refrain from drawing too sharp a line of distinction between archival documents and inscriptions of such documents on wooden boards and on steles. In his important essay on the recording of public documents in Greece, Wilhelm pointed out that the preservation of the originals in the archival repositories of Greek cities was handled as a routine matter, while their recording on whitened boards, on bronze, or on stone was expressly ordered by the governing bodies.

27. Théophile Homolle, *Les archives de l'intendance sacrée à Délos* (Paris, 1887), p. 13, n. 7.
28. *Ibid.*, pp. 13–14.
29. Wilhelm, "Über die öffentliche Aufzeichnung," p. 279.
30. *Ibid.*, p. 298.

Correcting his views, Günther Klaffenbach has shown that the formula *anagrapsai eis ta dêmosia* or *eis ta dêmosia grammata*—understood by Wilhelm to signify the publication of documents in public places or buildings—means what it literally says, namely an order to register or deposit a document in the archives.[31] The numerous cases in which instructions to that effect were given to the archon or to the secretary of the city council make it quite clear that the need for archival preservation of key documents was taken most seriously. Whether they were on papyrus or on wooden boards constituted no problem, because the archives personnel was used to handling both types of material. This makes it quite probable that occasionally the wooden boards that had been used for bringing official issuances to the attention of the people were transferred to and kept in the archives, particularly where they had been displayed before or in the *bouleutêrion* (the city hall) and where the city archives was located in the same building, as it was, for instance, on Delos. Klaffenbach says, in fact, that the copy of a document on a wooden board "was not always the mode of a temporary publication but was destined from the beginning to serve as the archives copy" and that "we are justified in presupposing a painted wall [for the publication of documents] at every archives since, as a rule, it was situated in the very center (*Brennpunkt*) of the city."[32]

It is surprising to find that writers frequently refer to the texts of inscriptions on steles, although the originals were presumably in the archives and although in general these inscriptions do not faithfully render the texts of the documents reproduced.[33] Klaffenbach adduces the following reason for what to the record-conscious person of today seems an anomaly: we must abandon the modern concept of authenticity (*Urkundlichkeit*) and the idea that a copy of a document cannot be accepted as a substitute for the original unless it corresponds to the

31. Klaffenbach, "Bemerkungen zum griechischen Urkundenwesen," pp. 5–25, 34.
32. *Ibid.*, pp. 22–25.
33. *Ibid.*, pp. 34–36.

original in every detail, including spelling and punctuation. To the Greeks deviations from the exact wording did not diminish the authenticity of the copied text; a record on imperishable stone was deemed of greater value than the perishable original in the archives; and, in addition, the text on the stele was easier of access, just as the text of the modern published law is easier to use than the original act in the archives.

Bearing in mind that wooden boards, primarily intended for publication, could find their way into the archives and that the inscription of the document on stone, although not the original, was considered an acceptable substitute for the archival document, what then did the public archives contain and how were they administered? As to their physical makeup, it appears that wooden writing tablets as well as papyrus were used for record-making purposes, though we know that the secretary of the council and people of Priene made it a practice to record the same document on papyrus and on parchment, the copy on parchment serving as a "security copy," and that he received particular praise for this wise precaution.[34] Wooden boards or tablets undoubtedly served particularly well for records that had to be consulted frequently or on which additional entries were to be made.

From Aristotle's description in the *Constitution of the Athenians* we learn that the commissioners for public contracts (*pôlêtai*) recorded on whitened wooden boards the budgeted income from property sold and from taxes that were farmed out annually, together with the dates on which payments were due; that on the respective due dates the boards, all of which were in the

34. Wilhelm, "Über die öffentliche Aufzeichnung," p. 272. On the use of leather and parchment see Wilhelm Schubart, *Das Buch bei den Griechen und Römern*, 2d ed. (Berlin and Leipzig, 1921), pp. 18–22. According to Herbert Hunger, "Papyrusfund in Griechenland," *Chronique d'Egypte*, XXXVII (1962), 415–416, the first papyrus fragments found in Greece proper were discovered in a grave near Thessalonica in 1962. Dating from the second half of the fourth century B.C., they stem from a papyrus roll that was burned on a pyre, together with the corpse of its owner. Only the charred edges of the roll have survived, and the texts on them have been published by S. G. Kapsomenos in his article "'Ο ὀρφικὸς πάπυρος τῆς Θεσσαλονίκης" [The Orphic Papyrus of Thessalonica], *Archaiologikon Deltion*, XIX (1964), 17–25 and plates 12–15. Earlier, two fragments were reproduced by Georges Daux, "Chronique des fouilles 1961," *Bulletin de Correspondance Hellénique*, LXXXVI (1962), 794.

custody of the secretary of the Council (*boulê*), were turned over to the receivers general (*apodektai*); and that the latter either struck off the amounts paid or noted the fact that payment was overdue and gave the reason for the delinquency. Finally, the receivers general apportioned to the different state agencies the amounts received, recording and adding them up on a board and reading them out before a meeting of the Council.[35] Also anyone who wanted to complain to the Reviewing Chamber (*euthynoi*) about an official whose account had been audited had to use a whitened board, entering thereupon his name, that of the official, the violation charged, and the penalty the complainant thought appropriate in the case.[36] In Delos the architect of the temple administration submitted his building plans and working drawings on wooden tablets that may have been coated for better wear.[37] All this makes reasonably certain that, as in Rome, much of the record material in the archival repositories consisted of wooden tablets.

We know very little about the premises in which archival holdings were preserved. The only establishment for which we have somewhat adequate information is the Metroon in Athens, and we cannot judge to what extent this information applies to other city archives. The location and history of the Metroon have been clarified by the American excavations of the Athenian Agora.[38] In the first place they have identified the remains of an

35. Livio Catullo Stecchini, ed. and trans., 'Αθηναίων Πολιτεία; *The Constitution of the Athenians*, 47, 48. See also Carl Curtius, *Das Metroon in Athen als Staatsarchiv* (Berlin, 1868), pp. 19–20.

36. Stecchini, 'Αθηναίων Πολιτεία, p. 48.

37. Homolle, *Les archives*, p. 13, n. 3.

38. The presentation of the history of the Metroon is based on Homer A. Thompson, "Buildings on the West Side of the Agora," *Hesperia*, VI (1937), 1–226, and on American School at Athens, *The Athenian Agora*. The authors of the latter publication have modified Thompson's interpretations in minor points. I refrain from referring regularly to the older literature concerning the Metroon, as for instance Walther Judeich, *Topographie von Athen*, 2d ed. (Munich, 1931), pp. 342–345, and Kurt Wachsmuth, *Die Stadt Athen im Altertum*, II (Leipzig, 1890), 315–344, because such literature has been superseded by the results of the American excavations of the Agora.

A paper by Professor Alan L. Boegehold on "The Establishment of a Central Archives at Athens" has been accepted for publication by the *American Journal of Archaeology*.

older layer of buildings on the west side of the Agora. These are the original Metroon, temple of the Mother of the Gods, built about 500 B.C. and presumably destroyed by the Persians in 480/79 B.C. and not used for archival purposes; the "Primitive Bouleuterion" or Council Chamber of the early sixth century B.C., erected as an administrative building and too small to serve as an assembly hall; and the "Old Bouleuterion," built on the same site soon after 500 B.C. as a meeting place for the newly organized Council of 500 (figure 23).

When a "New Bouleuterion" was built toward the end of the fifth century the old structure to the east of it became available and was presumably used for the storage of records, a purpose it may have partly served before. In fact, the main reason for replacing the Old Bouleuterion may have been that it could no

Figure 23. The Athenian Agora ca. 500 B.C.

longer accommodate both the Boule and its expanding archives.[39]

From then on the Old Bouleuterion served as an archival repository, and since the records did not take up all the space available, it also provided a place for the Mother of the Gods (*Mêtêr*), who had been without a home ever since her temple had been destroyed. Because of the respect in which she was held in all the countries of the Near East, the establishment received the name Metroon from the goddess, who thus became the protectress of the state's archives. Such divine protection must have seemed desirable and had its parallel in the role played by Pallas Athene in the Parthenon as the custodian of the state treasury. Exactly when the building began to be called Metroon we do not know. It must have been during the first half of the fourth century B.C., because in his speech against Aeschines (343 B.C.) Demosthenes referred to a document that "is in your public records in the Metroon."[40] We do not know either what the converted building looked like, because nothing has remained but the lower foundations of the outer wall and of the interior supports. These were almost completely overlaid by the Hellenistic Metroon, the construction of which may be placed in the second half of the second century B.C. In this four-room structure the archives may have occupied the first and third rooms from the south, while the room between them served as the sanctuary of the goddess. There her statue, not the work of Phidias but rather that of his disciple Agoracritus, had its place.[41] A fourth room on the northern end of the building, with a peristyle court and an altar in the middle, may have served as an official residence. This Hellenistic Metroon in turn suffered destruction during the Herulian invasion in A.D. 267 (figures 24 and 25).

39. American School at Athens, *The Athenian Agora*, pp. 49–50.

40. Richard E. Wycherley, *The Athenian Agora. III. Literary and Epigraphical Testimonia* (Princeton, N.J., 1957), p. 153. In 323 B.C. Deinarchos could say of the Mother of the Gods that she "is established as guardian for the city of all the rights recorded in the documents." Professor Thompson kindly called my attention to this publication, in which all known references to the Metroon have been conveniently assembled on pages 150–160.

41. Thompson, "Buildings on the West Side of the Agora," p. 206.

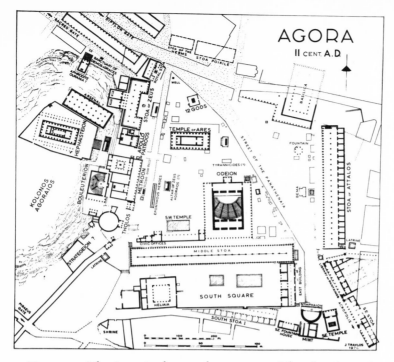

Figure 24. The Agora in the second century A.D. This plan shows the location of the Metroon in relation to other government buildings on the Agora.

Figure 25. West side of the Agora: southern part. On this plan, 7 indicates the Tholos, 8 the gateway to the New Bouleuterion, 9 the New Bouleuterion, 10 the Metroon, 59 the Strategeion.

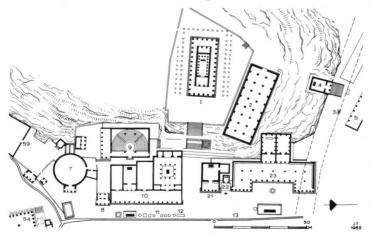

The interpretation of the Agora excavations has furnished us, then, with the following data:

1. The original Metroon had nothing to do with the preservation of archives.

2. Toward the end of the fifth century, the Old Bouleuterion became vacant, was converted to serve as an archival repository and as a home for the *Mêtêr*, and subsequently received the name Metroon.

3. In the second half of the second century B.C. this Bouleuterion-Metroon was replaced by the Hellenistic Metroon, in which the archives may have occupied two separate rooms.

4. This building seems to have lasted until the latter half of the third century A.D.

These findings are confirmed by literary and epigraphic evidence. That until about 409 or 408 B.C. records were kept in the Bouleuterion and not yet in a building called Metroon is suggested by the statement of Andocides at that time, who, defending himself, referred to a decree in his favor which "is still in the records in the Bouleuterion."[42] When the change from the Bouleuterion to the Metroon occurred is a much debated point. While Homer A. Thompson dated it between 411 and 405 B.C.,[43] Ulrich Kahrstedt saw a connection between the establishment of the Metroon and the work of the Commission for the Revision of the Laws of 403/2 B.C.[44] His hypothesis is indeed "most attractive, and is not contradicted by the history of the building."[45] On the other hand Kahrstedt's conclusion

---

42. Wycherley, *The Athenian Agora*, III, 129, referred to by Thompson, "Buildings on the West Side of the Agora," p. 215.

43. Thompson, "Buildings on the West Side of the Agora," pp. 215–216. His *terminus post quem* (411 B.C.) was taken from the Andocides story referred to above, his *terminus ante quem* from an episode in the life of Alcibiades, according to which Alcibiades went to the Metroon and, wetting his finger, erased from the bulletin board (*leukôma*) the indictment of a friend of his. This tale, however, is neither reliable nor specific enough to be used in connection with the history of the Metroon. Wycherley, *The Athenian Agora*, III, 152.

44. Ulrich Kahrstedt, "Das Athenische Staatsarchiv," appendix to his article "Untersuchungen zu Athenischen Behörden," *Klio*, XXXI (1938), 25–32.

45. Felix Jacoby, *Atthis: The Local Chronicles of Ancient Athens* (Oxford, 1949), p. 383, n. 27. See also A. R. W. Harrison, "Law-Making at Athens at the End of the

that no state archives existed in Athens before 403/2, that before
that date "the state wrote on either wood or stone or not at all,
and that prior to 403 B.C. steles were documents in the real sense
of the word, not just copies,"[46] seems wholly unjustified. It
would have been impossible to rule and administer Athens and
particularly its far-flung empire without the help of records, and
certainly the Boule, the state's central organ after the reforms of
Cleisthenes, had to rely on records, as did the many "administrative boards ... public and private associations, phratries,
phyles, demes or clans."[47] Even before 403/2 the Boule must
have had its archives and kept them in the Bouleuterion, as we
know from the Andocides story.[48] Very possibly the Commission for the Revision of the Laws of 403/2 found existing storage
conditions unsatisfactory, and its criticisms prompted the decision to build the New Bouleuterion and thus to obtain more
ample facilities for the records in the old building after its
evacuation by the Council.

It is doubtful that the years 403/2 B.C. were as important a
turning point in the history of the Athenian archives as Kahrstedt
thought. True, more space became available for the archives,
administrative arrangements could be improved, and the Mother
of the Gods found a refuge in the building which was renamed
in her honor and whose protectress she became. The character,
holdings, and functions of the repository, however, did not
change. It had been and remained the archives of the Council,[49]
it never served as the central state archives of Athens, and it
might at best be designated as a main state archives. A look at the
map of the Agora confirms the intimate relationship between
the Boule and the archives. The "Metroon-Bouleuterion

Fifth Century B.C.," *Journal of Hellenic Studies*, LXXV (1955), 26–35, and Klaffenbach, "Bemerkungen zum griechischen Urkundenweven," p. 29.

46. Kahrstedt, "Das Athenische Staatsarchiv," p. 31.

47. Jacoby, *Atthis*, p. 383, n. 27.

48. Kahrstedt, "Das Athenische Staatsarchiv, " p. 31, unconvincingly argues that it
refers to a stele and not to a document.

49. Ulrich von Wilamowitz-Moellendorff, "Der Markt von Kekrops bis Kleisthenes," in his *Aus Kydathen* (Berlin, 1880), 205–206, says emphatically that "the so-
called Metroon never lost its character as an archives of the Council."

complex," as Thompson has called it, was supplemented by the Tholos, where, according to the *Constitution of the Athenians*, "those members of the Council (Boule) who are acting as chairmen (*prytaneis*) first eat together . . . receiving pay from the city; they next arrange the meeting of the Council and the Assembly." [50] Even at night a number of members were always present to dispatch urgent business. Close by stood a building tentatively identified as the Strategeion, the headquarters of the ten generals. There was also, in front of the Middle Stoa, a building "designed to provide additional space for the public offices previously accommodated by the Tholos and Metroon," [51] and a latrine was not far away. Taken together, these structures formed a well-integrated center of government (figure 26), analogous to Washington's Federal Triangle, with the archives occupying a central position.

The character of the Metroon as the agency archives of the Boule is further confirmed by the arrangements for its administration and by the nature and scope of its holdings. In the Metroon there were to be found: [52]

Laws and decrees of the General Assembly.

Minutes of the meetings of the Council and of the General Assembly.

Records pertaining to the management of foreign relations.

Records pertaining to budgetary and financial matters subject to the Council's supervision.

Records of public trials, such as the trial of Socrates.

Contracts of the state with private individuals.

50. American School at Athens, *The Athenian Agora*, p. 45.
51. *Ibid.*, p. 57.
52. On the holdings of the Metroon, see Curtius, *Das Metroon*, pp. 15–20; Wachsmuth, *Die Stadt Athen*, II, 1, 334–338; Keil, *Anonymus Argentinensis*, p. 191; and Adolf Brenneke, *Archivkunde: Ein Beitrag zur Theorie und Geschichte des europäischen Archivwesens*, ed. Wolfgang Leesch (Leipzig, 1953), p. 180, where mistakenly in my opinion the Metroon is characterized as an *Auslesearchiv* (archives of a selective nature). In Athens as well as in other Greek cities special agencies called the *nomophylakes* (guardians of the laws) were at times charged with preserving the laws and watching over their observance. The guardians did not, however, develop into true archival agencies. See Georg Busolt, *Griechische Staatskunde*, I (Munich, 1920), 490.

Figure 26. Model of the west side of the Agora, from the southeast. The rotunda to the left is the Tholos, the building with the colonnade to the right of it is the Metroon, and the New Bouleuterion is seen behind the two buildings. In the background, on the hill of Kolonos Agoraios, is the Temple of Hephaistos.

Lists of the epheboi, the young men who at the age of eighteen were entered on the community rolls to undergo two years of civic and military training.

Official or record copies of the dramas of Aeschylus, Sophocles, and Euripides, probably kept in the Metroon as a result of a motion of the orator Lycurgus.[53]

Inventories of the temples and of the guaranteed measures and weights that were kept in the Tholos.

Clearly the holdings of the Metroon were confined to records originating from or related to the competence and supervision of the Boule as the center of state authority. In this the Metroon differed from the archival agencies of other Greek city-states; for, at least before the third century B.C., it did not receive, register, or validate private documents. Such a practice is mentioned for the first time in the will of Epicurus (who died in 270 B.C.), which referred to a deed of gift he had deposited in the Metroon. It seems that in this matter too, the bureaucratic government of Athens certainly lagged behind the general development"[54] and that it was only in Hellenistic times that the Athenians adopted *anagraphê* as their mode of publication.[55] This assumption is borne out by recent research on the recording of mortgages in Athens. Because there was no official system of registration, the "Athenians had recourse to the rather primitive system of setting out *horoi* [boundary stones] to provide the necessary publicity concerning liens on real property." Use of mortgage *horoi* seems to have terminated about the middle of the second century B.C., probably because at that time a system of *anagraphê* was finally instituted in Athens.[56]

53. Ptolemy III borrowed these record copies, paying as a guarantee of their safe return the considerable sum of fifteen talents, which he is said to have forfeited because he wanted to keep the record copies. Sir H. Idris Bell, *Egypt from Alexander the Great to the Arab Conquest* (Oxford, 1956), p. 139, n. 28, explains: "At the present rate of sterling, the silver value of a talent may perhaps be reckoned at about £400."

54. Keil, *Anonymus Argentinensis*, p. 192.

55. Steinacker, *Die antiken Grundlagen*, p. 48.

56. John V. A. Fine, *Horoi: Studies in Mortgage, Real Security, and Land Tenure in Ancient Athens*, in *Hesperia*, supplement IX (Baltimore, 1951), 52–54.

Administratively, the Metroon, together with the state treasury, was under the supervision of the *epistatês*, that is, the president of the Prytanes.[57] The Prytanes, consisting of the fifty representatives of one of the ten tribes that constituted the Boule, served for a tenth of the year as its executive committee, and they elected by lot the *epistatês*, who for a day—from sunset to sunset—kept the keys to the temples in which the treasury, the archives, and the state seal were stored.[58] Originally the secretary of the Boule had custody of the archives. Between 368/7 and 363/2 B.C., however, the secretariat was reshuffled, and a secretary of the Prytany appeared as the person in charge of the archives in the Metroon, the *grammateus ho kata prytaneian*. Aristotle describes the position of secretary-archivist as follows:

By lot is chosen also a secretary called Secretary of the Presidency. He has supreme powers over public records, keeps the texts of the decrees, keeps transcripts of all other business and sits in the meetings of the Council. Formerly he was elected by show of hands and the most illustrious and trustworthy citizens were appointed to the office. In fact, his name is inscribed on pillars at the head of the texts of alliances and of decrees granting to aliens citizenship or the status of guest of honor. At present he has become an official elected by lot.[59]

An assistant secretary-archivist, the *grammateus epi ta psêphismata* or *epi tous nomous*, was particularly concerned with recording and preserving laws and decrees. Neither he nor the *grammateus* of the Prytany could be expected to participate actively in the routine of the archives. They probably left it to an assistant, the *hypogrammateus*, who, in turn, had the actual work done by state slaves (*dêmosioi*). There was also an *antigrapheus*, a copy clerk

57. On the prytanes, their presidents, and their secretaries, see Busolt, *Griechische Staatskunde*, I, 476–480; R. Schultthess, "Γραμματεῖς," in Pauly-Wissowa, *Real-Encyclopädie*, VII, (1912), 1708–1780; Gustave Glotz, *La cité grecque* (Paris, 1953), pp. 219–225; and Sterling Dow, *Prytaneis: A Study of the Inscriptions Honoring the Athenian Councillors*, in *Hesperia*, supplement I (Athens, 1937).

58. Glotz, *La cité grecque*, p. 221.

59. As translated by Livio C. Stecchini, 'Αθηναίων Πολιτεία, p. 86.

who apparently provided the stone-cutter with copies of the decrees to be incised on stone,[60] when inscription on stone was ordered.

How the records were kept and arranged in the building we can only guess, particularly since we do not know what proportion of them was on papyrus and what on wood tablets. The tablets may have been stored in jars. This practice was certainly used by the arbitrators of civil suits, who in cases of appeal placed the records of the case in two separate jars, one for the plaintiff and one for the defendant, sealed them, attached the decision written on a tablet, and handed them "to the four of the Forties who handle cases for the defendant's tribe."[61] The records of the commissioners for public contracts, mentioned above, seem to have been stored on shelflike structures.[62] On the other hand, jars of considerable size must have been in the Metroon, because Diogenes the Cynic made his abode in such a jar in the building when he had trouble finding a place to live. But then, was his famous jar in the archives vaults or in the sanctuary of the goddess? We do not know.

For records on papyrus, niches such as those in library buildings of the period may have been provided. Thompson thinks that the similarity between the Pergamon library and the Metroon "not only in the disposition of space, but in the provision of a statue of the goddess is sufficiently striking to suggest some interdependence," and he thinks it possible "that the Athenian Metroon . . . was modelled on the earlier building" attributed to Eumenes II (197–159 B.C.).[63]

As to the arrangement of the material, whether on papyrus or wood, much can be said for the theory that records were kept in annual accumulations under the name of the *archôn*

60. Wycherley, *The Athenian Agora*, III, p. 160.

61. Stecchini, 'Αθηναίων Πολιτεία, p. 53.

62. In the *Constitution of the Athenians* Aristotle uses the term *epistylia*, which has been variously translated as niches, pigeonholes, and crossbeams. Wilhelm's translation seems quite acceptable: "Über die öffentliche Aufzeichnung," p. 248, *Wagrechte Holzbalken von Gestellen* (horizontal wooden beams of shelves), similar to the shelving frequently used for clay tablets.

63. Thompson, "Buildings on the West Side of the Agora," p. 217.

eponymos and thereunder according to the different prytanies. This has been inferred from the fact that copies of Metroon records, consisting of drafts without any dates or concluding formulas, have no dates either, and that the dates must have been obvious to the personnel simply from the place in which a document was kep̓t.[64]

Whatever the mode of storage and arrangement, reference service seems to have been efficient. There was of course no distinction between current and noncurrent material, and much of the service must have been to the Boule and its statutory needs. Records were used, for instance, when the Boule, or for that matter a private person, proposed a motion and wanted to adduce similar decrees, which were read aloud by a secretary,[65] or when in court one of the parties wished to call the attention of the judges to a law in his favor.[66] Holdings were also accessible for research purposes. Although we are not certain if Aristotle used them for his research,[67] we know that the Macedonian Krateros obtained from them the material for his collection of decrees of the Council.[68] Preservation as well as arrangement and reference service must have been satisfactory, for in 151/0 B.C. a decree proposed about 300 B.C. was produced without difficulty[69] and, even more surprising, during the third century A.D. the Roman Favorinus consulted Meletos' affidavit against Socrates in the archives.[70] On the other hand, the very combination of archives and sanctuary in a "multi-

64. Curtius, *Das Metroon*, pp. 23–24; Wachsmuth, *Die Stadt Athen*, p. 341. Glotz, *La Cité grecque*, p. 224, referring to the dignified position of the secretary of the Boule, says: "On the other hand, if the name of the secretary appears in the preamble and in the title of the decrees, together with the name of the tribe in charge of the prytany and that of the *epistates*, this is not for the purpose of honoring that dignitary; it is for the purpose of dating and authenticating the documents and of citing them according to their place in the archives."

65. The secretary of the city or secretary of the people (*grammateus tês poleôs or tou dêmou*), an elected official who had to have a clear voice (Glotz, *La cité greque*, p. 225).

66. Curtius, *Das Metroon*, p. 21.

67. Keil, *Anonymus Argentinensis*, p. 190.

68. Felix Jacoby, "Krateros," *RE*, XI (1922), 1617–1621.

69. Keil, *Anonymus Argentinensis*, p. 191.

70. Weiss, *Griechisches Privatrecht*, p. 401; Wycherley, *The Athenian Agora*, III, 153.

functional" building may have caused problems of control and safety, for Apellikon of Teos, a collector of books, was able to appropriate some old decrees of the Metroon and would have been brought to trial had he not fled the city.[71] An unusual defensive measure was directed against those who had eaten garlic, "supposed to be a specially exciting diet."[72] They were not allowed to enter the Metroon. This rule, however, may have been for the protection of those praying to the goddess rather than for the benefit of the archives personnel.

In Athens the evidential value of archives, and consequently the need to protect their integrity, was no doubt completely understood. A law was directed against bringing false documents into the Metroon, where the records enjoyed a sanctity comparable to that of the *Mêtêr*. And so, in 330 B.C., the orator Lycurgus addressed his listeners as follows: "Come now, gentlemen, if anyone went into the Metroon and erased a single law, and then alleged in defense that this law meant nothing to the city, would you not have put him to death? I believe you would have been justified in doing so, if you wanted to protect the other laws."[73]

Compared to the relative wealth of data we have for the Athenian archives, the information on archives of other Greek city-states is disappointing. Even the smaller city-states must have kept records, and, as pointed out earlier, the registration of business documents may have contributed to the practice. Dareste assumed that "in the majority of the cities, the public archives served as repositories for titles of property or indebtedness of private persons."[74] Similarly Ludwig Mitteis believed "that the well-organized system of archival administration that the Greek cities had had for a long time, made it possible to preserve the documents of property rights and other contracts

71. Keil, *Anonymus Argentinensis*, p. 190; Wycherley, *The Athenian Agora*, III, 152.
72. Jane E. Harrison and Margaret de G. Verrall, *Mythology and Monuments of Ancient Athens* (London and New York, 1890), p. 53; Wycherley, *The Athenian Agora*, III, 152.
73. Curtius, *Das Metroon*, p. 17.
74. Dareste, "Le χρεωφυλάκιον," p. 241.

in the city archives."[75] According to these authors, care of the official records preceded the care and registration of private material.

To what extent the temple archives also functioned as depositories for private documents we do not know. It is certain, nevertheless, that the temples were important centers of record-keeping. The temple administration of Delos has left us information about its purchases of papyrus and wood for record purposes,[76] and the priests of the Delphi temple certainly had an oracular archives for ready reference; for, although they deliberately made their responses ambiguous, they had to consult their archives if they wanted to maintain a consistent policy.[77] Temple archives played a particularly important role in connection with the liberation of slaves, which was effectuated by selling or dedicating the slave to the god of the temple. The document to that effect, on papyrus or a writing tablet, was kept in the temple archives.[78] Because of public interest in transactions of this kind, however, the temple authorities provided for their publication on stone. As a result of this practice, there have been preserved in Delphi records of the liberation of slaves from 201 B.C. to A.D. 126, more than a thousand of them.[79] These records were inscribed in prominent places outdoors, especially on the face of the great retaining wall of the terrace of the Apollo temple. Furthermore, the state kept a watchful eye on the administration of the temple treasures and seems to have ensured that the temples maintained careful records. We have on stone numerous inventories of temple

75. Steinacker, *Die antiken Grundlagen*, p. 50, referring to Mitteis, *Reichsrecht und Volksrecht*, p. 95.

76. Homolle, *Les archives*, p. 12, n. 1, 2, and p. 13.

77. Herbert W. Parke and D. E. W. Wormell, *The Delphic Oracle*, II (Oxford, 1956), xiii. It may be assumed that collections of oracles received were kept in the cities that had turned to the Pythia for advice.

78. According to Weiss, *Griechisches Privatrecht*, p. 358, the *autographon* remained with the temple, while another copy was sent to the slave's secular authority. The text of the copy on stone was derived from one of them "by means of simultaneous modification, abbreviation, and expansion."

79. Erich Ziebarth, *Kulturbilder aus griechischen Städten* (Leipzig, 1907), p. 4; Klaffenbach, "Bemerkungen zum griechischen Urkundenwesen," pp. 38–41.

treasures and equipment, frequently drawn up in connection with their transfer to the succeeding incumbent, that presuppose and reproduce originals on papyrus in the temple archives. In the temple of Hera on Samos equipment was controlled by means of a sealed inventory (*biblion sesêmasmenon*).[80] To give another example, seals originally attached to documents and hardened by fire were found in a back room of a Selinunte (Sicily) temple in which records seem to have been kept.[81]

What may have further increased the records of the temples was their practice of accepting deposits and lending money, particularly to the state.[82] In that capacity they competed with the private bankers, of whom there were many in Athens and other cities. The banker, called *trapezites* because of the *trapeza* (table or counter) he used, not only kept records pertaining to business with his clients but also accepted for deposit documents they wanted to entrust to him, particularly documents referring to payments to be made to third parties. Upon request, the *trapezites* issued certificates (*ekdosima*) from such documents. Athenian bankers had the "experience and facilities for the safekeeping of documents,"[83] and their reputation as record-keepers was such that "their accounts, when introduced in evidence, were accepted by the courts as *prima facie* evidence of the transactions therein entered."[84] Possibly because in Athens banks were used so widely for the preservation of business records, the Metroon for a long time had no facilities for keeping them, while other city archives did.

---

80. Otto, *Handbuch der Archäologie*, I, 229, 309.

81. Ziebarth, *Kulturbilder*, p. 8.

82. Ehrenberg, *Der Staat der Griechen*, I, 63.

83. On the equipment and bookkeeping methods of Greek banks, see Raymond Bogaert, *Banques et banquiers dans les cités grecques* (Leiden, 1968), pp. 376–384. Bankers preferred the use of wood tablets to that of papyrus, because the former were more difficult to falsify. Roman bankers and even those of the fairs of Champagne continued the use of the wax tablet (*ibid.*, p. 457). Contrary to the accepted theory, Bogaert (p. 382) thinks that "the books of the bank did not constitute an absolute proof, as has long been pretended." See also George M. Calhoun, *The Business Life of Ancient Athens* (Chicago, 1926), p. 102; Ludovic Beauchet, *Histoire du droit privé de la République Athénienne*, IV (Paris, 1897), 68; Steinacker, *Die antiken Grundlagen*, p. 52.

84. Calhoun, *Business Life of Ancient Athens*, p. 97.

In Athens as in other Greek cities archives administration assumed increasing prominence toward the end of the fourth century B.C. We have already referred to Athens' joining other cities in providing for the official registration of business transactions. At about the same time, the recording on stone of temple inventories and of accounts and other instruments of the temple treasurers fell into disuse. Seeking an explanation of the expanding archival consciousness, Klaffenbach mentions as a possible cause the influence of Alexander's expedition and reminds us "that the Persians, the youngest nation to dominate the world, which during the last 200 years before Alexander . . . ruled Egypt, inherited the Old-Babylonian record system (*Urkundenwesen*)." [85] There is much to support this hypothesis, as a look at Persian archives administration may prove.

85. Klaffenbach, "Bemerkungen zum griechischen Urkundenwesen," p. 41.

[4] Persia, Alexander the Great, and the Seleucid Empire

In dealing with the people of a subjugated country, most of the early autocratic rulers of the ancient Near East sought what we have learned to call a "total solution." Either the men were killed and the women and children enslaved or the entire population, what was left of it, was transferred to new seats of the conqueror's choice and under his effective control. Thus, for instance, the conquered Jews suffered the "exile" in Babylon. Among the great realms of the period the Persian Empire of the Achaemenid dynasty is exceptional in that it practiced, in principle at least, a "sound policy of decentralization"[1] by which the conquered population was allowed to remain where it was, and to retain, under Persian overlordship, its religious and other institutions. Founded by the great Cyrus, the empire was enlarged by the conquest of Elam, Babylonia, Syria, and Phoenicia and later included Egypt, all of Asia Minor with its Greek colonies, and the land eastward to the Indus River. It was indeed one of the most important political creations in the long history of the Orient.[2] So effective was the Persian rule and so appropriate were its governmental arrangements that the provinces or satrapies, except Egypt and Asia Minor, enjoyed at least three centuries of lasting peace.

It was truly a world-shaking event when this great empire was conquered by Alexander the Great and when as a result the vast reaches of the Orient were thrown open to Greek thought, Greek technical knowledge, and Greek administrative experience. Existing institutions were retained and adapted by the new masters, however, and in the field of archives particularly the practices and institutions of the Persian period were further developed and refined by Alexander and the Diadochoi, the

1. M. I. Rostovtzeff, *The Social and Economic History of the Hellenistic World*, I (Oxford, 1953), 83.

2. Eduard Meyer, *Der Papyrusfund von Elephantine: Dokumente einer jüdischen Gemeinde aus der Perserzeit und das älteste erhaltene Buch der Weltliteratur* (Leipzig, 1912), p. 23.

rulers of the successor states. Because of this continuity, Persian archival arrangements will be discussed along with those of the Hellenistic period of the Near East, but those of the Ptolemaic dynasty in Egypt, although they are mentioned, call for later consideration.

Based on the concept of governmental decentralization referred to above, the empire of the Achaemenids had to depend on a well-developed system of administrative communication. This system had its center in the royal chancery,[3] whose chief was responsible for drawing up royal proclamations and edicts, for handling diplomatic correspondence, and for retaining in a daily register a record of all actions of the king. Correspondence with the satraps or governors of the formerly independent countries demanded not only good roads but also an efficient postal service. This mail service, which served official needs only, was so admirably organized that it could transmit a message from Sardis in Lydia to Susa in Elam in seven days.

In conquered Elam the Persians had become acquainted with the use of the clay tablet for writing purposes. Cuneiform script, however, lent itself poorly to rendering texts in Persian. Furthermore, Persian could not properly serve as the administrative language of a multinational empire, and so from about the middle of the fifth century B.C. Aramaic, already the *lingua franca* of the region, replaced Persian as the official language of the empire.[4] Since perishable materials—leather and papyrus— were customarily used for preparing documents in Aramaic,

3. Arthur Christensen, "Die Iranier," in A. Alt and others, *Kulturgeschichte des alten Orients* (Munich, 1933), 266, 283.

4. Before Aramaic was adopted as an official language, it was necessary to write "unto the king's lieutenants, and to the governors that were over every province, and to the rulers of every people of every province, according to the writing thereof, and to every people after their language" (Esther 3:12). On the victory of the Aramaic language, see also Franz Altheim, *Alexander und Asien: Geschichte eines geistigen Erbes* (Tübingen, 1953), pp. 41–43, and Franz Altheim and Ruth Stiehl, *Die aramäische Sprache unter den Achaimeniden*, I (Frankfurt am Main, 1960). Written communication was supplemented by the use of royal inspectors, official watchdogs called "the king's eyes," and of police spies, the "ears of the king." Apparently the secretaries of the satraps were also supposed to report on the behavior of their superiors.

the quantity of Persian archives that have survived is small compared to the extant archives of earlier empires of the Near East.

For the period preceding the general adoption of Aramaic as the official language of the empire, we have records of subordinate officials and agencies only. These records are (1) the Elamite tablets of two revenue officials located in Susa, chiefly lists of objects they had received,[5] and (2) two groups of tablets that were found in Persepolis: the "fortification tablets," 510–494 B.C., and the "treasury tablets," 492–459 B.C. The Persepolis tablets, from two different fonds pertaining to an identical administrative function, document the payment of workers brought together from many lands to help with the building of Darius' and Xerxes' magnificent palace.

The fortification tablets, discovered in 1933 in the fortification walls at the northeast corner of the palace terrace, date from the twelfth to the twenty-eighth year of Darius (510–494 B.C.). Concerned almost exclusively with the collection, transportation, storage, and distribution of food, most of the more than 2,000 texts have so far remained unpublished.[6]

Except for a small number of tablets carried off and dropped by the plundering Macedonians, the so-called treasury tablets were found in Room 33 of the Persepolis Palace.[7] This large room (10.25 × 18.63 meters) housed the archives of the regional treasury of the Persis, the old Persian land of Parsa. Its roof was supported by two rows of columns (figure 27), and archaeological evidence makes it probable that above Room 33 there was a second level, also used for storing tablets. Most of the

5. Albert Ten Eyck Olmstead, *History of the Persian Empire, Achaemenid Period* (Chicago, 1948), p. 69. See also Altheim and Stiehl, *Die aramäische Sprache*, I, 109.

6. Richard T. Hallock, "Notes on Achaemenid Elamite," *Journal of Near Eastern Studies*, XVII (1958), 257. For further literature, see George G. Cameron, "Darius' Daughter and the Persepolis Inscriptions," *ibid.*, I (1942), 214–218. The fortification tablets have now been published by Richard T. Hallock as Oriental Institute Publication, vol. XCII (Chicago, 1969).

7. For the following see Erich F. Schmidt, *Persepolis. I. Structures, Reliefs, Inscriptions* (Chicago, 1953), pp. 173–175, and *Persepolis. II. Contents of the Treasury and Other Discoveries* (Chicago, 1957), pp. 4–7.

Figure 27. View of the Treasury Archives Room (Room 33) of the Persepolis Palace.

tablets were discovered in the corner of Room 33. "Others were scattered in the debris from the level of the floor to a height of 2 meters above it." The treasury archivists seem to have been unable to keep intruders out of the archival premises, for Room 33 and the subsidiary chamber 34 were also used for storing military equipment, furniture, and royal tableware. Erich F. Schmidt, famous excavator of the Persepolis Palace, found it "absurd to store administrative records, martial equipment, and tableware in the same rooms"; apparently he was not aware that empty shelves in archival repositories have always attracted unwelcome tenants.

The relationship of the fortification tablets to the treasury tablets has been the subject of much discussion. At first archaeologists considered the two groups to be one fond, and since the fortification tablets dealt with payments in kind while the treasury tablets specified payments in money, it was believed that about 492 B.C. the Persian government decided to change from the earlier mode of compensation to remuneration in money. Consequently Godefroy Goossens argued that when payment in money was introduced, the treasurer sent his earlier records to the fortification walls for dead storage. Were this assumption correct, we should have here a prime example of the separation of noncurrent from current records and of the removal of the former from "costly office space" to cheaper accommodations, with a resulting saving of thousands of shekels.[8]

We now know that the two sets of tablets represent two independent provenances: that of the royal storekeeper or *ambāra-bāra* and that of the treasurer of the Persis. George G. Cameron, abandoning his previous views as expressed in his great study of the *Persepolis Treasury Tablets*, no longer believes that the treasury tablets document the adoption of payment in coined money.[9] He now maintains that the fortification tablets,

8. Godefroy Goossens, "Artistes et artisans étrangers en Perse sous les Achéménides," *Nouvelle Clio*, I (1949), 39.

9. George G. Cameron, *Persepolis Treasury Tablets* (Chicago, 1948); "Persepolis

which deal with the receipt, inventory, and distribution of commodities in kind to workmen or royal messengers, were supplemented by other documents that were attached to them with strings (figure 28), and that these documents stipulated additional payments by the treasury in money. "Since none of these latter documents have been discovered at Persepolis for these years of Darius," he concludes, "the actual court treasury, for which they were destined, was at that time at some other, unexcavated spot on or below the Persepolis terrace."[10]

For the period beginning in 492 B.C., however, we do have the records of the treasury, which by that time had been able to move into its spacious quarters in the palace. Dealing exclusively with payment in money, these records had attached to them other documents listing the supplementary pay owed each salaried employee—the portion that was to be paid in kind, such as sheep, wine, beer, or grain.[11] We do not know the physical make-up of the documents attached to both the fortification and the treasury tablets. With the tablets were also found clay rings equipped with strings, rings that resemble the *bullae* found in Uruk,[12] and it is quite possible that these clay rings surrounded parchment or papyrus rolls, with a text undoubtedly in Aramaic. The texts on the tablets themselves are, with very few exceptions, written in Elamite. Elamite was used by the accounting and bookkeeping personnel in both the office of the storekeeper and that of the treasurer because, lacking indigenous qualified persons, the Persian kings may have recruited their accountants from an Elamite community in which public and private record-keeping had long flourished.

Although records written in Aramaic on parchment or papyrus, like those of Persepolis, were not likely to survive, the sands of Egypt have helped to preserve two accumulations

---

Treasury Tablets, Old and New," *Journal of Near Eastern Studies*, XVII (1958), 161–176, which article I am following.

10. Cameron, *Persepolis Treasury Tablets*, p. 164; fig. 1 there shows "Details of Tablet Manufacture."

11. *Ibid.*, p. 163.

12. See Rostovtzeff's description of these *bullae*, below.

Figure 28. Details of tablet manufacture.
A. *Cord from the inside of Fortification Tablet (Fort. 6751), magnified 5 times. B. Inside of Fortification Tablet (Fort. 6751), showing knot and impression of cord, magnified 3½ times. C. Oriental Institute "sealing" (A 3761) from Uruk (with roll of paper inserted in tube) showing impression left by cords which were tied around the parchment or papyrus roll and which protruded from the "sealings." D–G. Typical Fortification Tablet (Fort. 5903). D–E, obverse; F, edge; G, reverse.*

of Persian records. One of these is actually a mailbag or pouch containing "instructions of an official or semi-official nature issued by the Persian satrap of Egypt," ʾAršam, temporarily absent from his post, "or other high ranking Persian officers to subordinate Persian administrative officers in Egypt."[13] Since these instructions are directed to different recipients, they can hardly be considered "part of the archives of one of ʾAršam's officers in Egypt."[14] They are more likely the content of an official pouch that, for an unknown reason, never reached its destination. All of the documents are written on leather; they are in Aramaic and date from 411 to 410 B.C.

A second accumulation of documents, also in Aramaic but written on papyrus, was discovered in Elephantine, a Persian military outpost on the Nubian frontier of Egypt that was staffed with Jewish mercenaries. This accumulation, probably the archives of a Jewish family that included both soldiers and merchants, consists of official records, documents of the Jewish community, bills, letters, and private memoranda. Some promissory notes were found in their original condition—rolled and held together by a raffia cord that was secured by a clay sealing. These documents had been stored in clay jars, apparently imported from Phoenicia.[15]

No remnants of the central archives of the Persian kings have been discovered to date, but we can be sure that archival arrangements at the highest level of government were more than adequate. Royal archival establishments existed in Babylon and Ecbatana and probably also in Susa and Persepolis, the other royal residences. The assumption that the Babylon and Ecbatana archives were well-functioning offices is supported

---

13. Godfrey R. Driver, transcriber and ed., *Aramaic Documents of the Fifth Century B.C.* (Oxford, 1954), p. 2.

14. Driver, *Aramaic Documents*, p. 2. W. B. Henning, "Mitteliranisch," in *Iranistik* (Leiden and Cologne, 1958), p. 22, rightly speaks of a *Postsack* (mailbag). The place where this mailbag was found is not known.

15. Meyer, *Der Papyrusfund*, pp. 15–21; Karl Preisendanz, *Papyrusfunde und Papyrusforschung* (Leipzig, 1933), pp. 181–182; see also Bezalel Porten, *Archives from Elephantine: The Life of an Ancient Jewish Military Community* (Berkeley, 1968).

by biblical reference to the search for a decree of 538 B.C., in which the great Cyrus authorized the Jews to return to Jerusalem from their Babylonian captivity and to rebuild their temple. In 520 B.C. Tattenai, Persian governor of the land "Across the River," [16] asked the Jews to prove that they had actually been permitted to rebuild the temple. Referred by the Jewish elders to Cyrus' decree of 538 B.C., Tattenai asked of his superior that "a search be made in the royal archives which are there in Babylon to find out whether a decree was made by King Cyrus to build this house of God in Jerusalem, and let the King send us his pleasure regarding this matter." When the decree was not found in the house of archives in Babylon, in accordance with good reference practice the search was extended to Ecbatana in Media, where Cyrus had returned "before his first official year." In that city was found, not the decree itself, but an abstract of it in the "register roll." [17]

This register roll was the daily record of royal actions and activities, into which every royal decree was entered, a practice followed at the Persian court as well as the courts of Egypt, Babylon, and Assyria and the princely courts of Israel and Juda. This practice made it possible "to authenticate every precedent and every decision." [18] Similar registers, termed day-books (*ephêmerides*) by the Greeks, were certainly also kept by the satraps and other high officials. It was probably such a register or daybook that Xerxes (Ahasverus) had before him one night when he could not sleep and when "he commanded to bring the book of records of the chronicles" (Esther 6:1). Because the sleepless king could not be expected to handle and decipher cuneiform tablets in bed, the book was probably of parchment. These daybooks may have been the *diphtherai basilikai* (royal hides) that Ctesias pretended to have used as source material for his *Persica* (*Diodoros* ii, 32).

16. His superior was Hystanes, satrap of Babylon and "Across the River."

17. The preceding paragraph is based on Ezra 5:6–17, as paraphrased by Olmstead, *History of the Persian Empire*, pp. 139–140.

18. Eduard Meyer, *Geschichte des Altertums*, 3rd ed., IV (Stuttgart, 1939), 43–45.

Similar daybooks or registers and the royal archival establishments in the various capitals were to play a very important role when the empire succumbed to Alexander the Great. "We know with certainty that the administrative machinery of Alexander and his successors was practically a continuation of that of the Persian kings, and it is equally certain that no such continuation would have been possible without the help of the documents and information assembled in the Persian archives."[19] Much of the credit for this development may have been due to the experience and insight of Eumenes of Kardia, secretary (*grammateus*) of Alexander's father Philip and later first secretary (*archigrammateus*) of Alexander, chief of his chancery, and administrator of his records.[20] The most important of his own records Alexander had with him on his campaigns, and when they were destroyed by fire in Eumenes' tent, the king gave orders to have them reconstructed by obtaining from the satraps and military commanders copies of the instructions and other communications they had received. This was probably the first attempt ever made to reconstitute a destroyed archives, and it is evidence that preservation of the official documentation was a principle basic to the administration of the empire of Alexander the Great.[21]

Under Alexander the daily journals (*ephêmerides*)—probably kept by, or under the special supervision of, Eumenes' subordinate, Diodotos—became a comprehensive record of everything that happened at court and in the entire empire. The journal "reflected in a magnificent fashion the genesis and steady growth of the giant organization; it also enabled the administration itself to exercise control and to draw precedents from earlier events and measures."[22] Entries must have been detailed,

19. Rostovtzeff, *History of the Hellenistic World*, II, 1034.

20. On Eumenes' prominent role as one of the king's companions (*hetairoi*), on his futile efforts to keep the empire intact after Alexander's death, and on his tragic end, see Helmut Berve, *Das Alexanderreich auf prosopographischer Grundlage*, II (Munich, 1926), 156–158, and the literature referred to there.

21. Berve, *Das Alexanderreich*, I, 54.

22. *Ibid.*, I, 50–51. The entire organization and functioning of Alexander's chancery is discussed on pages 42–55 of Berve's extremely helpful book.

for after Alexander's death the journal served as the main source of information about the last days of the king.[23]

Once Babylon had been established as Alexander's royal residence, it became the seat of the archives of the realm. The archives contained the correspondence of the king, including his orders and decrees, and, a matter of particular importance, official reports from the field that retained their value after the king's death. It has been surmised that abstracts from these reports, possibly prepared by the archives staff, were made available to interested persons. As a result of the organization of the archives undoubtedly initiated by Alexander, it was possible for the scientific results of his conquests to have their full impact on the Greek mind.[24] After Alexander's death the Babylon archives was administered by Xenokles, who had the title of *gazophylax.*

Our knowledge of archives administration in the successor states is very uneven, except for Ptolemaic and Roman Egypt, where record-keeping developed into such an elaborate system of practices and institutions that it deserves a separate discussion. The only other state for which we possess any relevant information is the Seleucid Empire, the heir of Persia in the Near East, and even in this case "almost all is complete darkness."[25] Only one archival installation has been discovered and no archival documents have come to light, except for some parchments and papyri from the fortress Dura-Europos on the Euphrates River.

Despite this scarcity of archival remains, there is no doubt

---

23. Julius Kaerst, "Ephemerides," Pauly-Wissowa, *Real-Encyclopädie*, V (1905), 2749–2753. Alexander's journals must not be confused with the royal projects or plans pertaining to the building of vast roads, huge fleets, and gigantic temples, plans that after Alexander's death were submitted to the Macedonian army, which refused to sanction them (Berve, *Das Alexanderreich*, I, 52). A special group of the chancery, a survey staff called the *bêmatistai*, was in charge of keeping a record of distances and other pertinent data for strategic, logistic, and administrative purposes. These data furnished the basis for an official journal entitled *Stathmoi Asias* (Asiatic road stages or distances).

24. Berve, *Das Alexanderreich*, I, 54.

25. M. I. Rostovtzeff, *Seleucid Babylonia: Bullae and Seals of Clay with Greek Inscriptions* (New Haven, 1930), p. 57.

that the rulers of the Seleucid Empire retained the administrative system of their great predecessor, including its provision for the care of records. They may have done so mainly for fiscal reasons, which would account for the development in the Seleucid Empire of state offices for the registration of business transactions. In the city-states on the Greek peninsula such registration had become the accepted practice when the institution of the *syngraphophylax* was superseded by the setting up of official registry offices,[26] and registry offices undoubtedly also existed in the Greek cities in Asia Minor. Under the Seleucids, the city registry office (*chreophylakion*) became a state office headed by the *chreophylax*, an officer of the crown.[27] State-controlled registration of business transactions must have seemed desirable because it made it easier to collect the many new taxes that the Seleucid government had imposed. *Chreophylakia*, in which certified copies or at least abstracts from registered contracts were preserved, are attested to in Susa, Seleucia on the Tigris and Dura-Europos, and in Orchoi, the ancient Sumerian and Babylonian city of Uruk.[28]

Figure 29. Location of the Dura-Europos chreophylakion in Block G3, Rooms A1–A5. Part of restored plan of Section G in its final state.

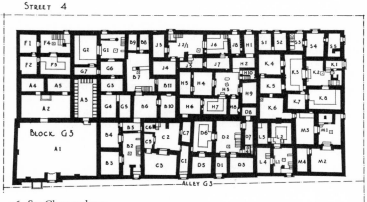

26. See Chap. 3 above.

27. Rostovtzeff, *Seleucid Babylonia*, p. 63, points out that the *chreophylax* of Orchoi undoubtedly was a crown officer and that we can assume that elsewhere too the *chreophylax* was a state officer "more or less like the agoranomoi of Egypt."

28. E. Bikerman, *Institutions des Séleucides* (Paris, 1938), p. 209.

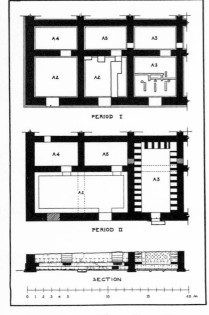

PERIOD I

PERIOD II

SECTION

0 1 2 3 4 5   10   15   20 M.

Figure 30. The Dura-Europos chreophylakion, Block G3, A2–5. Periods I and II. Restored plans.

Figure 31. The Dura-Europos chreophylakion, Block G3, F–A, final state. Restored plan.

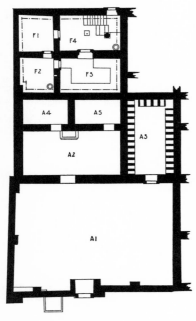

The excavations of the agora and bazaar of Dura-Europos, conducted since 1928 by Yale University and the French Academy of Inscriptions and Letters, have yielded a great deal of information about the physical arrangement of a state registry office. In Dura the office was housed in Block G3, where it occupied Rooms A1 to A5 (figure 29). The recording of business transactions may have started about 300 B.C., when the city government was organized, but before 128–129 B.C. the holdings of the registry office were kept elsewhere. At that time the premises in Block G3, originally used as shops, were fitted out for the business and the records of the *chreophylakion*. "The central location on the market place was appropriate to this function," and "the permanent character of this group of rooms as a public bureau is sufficiently indicated by the fact that they alone of all the structures in the area of the original agora buildings remained essentially unchanged throughout the subsequent history of the city."[29] Room A2 probably served for transactions with the public, while A4 and A5 were used as offices by the *chreophylax* and his assistants (figures 30 and 31).

A3 (figure 32) was the archives room proper, equipped as follows:

Against the east, north, and west walls of the room on a plinth of

29. M. I. Rostovtzeff and others, eds., *Excavations at Dura-Europos . . . Preliminary Report of the Ninth Season of Work, 1935–1936*, pt. I (New Haven, 1944), 30. For the following see also *ibid.*, pp. 169–176; M. I. Rostovtzeff, ed., *Preliminary Report of the Fifth Season of Work, October 1931–March 1932* (New Haven, 1934), p. 82; and C. Bradford Welles and others, *Final Report V*, pt. I, *The Parchments and Papyri* (New Haven, 1959), pp. 4–5, 13–14, and 84–98. The location of the office is shown in Figure 29. Figures 30 and 31 tell the architectural history of the building which originally housed shops (Period I) and later was converted to use as a registry office (Period II). In a still later development period (Figure 31) the monumental courtyard A1 in front of the building was added. This may have been done to provide better protection for the archives Room A3 which had been accessible from the street. That it could not be entered directly from the offices also seems a poor arrangement. Does this prove that even at that early period the conversion of existing premises to archival use was not satisfactory? C. Bradford Welles, "Die zivilen Archive in Dura," in Walther Otto and Leopold Wenger, eds., *Papyri und Altertumswissenschaft* (Munich, 1934), pp. 379–399, discusses individual documents rather than the archival situation in general. M. I. Rostovtzeff's "Das Militärarchiv von Dura," *ibid.*, pp. 350–378, has to do with military archives of the Roman period.

mud brick mortared and rendered with plaster and 0.31m. high were built the tiers of deep square bins or compartments described in Rep. V, p. 82. The tiers were built up on a lozenge system of partitions at an angle of 45°. Each compartment was 0.80m.–0.85m. deep, 0.50m. across, and 0.35m.–0.36m. on a side save in the bottom tier and at the ends, where gabled shapes and half compartments occurred. These dimensions were determined by the fact that the framework of the compartments was as far as possible constructed of undivided mud bricks 0.35m.–0.36m. or 1 foot square set on edge and heavily mortared with plaster, the angle joints being packed with clay ... There were ... twenty-five compartments in each tier about the room and at least four complete tiers, as indicated by the compartments found standing to this height in the north end of the room.[30]

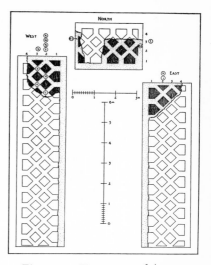

Figure 32. Equipment of the Dura-Europos chreophylakion.

As a cheap type of shelving, the storage equipment was not unsuitable for the storing of papyrus rolls; they could easily be extracted since each was identified by its protruding *coda*.

To the right of the diamond shaped compartments are groups of numbers that refer to their contents, and some of them are followed by the symbol or monogram ⳤ, said to be "the familiar abbreviation for χρ(εοφύλαξ), χρ(εοφυλάκιον), χρ(εοφυλκικός)." The numbers indicate years of the Seleucid era, beginning with the autumn of 312 B.C., and give the inclusive dates of the material stored in the individual compartments. Frank E. Brown, who wrote this part of the Dura-Europos *Ninth Report*, believed that "the registrar kept copies of all documents drawn up for registration in his office, and combined them in the form of an expanding roll, attaching the sheets of parchment or (after the arrival of the Romans in the sixties of the second century, which does not seem to mark a change in the procedure) papyrus together edge to edge by stitching or gluing."[31]

None of the records of the office were discovered *in situ*. Some legal documents "were found in the city towers and along

30. Frank E. Brown in *Preliminary Report of the Ninth Season*, I, 29–30.

31. *Ibid.*, p. 174. "When the building in Block G was taken over by the *chreophylax*, the earlier files were placed in the lowest tiers, that is, in the least desirable space, probably for the simple reason that they were rarely used" (p. 176). Obviously the *chreophylax* had little reason to expect reference use of the old record.

the walls as they had been dropped, brought in with the fill, or blown by the wind in the last months of the city's existence."[32] One of them, a fragment of a roll of copies of the second century B.C.,[33] is the complete text of a sales document, not just an abstract of its contents, and the same is true of such rolls of the Roman period. Just what the procedure of the record office was is not entirely clear. Since a registry roll of the second century B.C. was found in Dura-Europos, one might infer that the rolls were kept indefinitely by the office and were not, as had been surmised originally, forwarded to some central archives at Antioch, Ctesiphon, or some other city.[34] The scanty evidence available suggests that the originals of a transaction were not retained in the registry office. Those found in Dura in various other places "are without exception double, that is to say, the text of the agreement or transaction was copied twice on the same sheet of parchment or papyrus. Typically the upper version was fastened shut in some fashion while the lower version, reinforced by signatures of principals and witnesses, remained open for convenient perusal."[35]

In Uruk the registry office was located in the temple of Anu.[36] In this case we do not know what the installation looked like nor do we have any documents that were kept there, but we have the clay rings (*bullae*) that were used to secure the documents. M. I. Rostovtzeff has described the *bullae* as follows:

On the lump of clay which surrounded the document and which may be compared with a wrapper such as is used for mailing newspapers, or with a napkin ring, seals were impressed by witnesses, and perhaps by the contracting parties also. Within its clay ring, the document was deposited in the official or temple archives . . . A description of the contents of the document may have been written on an at-

---

32. *Final Report V*, pt. 1, p. 4.

33. *Ibid.*, no. 15, pp. 84–91; on p. 89 the pertinent literature is referred to. Nos. 16 and 17 are fragments of similar rolls of copies of the first and second centuries A.D. In its original form no. 17 combined the texts of four different documents.

34. *Preliminary Report of the Ninth Season*, I, 174.

35. *Final Report V*, pt. 1, p. 14.

36. Bikerman, *Institutions des Séleucides*, p. 209.

tached label or on one of the protruding ends of the parchment or papyrus.[37]

Since we have nothing but the *bullae*, we cannot be sure of the types of documents that were registered, and whether for certain kinds of business transactions registration was required.[38] Transactions involving the sale of slaves undoubtedly had to be registered. For other transactions registration may have been optional. Even if not required, registration must have been considered a desirable precaution because the official seal of the *chreophylax* gave "a valuable protection of the rights acquired by means of these documents."

Sealings similar to those of Uruk were discovered in Seleucia and enable us to form some idea of how private archives may have been stored under the Seleucids. These sealings—all that remains of the records of a firm of wholesale salt merchants—were found in the archives Rooms A and B of the "Great House" in Seleucia. In Room A the sealings lay in a corner and possibly had been maliciously broken into pieces. Those in archives Room B, however, were found on two platforms along the eastern and western walls of the room. With them were found fragments of charred wood, iron nails, and bronze straps, some of them perforated and with iron nails in the holes. These might be fragments of wooden shelves or of chests in which the documents were kept. Among the debris, charred small grain was discovered. Was it possibly placed in the containers with the documents to absorb excess moisture?[39] And were containers rather than "open shelving" of the Dura type used in the other city record offices?

The *chreophylakia* were urban institutions. Did similar record offices exist for the rural parts of the country? There is evidence to prove they did. A frequently cited inscription in the temple of Apollo in Didyma has preserved the texts of official documents

37. Rostovtzeff, *Seleucid Babylonia*, p. 24.

38. *Ibid.*, p. 65.

39. Robert H. McDowell, *Stamped and Inscribed Objects from Seleucia on the Tigris* (Ann Arbor, 1935), pp. 11–12.

created in 254/3 B.C., when King Antiochus II sold to his divorced Queen Laodice the village of Pannus in the Lydian Satrapy.⁴⁰ In one of these documents the strategos Metrophanes informs a certain financial officer that he has "written to Temoxenus the archivist (*bibliophylax*) to file the deed of sale and the survey in the royal records at Sardes, as the King has directed."⁴¹ What is meant by the royal records (*hai basilikai graphai*)? Rostovtzeff maintains that they were a special cadastre of royal land, a *Grundbuch* of royal land kept by a special record officer.⁴² Similarly, Franz Dölger is inclined to think of a cadastre for the crown land that had to be maintained by the Sardes archives office headed by a *bibliophylax*⁴³ rather than a *chreophylax*. Bradford Welles seems to beg the question when he writes of a royal record office for documents relating to the crown land, in this case the office for Asia Minor north of the Taurus.⁴⁴ Another writer goes considerably further by assuming an entire hierarchy of land registries: a land office in each hyparchy, which gave the boundaries of villages and properties; a register of the satrapy, kept by a registrar in the capital in a bureau called the royal records; and, compiled from the satrapal registers, a central register for the use of the king.⁴⁵

If there was this hierarchy of land record offices it would have paralleled the system developed by the Ptolemaic kings of Egypt. There, during the second century B.C., the *grapheion* in the *kômê* and the *agoranomeion* in the capital of the nome came into existence and served as offices for the legalization of certain business transactions and for the preservation of pertinent

40. These documents are published as nos. 18–20 in C. Bradford Welles, *Royal Correspondence in the Hellenistic Period: A Study in Greek Epigraphy* (New Haven, 1934), where on pp. 89–90 the extensive literature pertaining to them is listed including William L. Westermann, "Land Registers of Western Asia under the Seleucids," *Classical Philology*, XVI (1921), 12–19.

41. Welles, *Royal Correspondence*, p. 101.

42. Rostovtzeff, *Seleucid Babylonia*, p. 71.

43. Franz Dölger, *Beiträge zur byzantinischen Finanzverwaltung, besonders des 10. und 11. Jahrhunderts* (Leipzig, 1927), p. 92.

44. Welles, *Rôyal Correspondence*, p. 98.

45. William W. Tarn, *Hellenistic Civilization*, 3d ed., rev. by the author and G. T. Griffith (London, 1952), p. 133.

records. Since these institutions furnished the basis on which the Roman conquerors built their elaborate system of public record-keeping and since there seems to be no sharp dividing line between what the Romans found and what they added, the archival history of Ptolemaic Egypt and that of Roman Egypt will be considered together.

Greco-Roman Egypt offers to the historian of archives administration a nearly perfect example of a bureaucratic autocracy whose functioning was based on intensive use and remarkable care of the written record. The country, conceived like the Egypt of the Pharaohs as the king's estate, was governed for the financial benefit of its rulers—the Ptolemies and later the Roman emperors—with the clear intent of extracting the maximum amount of revenue from the subjects, incurring a minimum of expenses, making the fewest possible changes in the existing order, and taking the fewest possible risks; "the root conception was maintained that Egypt was a cow to be milked for the benefit of Rome. The cow was no doubt rich in milk, but Rome systematically overmilked her." [1]

To carry out this process, the centralizing character of Egyptian government, obvious under the Pharaohs, was not only preserved but intensified, so that Egypt under the Romans has been described as the biggest business organization of the Ancient World. [2] Alexandria became the seat of the government and of its chief officers. These were the principal minister—probably, like his opposite number at the Seleucid court, called "the man over business"—the powerful *dioikêtês* in charge of fiscal administration, and the *archidikastês*, the chief justice. [3] As in the days of the Pharaohs, the country was divided into regions (nomes), in which a civilian officer, the nomarch, was slowly being replaced by the strategos as the chief civil and military officer. [4] Within the nome, the *topos* (district) and the

1. Sir Harold Idris Bell, *Egypt from Alexander the Great to the Arab Conquest: A Study in the Diffusion and Decay of Hellenism* (Oxford, 1948), pp. 56, 76.

2. M. I. Rostovtzeff, "Roman Exploitation of Egypt in the First Century A.D.," *Journal of Economic and Business History*, I (1920), 337.

3. Pierre Jouguet, *Macedonian Imperialism and the Hellenization of the East* (London and New York, 1928), p. 299.

4. On this process—the acquisition of all powers in the nome by the strategos—see Hermann Bengtson, *Die Strategie in der hellenistischen Zeit: Ein Beitrag zum antiken Staatsrecht*, III (Munich, 1952), pp. 43–48. Bengtson considers the strategos "the specifi-

kômê (village) formed the lower levels of government, administered by the toparch and the komarch respectively.

In this strictly centralized structure, attention to official
documentation, including the recording of transactions of all
kinds and the arrangements for preserving records and providing
access to them, became all-important. Reverence for the written
record had been characteristic of Pharaonic Egypt. When under
the Ptolemies a steady stream of Greek immigrants came to
Egypt, they furnished the administrative talent and the technical
knowledge that the new rulers needed in order to remake the
Pharaonic state into "the logical and complete absolutistic
bureaucracy of the Ptolemies."[5] These experts with their
superior training and ability brought with them techniques
and practices that could be grafted upon existing procedures
and resulted in an ever increasing amount of paper work, or
rather papyrus work. We owe to them some 100,000 papyri,
or fragments thereof, in the form of letters, accounts, legal
documents, and the like,[6] and these are surely only a fraction
of the enormous output of records. For example, in a single
office of the *dioikêtês* Apollonius as many as 60 rolls of papyrus
were used in ten days, and in 258/7 B.C. some offices of Apollonius
utilized 434 rolls in thirty-three days.[7] The obvious satisfaction

cally hellenistic element" that the Ptolemies instituted in the administration of Egypt and
that the Romans retained with minor changes (pp. 2–10).

5. William Linn Westermann, "The Greek Exploitation of Egypt," *Political
Science Quarterly*, XL (1925), 530. See also his "The Ptolemies and the Welfare of Their
Subjects," *American Historical Review*, XLIII (1938), 270–287. C. Bradford Welles,
"The Ptolemaic Administration in Egypt," *Journal of Juristic Papyrology*, III (1949), 47,
suggests that in Egypt "Ptolemy took over a going concern, and did not change it
very much, except as was necessary to adapt it to Macedonian control and to the Greek
monetary economy." This adaptation was facilitated by the fact that, according to
Werner Schur, "Zur Vorgeschichte des Ptolemäerreiches," *Klio*, XX (1925–1926),
270–288, the use of Greek mercenaries and financial advisers by the last Pharaohs had
already begun the Hellenization of Egypt.

6. Claire Préaux, *Les grecs en Egypte d'après les archives de Zénon* (Brussels, 1947),
p. 3.

7. Claire Préaux, *L'économie royale des Lagides* (Brussels, 1939), p. 193, as cited by
Černý, *Paper and Books*, p. 23. The usual papyrus roll consisted of twenty sheets, but
some rolls had as many as fifty. Referring to Ulrich Wilcken, ed., *Urkunden der Ptolemäerzeit (Ältere Funde)*, I (Berlin and Leipzig, 1927), C. Bradford Welles, *Royal Corre-*

felt by Egyptian officials in creating records is splendidly illustrated by that royal scribe of a nome, called the *basilicogrammateus*, who in his temporary capacity of acting strategos
addressed a letter to himself as *basilicogrammateus* urging that he
conscientiously send in his monthly grain reports.[8]

The value of the Greco-Roman papyri is greatly enhanced
by their "precious quality of constituting dossiers, for many of
them stem from the cartonnages of mummies that the embalmers
made with out-of-date administrative papers. And these papers
had remained almost classified in the stucco from which one
detaches them sheet by sheet, or in the bodies of the mummified
crocodiles that were stuffed with them."[9] Selling records to
the embalmers was one way of disposing of useless papers.
Also, to avoid an excessive accumulation of records and the
resulting space problems, scribes often wiped the writing off old
papyrus rolls, cut them up, and pasted them together again
for further use.[10]

A system so dedicated to the importance of written communication could not function without a well-staffed clerical apparatus. In the office of the *dioikêtês* Apollonius, for instance, there was

---

spondence in the Hellenistic Period: A Study in Greek Epigraphy (New Haven and Prague,
1934), p. xxxviii, emphasizes "the complicated process by which the chancery of the
finance minister in Egypt prepared two executive orders in compliance with instructions
from the king. The matter at issue involved no large sum of money, but several experts
were consulted concerning the technical details of each order, drafts of each were
separately prepared and submitted to the *dioecetes*, and only after his approval had been
given were the clean texts prepared, checked for their correctness, and finally returned
to him for his signature."

8. Oscar William Reinmuth, *The Prefect of Egypt from Augustus to Diocletian* in *Klio*,
supplement XXXIV, new ser., no. 21 (Leipzig, 1935), 41. See also the communication
"Hephaestion also called Ammoninus, royal scribe of Nesut," as acting strategos
addressed to himself, "Hephaestion also called Ammoninus, [his] most dear friend,"
in Arthur S. Hunt and C. C. Edgar, eds., *Select Papyri*, II (Cambridge, Mass., and London, 1934), 313–315. P. W. Pestman, "A Family of Egyptian Scribes," *Bulletin of the
American Society of Papyrologists*, V (1968), 61, shows that the office of the *basilikos
grammateus* of Ptolemaic times goes back to the office of the "scribe of Pharaoh"
before the conquest, "which illustrates the policy of the first Ptolemies to continue
certain existing Egyptian functions."

9. Préaux, *L'économie royale*, p. 12.

10. Wilhelm Schubart, *Ägypten von Alexander dem Grossen bis auf Mohammed*
(Berlin, 1922), p. 199.

an office called the *hypomnêmatographeion*, charged with keeping the daybooks (*hypomnêmatismoi*),[11] and another office, the *epistolographeion*, to take care of the minister's correspondence. In addition, at least seven accountants served in the accounting office, each with the help of assistants, as many as ten working under just one accountant.[12] Mistrust of the honesty of officials in general and particularly of financial officials led to the system of assigning to each of them a "counter-scribe" or checker. When a peasant took his produce to the barn he got no receipt until this checker had verified the barn-master's weighing.[13]

The Romans, with their talent for organization, perfected the administrative arrangements they found in the conquered country.[14] In the chancery of the prefect of Egypt, which resembled that of the emperor, the *eisagogeus* served as director of the registry office. His was the job of organizing the records so that separation in accordance with a definite scheme was followed. Records were assembled into *tomoi synkollêsimoi* (figure 33) produced by pasting together into composite volumes (that is, rolls) documents of the same kind. Other chancery officials, the *hypomnêmatographeis*, had to keep the daybooks or *commentarii* of the prefect, recording that official's transactions and entering abstracts and occasionally the full wording of all the documents that left the office, in short, the *epistolae* of the official. The *commentarii* were meant not solely for official use and later preservation in the state archives. Before they were accessioned in the prefectorial record office, they

11. There is considerable literature on the *hypomnêmatismoi* and their Roman equivalent, the *commentarii*. I have mainly relied on the still fundamental article by Ulrich Wilcken, "Υπομνηματισμοί," *Philologus*, LIII (1894), 80–126. For other literature, see A. V. Premerstein, "Commentarii," *RE*, IV (1901), 726–759, and Leopold Wenger, *Die Quellen des römischen Rechts* (Vienna, 1953), pp. 417–419.

12. Préaux, *Les grecs*, pp. 74–79.

13. William W. Tarn, *Hellenistic Civilisation*, 2d ed. (London, 1936), p. 196.

14. The following is based on Arthur Stein, *Untersuchungen zur Geschichte und Verwaltung Ägyptens unter römischer Herrschaft* (Stuttgart, 1915), pp. 187–192, and on Reinmuth, *Prefect of Egypt*, p. 41. N. Lewis, "'Greco-Roman Egypt': Fact or Fiction?" *Bulletin of the American Society of Papyrologists*, V (1968), 49, warns against overestimating the degree of "continuity in governmental structure" between Ptolemaic and Roman times.

Figure 33. Part of a tomos synkollesimos *consisting of census declarations of the Egyptian village of Thelbonton Siphtha (P. Bruxelles Inv. E7616).*

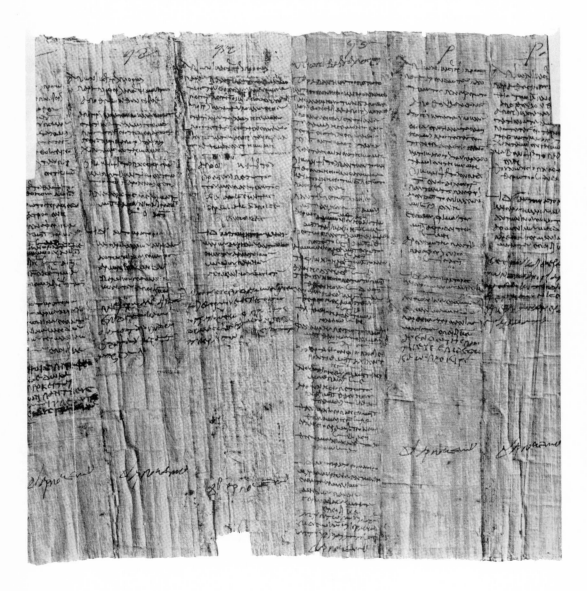

were publicly displayed, and they remained open for inspection by interested parties even after they had been taken over by the head of the record office (the *bibliophylax* of the *hêgemonikê bibliothêkê*). In that office, upon demand, they were produced by the *proairetês*, the person in charge of reference service.[15] A *biblion*, it should be remembered, signifies a roll of papyrus regardless of the content of the writing that appears on it; hence a *bibliothêkê* is a container for papyrus rolls and, in a wider sense, an institution or agency that preserves such rolls, whether of literary or business character. Thus a *bibliothêkê* may be a repository for books, that is, a library, or a repository for records. In our context it is the latter: a record office or archival agency.

Hypomnêmatismoi or *commentarii* were also to be kept by the strategoi in the regions and, at least in Roman times, by lesser officials and municipalities. If a strategos was in charge of two nomes, he kept separate records for each of them. Aurelius Leontas, who was in charge of Omboi and Elephantine, prepared and registered his records in the following manner: For each inspection trip into the area of Elephantine there is a separate column, and apparently never more than one column. Official acts of the strategos were entered in the third person with a new line for those of each day. At the end of each entry, the official signed: "I have read it." Upon his return to the capital of the nome, a fair copy was made, approved by the strategos, and transferred to the record office. There an official certified the accession by entering: "I, N.N., have registered the above for purposes of publicity." Later on one copy was deposited in the regional state archives and one in the central archives in Alexandria.[16]

15. Ulrich Wilcken, "Papyrus-Urkunden," *Archiv für Papyrusforschung*, VII (1924), 97.

16. Wilcken, "Ὑπομνηματισμοί," pp. 97–102. Eric G. Turner, *Greek Papyri* (Princeton, 1968), p. 138, gives the following specimen from the journal of the strategos Aurelius Leontas:

[Date]. The strategos after working at the Caesareum on matters of business sat at the office attending to public affairs.

[Signed] Read [Date]

Apart from what they contributed to official record-making and record-keeping,[17] Greek and Macedonian settlers brought to Egypt practices and institutions that on the peninsula and in the coastal cities of Asia Minor had been developed in order to validate officially the records of private transactions.[18] Institutions of this kind were established in the Seleucid Empire,[19] and the same development, in more elaborate form, occurred in Egypt. Under the Ptolemies the six-witness contract, an instrument guaranteed by six witnesses, was taken over from Greece. This contract was prepared in duplicate—that is, it consisted of an interior and an exterior text on rolled-up papyrus—and was sealed by the witnesses, one of whom might

---

[Date]. The strategos after holding an examination of the tax collectors at the office departed to the other nome, the Ombite.

    [Signed] Read [Subscribed] Registered by me, Aurelius Dionysodorus, assistant, after being publicly displayed.

17. On the archives of the Ptolemaic period, see Erwin Seidl, *Ptolemäische Rechtsgeschichte*, 2d rev. ed. (Glückstadt, Hamburg, and New York, 1962), especially the sections entitled *Die Archive*, pp. 15–49, and *Urkundenlehre*, pp. 49–68. The former discusses from the legal point of view family archives, business archives (*Buchführungsarchive*), and public archives. Seidl points out (p. 16) that legal documents have greater meaning "if we can determine: 1. Who has preserved them? 2. Why has he preserved them? 3. What do the documents discovered together with them contribute to their interpretation?" This leads him to the conclusion that "archival research is a field of activity especially for the jurisprudent." For the archives of the Roman period, Sir Harold Idris Bell, "The Custody of Records in Roman Egypt," *Indian Archives*, IV (1950), 116–123, is invaluable.

18. The literature pertaining to the making and notarizing of private business documents is voluminous and in part controversial. For the historical scholar, Harold Steinacker's *Die antiken Grundlagen der frühmittelalterlichen Privaturkunde* (Leipzig and Berlin, 1927) is particularly helpful. The basic work in the field is still Ludwig Mitteis and Ulrich Wilcken, *Grundzüge und Chrestomatie der Papyruskunde*, pts. 1 and 2 in 4 vols. (Leipzig and Berlin, 1912). Other helpful literature includes Otto Eger, *Zum ägyptischen Grundbuchwesen in römischer Zeit* (Leipzig and Berlin, 1909); Friedrich Preisigke, *Girowesen im griechischen Ägypten* (Strassbourg, 1910), and his "Das Wesen der βιβλιοθήκη 'εγκτήσεων," *Klio*, XII (1912), 402–460; Friedrich von Woess, *Untersuchungen über das Urkundenwesen und den Publizitätsschutz im römischen Ägypten* (Munich, 1924); and Giuseppe Flore, "Sulla βιβλιοθήκη ἐγκτήσεων," *Aegyptus*, VIII (1927), 43–88. A brief statement of the different opinions regarding the purpose of the *bibliothêkê enktêseôn* is found in Raphael Taubenschlag, *The Law of Greco-Roman Egypt in the Light of the Papyri, 332 B.C.–640 A.D.*, 2d rev. ed. (Warsaw, 1955), pp. 222–224. The archival reader will first turn to Bell, "The Custody of Records"; he might also consult Turner, *Greek Papyri*, pp. 134–138.

19. See Chap. 4 above.

be the *syngraphophylax*, the man who assumed responsibility for the custody of the document. In addition to the six-witness contract, a far more informal instrument, the chirograph or deed of hand, was widely used. Because this deed lacked the authentication of witnesses, and because there was no provision for its safe preservation, its legal value was subject to doubt. Still a third way of completing a business transaction (also used in Greece) was the *diagraphê trapezês*, a document prepared by the owner of a bank. Originally of a purely private character, it acquired increased legal value because of the quasi-public status of banks which, in Egypt, to a certain degree constituted a state monopoly.[20] The text of a transaction entered in the bank's register was considered the original.

Superior to the above methods of completing business transactions was the system of official registration that developed in the second century B.C., when the Ptolemies, wishing to control transactions in which the state was financially interested, established public registration offices. To facilitate the collection of its sales tax, the government in 264 B.C. created *kibôtoi* (file cabinets) to which all sales documents in Demotic, that is, Egyptian, had to be submitted. The head of a *kibôtos*, in addition to preserving these documents, also prepared an inventory of them.[21] The system was reorganized and expanded in 145 B.C. when King Philometor substituted offices called *grapheia* for the *kibôtoi*. In these offices transactions written in Egyptian as well as in Greek had to be registered unless they had been prepared by the *agoranomos*, a notarial officer in the nome capital. How the *agoranomos*, first appointed by the Ptolemies and, as his title indicates, an overseer of the market (*agora*), came to assume notarial functions, we do not know; nor have we learned much about his way of transacting business and keeping the pertinent records.[22]

<hr />

20. William Linn Westermann, "Warehousing and Trapezite Banking in Antiquity," *Journal of Economic and Business History*, III (1931), 30–54.

21. For the following see Seidl, *Ptolemäische Rechtsgeschichte*, pp. 63–65, where the earlier literature is referred to.

22. A list of *ágoranomoi*, private notaries, and other registration personnel is found in

On the *grapheion*'s practices and techniques of record-keeping, however, we are quite well informed, for we have, although for a later period, substantial parts of the archives of the *grapheion* of Tebtunis and Kerkesoucha Oros. These are probably typical of the other village record offices in the Fayyûm, and perhaps throughout Egypt as a whole.[23] From at least A.D. 43 to 52 the office was in the hands of a certain notary (*nomographos*), Kronion and his partner Eutuchas. Kronion, the senior partner, kept the financial records of the office, which he may have taken over from his father, Apion. Records of Apion's office from A.D. 7 on were found with those of the two partners, kept either in the *grapheion* or in Kronion's house. In fact, the latter may have served as the office of the *grapheion*. It was staffed with some clerks, including night clerks and others able to write Egyptian. In all probability Kronion and his partner held the office on a commission basis.

About the functions of the *grapheion* the following can be said with certainty: it assisted its clients in a notarial capacity by completing their business transactions; it drew up the necessary contracts and other documents and gave copies (*ekdosima*) to the parties; it prepared tax records, petitions, reports, and the like for its clients who paid a writing fee (*grammaticon*); and it served as an archival institution.

Provisions for the control of records were elaborate, although presumably these were not always faithfully carried out. Down to the days of Emperor Claudius at least, the originals of the contracts remained at the *grapheion*. Every four months the head of the office had to draw up a composite roll of them, a *tomos synkollêsimos*, to condense the contents of the documents

Willy Peremans and E. van t'Dack, *Prosographia Ptolemaica*, III (Louvain and Leiden, 1956), 265–298.

23. On the *grapheion* at Tebtunis, see Arthur E. R. Boak's introductions to *Papyri from Tebtunis*, I ("Michigan Papyri," II [Ann Arbor, 1933]), and II ("Michigan Papyri," V [Ann Arbor and London, 1944]). Among the literature referred to there, Ulrich Wilcken's "Griechische Vermerke auf demotischen Verträgen aus Memphis," in his *Urkunden der Ptolemäer Zeit . . . Ältere Funde*, I (Berlin and Leipzig, 1927), is still of basic importance. A useful discussion of the organization and functions of the *grapheion* is found in D. Cohen, *Schets van het notariaat in het oude Egypte* (Amsterdam, 1955).

processed in abstracts (*eiromena*), and to prepare a chronological list or register of them, (the *anagraphê*). We cannot say with certainty whether the original documents were actually enrolled—that is, pasted together into composite rolls—but it has been assumed that "at least as a rule and especially during the first two centuries of the empire, the documents were not pasted together and enrolled, but were preserved loose, as for example the Pap. Fuad and the Pap. Michigan."[24]

The abstracts or résumés were chronologically arranged. The first word of each résumé begins with a capital letter and is written to the left of the usual left-hand margin; since this word identifies the type of document abstracted, a clerk would have little trouble finding the abstract he was looking for. A typical abstract reads as follows:

> Hermias, son of Cheos, about forty years old, having as distinguishing marks a mole and a prominent eye on the left side, acknowledges to Soterichos, son of Kronides, about thirty years old, with a scar on his neck to the left, that he has received from him in cash from hand to hand out of the house 100 silver drachmas, and in place of paying the interest and in return for clothing I will present myself daily for one year from the month Sebastos of the third year to render him service and perform all the aforesaid tasks, and Soterichos is to suffer no prejudice therefrom in his right to the capital sum of silver drachmas which I owe him in accordance with a contract of service.
>
> Onnophris, son of Pakebkis, about thirty-two years old, with a scar on his right knee, wrote for him.[25]

In most instances, the details in the résumé must have made it unnecessary to consult the document itself and to unroll for that purpose an entire papyrus roll; thus the résumés can well be compared to calendars such as those of the British State Papers, Foreign and Domestic. To facilitate the finding of a

---

24. Angelo Segrè, "Note sul documento greco-egizio del grapheion," *Aegyptus*, VIII (1927), 107, n. 1. Boak calls Segrè's conclusions "most important" (*Papyri from Tebtunis*, I, 2).

25. Boak, *Papyri from Tebtunis*, I, 75. It stems from papyrus no. 121 recto; in the publication, pp. 20–80. There is a register on the verso of the same papyrus (*ibid.*, pp. 7–20).

résumé, an alphabetic index would have been most appropriate. However, the *grapheion* adhered to the ancient method of preparing another straight chronological finding aid, the register, as the following example shows:

[Month of Tubi, the] 17. Agreement of Horos and his wife with Eutychos concerning a deposit of 220 silver drachmas and $12\frac{1}{2}$ artabas[26] of wheat. 7 drachmas.
Confirmation of Panesneus for Horos of the receipt of an agreement about 220 silver drachmas. 6 drachmas.
Leasing by Harmiysis to Onnophris of 9 arouras of pasture.
Leasing by Leon to Heracles of 5 arouras of grazing land. He owes the writing fee.
And of Kronion, son of Didymos, for the rent he owed the 13th [of the month] of Phaopi. 4 drachmas.
Agreement of Thenpasos and her husband with Pasepsemis concerning compensation for the nursing of a slave child.
[Month of Tubi, the] 19. Loan by Pasepsemis of 100 silver drachmas to Kollouthos and his wife.[27]

for these two
4 drachmas

   Although elaborate, the techniques for the control of documents were not perfect, as appears from a memorandum probably written by a clerk of the *grapheion* as a reminder to search for a missing document: "See where the contract of Alexander with the son of ———— has gone."[28]
   Because the higher authorities must have believed that the originals were not safe in the custody of the notarial offices, at least from Roman times on official copies were sent to the regional state archives in the nomes for better protection and also for centralizing in one place information concerning all

26. The *artaba*, a word of Persian origin, holds 39,29 liters. The *aroura* amounts to 2,756 square meters. M. David and B. A. van Groningen, *Papyrological Primer*, 4th ed. (Leiden, 1965), p. 38.

27. Boak, *Papyri from Tebtunis*, I, 130, part of the *grapheion* register on papyrus no. 123 recto, *ibid.*, pp. 87–178. The same example is used by Cohen, *Schets van het notariaat*, p. 96, whose translation into Dutch I have consulted. Plate IV in Boak, *Papyri from Tebtunis*, I, reproduces Column II of the register. The month of Tubi runs from December 27 to January 25.

28. Boak, *Papyri from Tebtunis*, II, 74–75.

property transactions within the region. These archival agencies probably do not go back to Ptolemaic times. The Romans certainly had in each nome capital a public archives, called the *dêmosia bibliothêkê*. It received and administered accessions from the offices of the strategos and from other agencies, including census rolls, copies of the cadastre, records of village officials, and records of the *grapheia* and *agoranomeia*. In the long run, administration by one and the same agency of both official records and semi-public records pertaining to private property must have seemed impractical or inappropriate to Roman officials. Considerations of this kind probably prompted them to separate the two types of records and the administrative responsibility for them by limiting the public archives to official records and establishing a property record office (*bibliothêkê enktêseôn*[29]) for the preservation and management of nonofficial records. We do not know the extent and decisiveness of this separation action. In all probability the two establishments functioned as subdivisions of the same agency, each of them headed by a *bibliophylax* or archivist appointed for a concurrent term.[30] Most of the evidence we have refers to the *bibliothêkê enktêseôn*, which might be called a land office except that slaves were considered real property and that accordingly the *bibliothêkê* also preserved legal instruments relating to their sale and acquisition.

Apparently the functional separation of the two offices took place gradually, over an extended period of time. In the Arsinoe nome, as the Fayyûm was called in Greco-Roman times, it occurred between A.D. 67 and 72, and this is the first case of which we know. We need not here enter into the much debated

29. The word *enktêsis* means property, and usually real property. See Friedrich Preisigke and E. Kiessling, *Wörterbuch der griechischen Papyrusurkunden*, I (Berlin, 1925), 414.

30. Here I am following Paul M. Meyer, *Juristische Papyri* (Berlin, 1920), p. 196, who points out that the two *bibliothêkai* together constitute the *bibliophylakion* of the nome, and B. A. van Groningen, "Un conflit du IIe siècle de notre ère," *Chronique d'Egypte*, XXII (1947), 317. Mitteis and Wilcken, *Grundzüge*, II, 1, 94, suggest that quite possibly the *bibliothêke enktêseôn* remained just "a special department of the older archives."

question of whether and to what extent the property record office was to serve the purpose of the German *Grundbuch* or of the Australian Torrey System, for we are solely concerned with the archival function and techniques of the institution, and these are on the whole reasonably well understood. The property record office was, in the first place, the repository for all the documents related to a person's property rights. These records, kept together under his name in a pigeonhole or fascicle, included: the declaration of intention to sell (*prosangelia*), filed by the seller; the approval of the sale (*epistalma*) by the property record office, issued, we must assume, after the seller's right of ownership had been ascertained; the *apographê*, the purchaser's declaration of the property acquired, to which the purchase contract was attached; and documents specifying possible encumbrances of the property involved. Records were arranged under the name of the place, thereunder according to type of property (land, house, slave), and thereunder by the name of the purchaser. Thus the documents pertaining to a house that X had bought in the village Karanis would be found under Karanis, real property, X.[31]

Because of the quantity of records on hand, the property record office needed a device to serve the dual purpose of controlling the holdings and of determining at a glance all the property rights of the inhabitants of the nome. This purpose was met by the *diastrômata* or abstracts.[32] Arranged by village, and in the case of the provincial capitals by districts, the *diastrômata* listed on separate rolls for each letter of the alphabet all the property owners of the village or district, assigning a column to each of them. Under each owner, his or her properties, wherever located, were listed and identified as to type (house, building plot, vineyard, agricultural land, shares, and so forth). Clearly, as finding aids the *diastrômata* were vastly superior to the abstracts and registers of the notarial offices, with their

31. Preisigke, *Das Girowesen*, pp. 488–495.
32. Bell, "The Custody of Records," p. 121, uses the term abstracts for *diastrômata*. The German translation *Übersichtsblätter* seems to convey the idea somewhat better.

strictly chronological arrangement. To keep the *diastrômata* up-to-date was obviously of great importance. An edict of Prefect M. Mettius Rufus of the year A.D. 89 instructed "the keepers of the record office to renew the abstracts every five years, transferring to the new lists the last statement of property under each rubric, arranged by village and class."[33]

Although quite admirable, the institution of the property record office and its procedures could not be relied upon to furnish evidence in all cases of change of property ownership and thus to prevent illegal transfers and to avoid litigation in court. This was so because transfer of property by deed of hand was not forbidden; and, since the official registration process was time-consuming and costly, the deed of hand remained in use. If at some later date the parties concerned wanted to obtain for the deed of hand the publicity, protection, and validity of a contract approved by and filed in the property record office, they had to institute publicity (*dêmosiôsis*) proceedings in the office of the chief justice (*archidikastês*) in Alexandria; hence in the long run they might not save any money.[34]

Because the records as well as the abstracts were organized by names of property owners, they could not and did not take the place of a cadastre—a topographical register designed to furnish data on the location, area, land use, and tax rate of a given piece of ground. A record of this kind existed in Ptolemaic times and most certainly had its roots in the days of the Pharaohs. It was prepared by the village scribe (*kômogrammateus*), kept up-to-date by means of an annual inspection (*episkepsis*), and

33. As translated by Bell, *ibid.* For a detailed discussion of the *diastrômata* see, for instance, Von Woess, *Untersuchungen*, pp. 98–102. Mitteis and Wilcken, *Grundzüge*, II, 2, 213–215, shows the entry for a certain Sarapion on the *diastrôma* of the city Oxyrhynchus. See also Von Woess, *Untersuchungen*, p. 124, n. 2.

34. The chief justice, who has been compared with the British Master of the Rolls, maintained two offices for processing validation requests, the *dialogê*, which examined the documents submitted, and the *katalogeion*, which carried out the process of *dêmosiôsis*. Neither office retained the documents that had been validated. A party could also obtain ex post facto validation of a deed of hand by the *ekmartyrêsis* procedure, that is, by filing with the competent archival agency a supporting document designed to confirm a deed of hand. See Wenger, *Die Quellen*, p. 741, and the specialized literature he refers to.

supplemented by a cadastre of the buildings constructed on the land. The cadastre was continued by the Romans, and so, of course, was the census taken at intervals of fourteen years and, according to one author, instituted by Ptolemy IV Philopater "to exact the maximum of taxes when he introduced the poll tax at the beginning of his reign."[35] The requirement that census returns be filed in four or five different offices imposed a heavy burden on householders and landlords. Copies of the cadastre and of the census records, or at least summaries of the latter, were sent to the public archives of the nome for safe-keeping, and presumably summaries of the cadastre were also sent to the central archives in Alexandria to be available to the high officials responsible for the financial administration, or rather exploitation, of the country.[36]

In Roman times the prefects of Egypt seem to have taken considerable interest in matters pertaining to both the property record office and the regional state archives. It is evident in the often cited proclamation of Prefect M. Mettius Rufus of A.D. 89, which criticized negligence in keeping the abstracts (*diastrômata*) in the property record offices and prescribed their renewal every five years. And no one could show better understanding of the primary needs of an archival establishment than Prefect Minicius Italicus, who on May 19, 109, instructed the three strategoi of the Arsinoe nome to construct a new building for the property records because in the existing one they were perishing and most of them could not even be found. When the building was ready, the strategoi were to transfer to it "the records of earlier dates which . . . are partially destroyed and sealed up, since no one can make them available, because the parties to them have long been dead." Upon completion of the transfer, the

35. Sherman LeRoy Wallace, *Taxation in Egypt from Augustus to Diocletian* (Princeton, 1938), p. 96. Contrary to Wallace's opinion, Marcel Hombert and Claire Préaux, *Recherches sur le recensement dans l'Egypte romaine* (Leiden, 1952), 50–52, believe that the existence of the periodic census cannot be proved before A.D. 34. On the officers to whom census returns had to be sent and on the copies needed for the purpose, see *ibid.*, pp. 84–87. Figure 33, showing some census returns pasted together into a *tomos synkollêsimos*, reproduces part of a plate included in this authoritative work.

36. Mitteis and Wilcken, *Grundzüge*, I, 1, 178, and Wallace, *Taxation*, p. 9.

records were to be registered "in the presence of the proper persons," and the register was to be filed. The cost of the new building was established at 3,282 drachmas and three obols, a surprisingly precise estimate.[37]

Staffs of the nome public archives and the property record office—assuming that these were subdivisions of one and the same agency—normally consisted of an archivist in charge (*bibliophylax*), a chief clerk, and other personnel. From what we know, the performance of both offices left much to be desired, although the prefects kept a watchful eye on the archives during their inspection trips. What, however, could be expected of the archivists when they had to assume their duties as a *leitourgia*, a service imposed upon the well-to-do citizens of the nome? Although relieved of the actual work, which was performed by the chief clerk and his staff of clerks and servants, the archivist *malgré lui* had to sign certain letters and lists and had to be present when needed. And, most important, the nome archivists had to "pay the necessary expenses [of the office] and . . .[be] responsible toward the government with their private fortune. To the necessary expenses belongs also, when necessary, the building of a new store house for the records."[38] And if the archivists died—and most of them as men of means must have been elderly persons—their heirs, widows as well as children, were responsible for the archives. Burdened with a task that might have disastrous financial consequences for them and their families, archivists could hardly be expected to assume and perform their duties with enthusiasm.

No wonder, then, that conditions in the state archives seem to have been fairly bad, judging by complaints that have a familiar ring to us. The strategoi and their scribes, we are told,

37. Both documents referred to in this paragraph are reproduced in full by Bell, "The Custody of Records," pp. 121–123.

38. B. A. van Groningen, ed., *A Family-Archive from Tebtunis* (Leiden, 1950), p. 107. See also the same author's "Un conflit du IIe siècle de notre ère," pp. 313–332; and, on the institution of the liturgy, Friedrich Oertel, *Die Liturgie: Studien zur ptolemäischen und kaiserlichen Verwaltung Ägyptens* (Leipzig, 1917). According to Oertel, p. 288, archivists had to serve for about three years.

sent the records to the state archives regardless of their condition; many of them were "piled up in confusion"; the papyrus rolls were frail and damaged from heavy use; and they were "eaten away at the top," or lost their beginning, or fell to pieces because of excessive heat in the depositories. These defects came to light and often led to litigation when the previous incumbent of the archives job, or more frequently his heirs, wanted to get rid of the archives by transferring them to a newly appointed archivist and when the recipient, in his own interest, did not want to accept any rolls not in good condition. In the Arsinoe nome, the problem of who in such a case should pay for repairing the damaged records was the subject of a lawsuit that lasted from A.D. 90 to 124.[39]

Conditions in the central archival establishments undoubtedly were better than those in the nomes, for it is quite certain that they were staffed with regular civil servants. We know of three such establishments: the *bibliothêkê en Patrikois*, that is, the record office in the Patrika section of Alexandria; the Hadriane, which may have been founded by the Emperor Hadrian; and the Nanaion, probably housed in the Nana temple. At one time the keeper of the Nanaion was subordinate to the chief of the Hadriane, for an edict of Prefect T. Flavius Titianus of A.D. 127 instructs the keeper of the Nanaion to allow no one, the keeper included, to lend documents entrusted to his custody or even to grant access to them without the consent of the head of the library of Hadrian. This restriction had become necessary, because the keeper of the Nanaion had attempted to tamper with the records.[40]

Responsibilities were divided between the Patrika record office on the one hand and the Hadriane and Nanaion on the

39. The documents pertaining to the lawsuit are found in Van Groningen, ed., *A Family-Archive*, pp. 44–62 and 85–108. His article in *Chronique d'Egypte* supersedes Wilhelm Schubart, "Die Bibliophylakes und ihr Grammateus," *Archiv für Papyrusforschung*, VIII (1927), 14–24.

40. Bernard P. Grenfell and Arthur S. Hunt, eds., *The Oxyrhynchus Papri*, pt. 1 (London, 1898), 70. See also Ulrich Wilcken, "Papyrus-Urkunden," *Archiv für Papyrusforschung*, I (1901), 124.

other. To the latter two institutions the clerks in the nome
property offices were to send, in accordance with established
practice, lists of contracts deposited, with a short description of
the contents of each. Similarly, the *archidikastês* sent the documents pertaining to the *dêmosiôsis* of deeds by hand to the
Hadriane, with a copy going to the Nanaion. Additional light is
thrown on the function of the Hadriane by another edict of
Prefect T. Flavius Titianus five months later, in which he criti-
cizes the nome officials of Egypt for not sending their reports to
the Library of Hadrian, which was established for the purpose
of preventing the concealment of any irregularities. Further
violations, he threatens, will be appropriately punished.[41]
From the above it appears that the Hadriane was the younger
of the two institutions, designed to prevent irregularities and
abuses that had been discovered in the older Nanaion.

If on the central level Nanaion and Hadriane corresponded
to the property record offices in the nomes, the Patrika record
office was the central repository for public records for which in
the nome the *dêmosia bibliothêkê* was responsible. We know
nothing about its personnel, its functions, and its techniques.
There certainly was an established procedure for the transfer
of records to the archives, for we have a letter dated A.D. 136,
with which the strategos of the Mendesian nome transmits to
the Patrika state archives four rolls of his daybooks, identified
by their inclusive dates. The letter of transmittal shows what
seems to be the receipt of the messenger who was to deliver
the records in Alexandria, and a second receipt, that of the
director of the archives. When the transfer document with the
director's receipt was received at nome headquarters, it was on
the verso identified as "Receipt of the Director of the Patrika
State Archives for records covering the period from the 21st
of Hadrianus to the 4th of Phamenoth contained in four rolls."[42]
No doubt the high officials residing in Alexandria also sent their

---

41. Grenfell and Hunt, *Oxyrhynchus Papyri*, pp. 70, 74; Wilcken, "Papyrusurkunden," p. 125.
42. Preisigke, *Das Girowesen*, pp. 410–411; Bell, "The Custody of Records," p. 123.

noncurrent records to Patrika. As already noted, it would be logical to assume that in one form or another cadastres and census returns had to be available in Alexandria and that the Patrika archives would have been the appropriate repository.

We do not know what the archives buildings in Alexandria and in the nomes looked like. The latter were undoubtedly rather modest. Those in Alexandria might have been more substantial structures; and, since the physical make-up of archives did not differ from that of library material, the remnants of Hadrian's library in Athens and those of the Ephesus library may give us some idea of the arrangements in the Alexandria archives. A large reading room, such as existed in these two libraries, was of course not needed for those consulting the archives; but the storage facilities—niches or pigeonholes in the walls—were probably similar to those still to be seen in Athens and Ephesus.[43]

Strictly controlled by the state, the temples could not avoid contributing their share to the process of enormous record production that characterized Ptolemaic and Roman Egypt. The Roman government required each temple to submit an annual report on the number of priests on its "staff" and also an inventory of the establishment. Copies went to at least five different officials, among them the strategos, the scribe of the nome, and the *bibliophylax* of the state archives. And, needless to say, copies were retained in the temple archives, as they were, for instance, in the temple of the crocodile god Soknobraisis at Bacchias.[44]

In a country in which the government urged its subjects to seek official documentation of their business affairs and in which

43. Franz Miltner, *Ephesos, Stadt der Artemis und des Johannes* (Vienna, 1958), pp. 55–58. According to Wilhelm Alzinger, *Die Stadt des siebenten Weltwunders* (Vienna, 1962), p. 117, the capacity of the Ephesus library has been estimated at about 12,000 papyrus rolls. On the library of Hadrian, see M. A. Sisson, "The Stoa of Hadrian at Athens," in *Papers of the British School at Rome*, XI (1921), 50–72. Christian Callmer, "Antike Bibliotheken," in Institutum Romanum Regni Sveciae, *Opuscula Archaeologica*, III (1944), pp. 145–193, is one of the best studies of classical libraries.

44. Elizabeth H. Gilliam, "The Archives of the Temple of Soknobraisis at Bacchias," *Yale Classical Studies*, X (1947), 191, 197.

the government itself required and accumulated a multitude of data for the transaction of its business, the inhabitants must have become as conscious of the importance of record-making and record-keeping as had been their ancestors in the days of the Pharaohs. It is not surprising that, insofar as conditions of climate and soil did not prevent their preservation, a great number of family and personal archives have survived. As is frequently the case with modern archives of this type, they include purely personal documents together with business records and records of offices held by the archives creators. Thus, the archives of a certain Aurelius Isidorus consist of his and his family's personal papers, documents accumulated by him as a landholder and as a tenant, and records of the ten liturgical offices to which he was assigned during the twenty years from A.D. 289/9 to 318/19.[45]

The combination of official and private archives is also represented by the archives of Apollonius, strategos of the nome of Apollonopolis Heptakomia during the end of Trajan's and the beginning of Hadrian's regime. When he retired to his property in Hermopolis, Apollonius took with him his almost 150 papyri. They cover the routine business of his office, the administration of the census, the proceedings of his court of first instance, and the affairs of his family circle.[46]

Of outstanding importance among the private archives is that of Zenon, businessman and manager in the modern sense of the word, who administered the great estate of Apollonius, minister of finance of King Ptolemaeus Philadelphus, in the newly founded development Philadelphia in the Fayyûm.[47]

45. Arthur E. R. Boak and Herbert Chayyim Youtie, eds., *The Archive of Aurelius Isidorus in the Egyptian Museum, Cairo, and the University of Michigan* (Ann Arbor, 1960). See also Turner, *Greek Papyri*, p. 83.

46. C. H. Roberts, "The Greek Papyri," in S. R. K. Glanville, ed., *The Legacy of Egypt* (Oxford, 1942), pp. 276–281; and John Garrett Winter, *Life and Letters in the Papyri* (Ann Arbor, 1933), p. 66, where the reader is referred to A. G. Ross's publication of the Apollonius correspondence in "Apollonius, strateg van Heptakomia," *Tijdschrift voor geschiedenis*, XXXVII (1922), 1–40, 129–146.

47. On Zenon, see M. I. Rostovtzeff, *A Large Estate in Egypt in the Third Century B.C.: A Study in Economic History* (Madison, 1922). Seidl, *Ptolemäische Rechtsgeschichte*,

Though found in Philadelphia, Zenon's records date back to a period when he spent part of his time in Alexandria and part in the Syrian provinces of the Ptolemies and when he was traveling a great deal, already serving as an agent of Apollonius. Appointed by the latter to serve as manager of his estate in Philadelphia, Zenon brought with him a four-year accumulation of his papers, and to these he added systematically his managerial correspondence in which "every rank of society is represented among the correspondents, from the chief minister of the Kingdom down to the native swineherd writing from prison."[48] In the best tradition Zenon must have realized the wisdom of clearly identifying each letter before filing it, for, after he had opened and read it, he had the document folded up again and on the outside, to the left of the address, were entered the date and sometimes the place of its reception, the name of the writer, and the subject matter.[49] Unfortunately we do not know where and how Zenon kept his archives, because the dealers who disposed of the documents did not disclose the source of their supply. Quite possibly, however, the papyri were found in the ruins of Zenon's house.[50]

In addition to the Zenon archives many other bodies of private papers have survived. Those of the Ptolemaic period have been dealt with by Erwin Seidl,[51] who discusses the contents of twenty-five private archives. With few exceptions these archival bodies are now dispersed, for, even if the native diggers

pp. 34–43, deals in detail with the contents of the Zenon Archives, which somewhat narrowly he terms a *Buchführungsarchiv*. Rightly, it seems, he distinguishes its six components: (1) Zenon's papers predating his being sent to Philadelphia; (2) the papers of his predecessor Panakestor, which Zenon took over; (3) Zenon's administrative records during his term of office as an administrator of Apollonius' estate; (4) Zenon's papers pertaining to public affairs; (5) the papers of Eukles, who succeeded Zenon as administrator of the Philadelphia estate; and (6) Zenon's papers of the period following his dismissal. Seidl thinks that possibly Zenon assisted his successor and that therefore the entire archives remained in Zenon's hands and in Philadelphia, where he had his residence.

48. Campbell C. Edgar, *Zenon Papyri in the University of Michigan Collection* (Ann Arbor, 1931), p. 3.

49. *Ibid.*, p. 59.

50. Rostovtzeff, *A Large Estate*, p. 5, n. 9.

51. Seidl, *Ptolemäische Rechtsgeschichte*, pp. 17–34.

found them fairly intact, they were sold piecemeal and are now in the possession of institutions in many lands. The archives of the embalmer Psemminis, however, were found untouched in two earthen jars, and the jars and their contents remained together until they reached responsible custody. Another private archive that has remained intact is that of a certain Horos.[52] It came into the hands of Elkan N. Adler as "a potful of Papyri" and stems from the area of the villages of Pathyris and Krokodilopolis, south of Thebes, where a number of private archives of the period from about 150 to 88 B.C. have come to light. This group includes the papers of Peteharsemteus, consisting of documents that were successively in the custody of a certain Totoês, his oldest son, and his oldest grandson, each of whom also kept the documentation of his brothers and sisters and of his wife.[53] The other private archives that Seidl has identified represent a laudable effort on his part to reconstruct on paper archival accumulations, or parts of them, that have become dismembered.

To name but a few of the private archives of the Roman period, there have been preserved the archives of the Flavius family, which, the records reveal, had its own prisons, postal service, racing stable, public baths, hospitals, counting houses, Nile boats, and monasteries, together with the necessary staff of secretaries, accountants, and tax collectors;[54] the archives of the mortician and embalmer Petesis, preserved by several generations of his family;[55] the records of the notary Flavius Dioskoros, of the later period of Justinian and Justin II, consisting of business records and poetical elaborations written on the verso of records that apparently he had acquired as waste paper;[56] and the records of Heroninos, administrator during the

---

52. Elkan N. Adler and others, eds., *The Adler Papyri* (London, 1939).

53. P. W. Pestman, "Les archives privées de Pathyris à l'époque ptolémaique: La famille de Pétéharsemtheus, fils de Panebkhdunis," in *Studia Papyrologica Varia* (Leiden, 1965), pp. 47–105.

54. Bell, *Egypt*, p. 122.

55. Karl Preisendanz, *Papyrusfunde und Papyrusforschung* (Leipzig, 1933), p. 84.

56. *Ibid.*, pp. 214–217.

third century A.D. of an imperial estate in Theadelphia.[57] It has been surmised that families kept their important documents in earthen vessels and stored these in the family tombs, where the family congregated every year.[58]

Record-keeping, however, was not solely a concern of the educated and the mighty, for also extant are the archives of a Philadelphia servants' club, which had one of its meetings in the harness room next to the stables and another in the storeroom or granary. Such social clubs were quite common in every Egyptian town, and there are many records left of them.[59] Even persons who, because of their purpose in life, would not be expected to care about good record-keeping, might keep a file of "letters received," as did Paphnutius, an anchorite of special fame, highly regarded for his sanctity. Living about the middle of the fourth century A.D., he made it a practice to keep the requests of those who, unable to visit him in person, asked him to intercede for the salvation of their souls or for their recovery from illness.[60]

People in the lower walks of life used papyrus sparingly as writing material. Although a native product, under the Ptolemies the sale of first quality papyrus was a state monopoly, and the export of papyrus was subject to a duty so high that on the island of Delos a roll of papyrus was two or three times more expensive than in Egypt.[61] To avoid using such costly writing material, the Greeks had resorted to potsherds (ostraca) for everyday purposes, and they may have brought this practice with them

57. *Ibid.*, p. 224.

58. *Ibid.*, p. 113.

59. Campbell C. Edgar, "Records of a Village Club," in *Raccolta di scritti in onore di Giacomo Lumbroso, 1844–1925* (Milan, 1925), p. 372. According to Franz Poland, *Geschichte des griechischen Vereinswesens* (Leipzig, 1909), p. 467, Greek associations needed a facility "that would serve especially to house their records, although in most cases one should hardly think of a separate archives building."

60. Sir Harold Idris Bell, ed., *Jews and Christians in Egypt* (London, 1924), pp. 100–120, and H. Leclercq, "Paphnuce," in *Dictionnaire d'archéologie chrétienne et de liturgie*, XIII (Paris, 1936), 1358–1361. Paphnutius has been immortalized in Anatole France's *Thaïs* (Paris, 1890).

61. N. Lewis, *L'industrie du papyrus dans l'Egypte gréco-romaine* (Paris, 1934), pp. 125–133 and 150–153.

to Egypt, where the ostracon cost nothing.[62] Well-to-do people considered the use of the ostracon unfashionable, and so it remained the "paper" of the little fellow. Though it was plentiful, he conserved it carefully, possibly wiping off the original writing (palimpsest), writing on the verso (epistograph), or making more than one entry on the same ostracon. For official use it was not admissible in interagency correspondence, but it served well in communication with the public, as for instance in tax receipts. It is thought that, though methods of storing the awkward ostraca must have differed, they were often, like papyrus rolls, kept in big earthen vats. "An archives of this kind must have looked like a wine cellar."[63] Whole ostraca archives have indeed been found. One of them is the business archives, or at least part of the business archives, of a transportation enterprise in Coptos, owned by a certain Nikanor and members of his family. It consists of receipts for the delivery of goods that the firm had shipped to their destination. Covering the period from A.D. 6 to 62, it records fifty-six years of the activities of this family business.[64]

The prostitute Thinmareine thought equally well of the importance of her business records, for she kept the following document issued to her on an ostracon: "Ammonios and his colleagues, farmers of the courtesan tax, [wish] joy to Thinmareine. We have granted you permission to ply your trade the 26th of Thot of the sixth year of Antoninus Caesar our lord."[65]

62. Ulrich Wilcken, *Griechische Ostraka aus Ägypten und Nubien*, I (Berlin and Leipzig, 1899), 9. Few ostraca dating from pre-Ptolemaic times have been found in Egypt. A regular ostraca archives was found in Philadelphia. It relates to the administration of an estate during the third century B.C. See Seidl, *Ptolemäische Rechtsgeschichte*, p. 43.

63. Wilcken, *Griechische Ostraka*, p. 19.

64. John G. Tait, ed., *Greek Ostraka in the Bodleian Library at Oxford and Various Other Collections*, 2 vols. (London, 1930–1955). See also Alexander Fuks, "Notes on the Archive of Nikanor," *Journal of Juristic Papyrology*, V (1951), 207–216.

65. Wolfgang Müller, ed., "Griechische Ostraka," *Archiv für Papyrusforschung*, XVI (1958), 212–213.

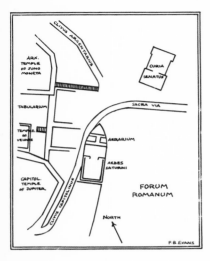

Walking up to the Campidoglio, Rome's Capitol Hill, the visitor finds himself in front of the Senatorial Palace. In all probability he will not realize that the rear of the building, which faces down toward the Forum Romanum, includes what is left of the Tabularium, once the state archives of Rome (figure 34). From an arcade, only a part of which has been restored to its ancient beauty, the spectator still enjoys a sweeping view of the Forum and the Palatine. Turning toward the interior of the structure, however, he will find no traces of the purpose the building was to serve when it was erected in 79 B.C. He will not be able to identify office space and stack areas, nor will he find any of the equipment used for storing the records. And so it is that, while we can still admire part of the glory of the Roman archives, we must turn to literary evidence if we wish to explore the archival practices of ancient Rome. Fortunately, Roman authors have frequently referred to the archives, a few of them have actually used them, and copies of archival documents have been preserved on tablets of bronze and stone. Thus there has come down to us a considerable body of data that enables us to piece together in broad outline the history of Roman archives administration. Logically this history is divided into two periods: that of the archives of the Republic and that of the records of imperial Rome down to and including the legislation of Justinian.

In his *Georgics* Vergil praises as lucky the man of the golden age who earned the fruits his fields had borne and who did not have to "behold the iron laws, the Forum's madness, or the public archives," [1] and, indeed, for a long time Roman government appears to have been oral government. Even for the publication of laws, *renuntiatio*—that is, promulgation through a herald—was the only known device. When writing began to

Figure 34. Sketch of the western part of the Forum Romanum in Republican times.

1. The *Georgics* ii.502, cited in C. Dziatzko, "Archive," in Pauly-Wissowa, *Real-Encyclopädie*, II (1896), 554; *Real-Encyclopädie* is hereafter cited as *RE*.

Figure 35. *The location of the former Aerarium east of the steps leading to the pronaos of the Temple of Saturn, with the marble threshold of the door still in place.*

be used for official purposes, methods of making and preserving records differed materially from those practiced at that time in other parts of the ancient world, for in Rome record-making as a relatively original and national phenomenon was already fully developed when papyrus, the preferred writing material of the East, became available. Instead, the wood tablet (*tabula*) remained in use, and the Romans stuck to it with truly Roman tenacity, because, although inconvenient, it had its advantages, if only that wood was cheap and easily obtainable in Italy.

The wood tablet was either an *alba*, that is, a tablet covered with white paint or gypsum that could be written or painted on, or it was a *tabula cerata* or *cera* covered with a layer of wax that was protected by a surrounding profile and could be written on with a stylus.[2] A number of tablets of either kind could be hinged together and thus would form a diptych (two tablets), a triptych (three tablets), or, if there were even more of them, a polyptychon. A whole cluster of tablets was called a *caudex* or codex, literally translated, a block of wood, and later assuming the more specific meaning of a block of wood that had been split or sawed into leaves or tablets. Except for its bulkiness, the codex could be compared to a file consisting of paper documents held together by a metal fastener. Documents in a codex were referred to by identifying the *tabula* within the codex and the *cera* (page) of the *tabula*. Codices of this kind can be seen on one of the so-called *Anaglypha Trajani*, marble barriers now in the Senate Building (*Curia Senatus*) on the Forum. One barrier records the burning of tax records pursuant to an amnesty granted by Emperor Hadrian. It shows men in semi-military garb carrying bundles of wooden tablets and stacking

---

2. For details on the wood tablet, see Erich Sachers, "Tabula," *RE*, ser. 2, vol. IV (1932), 1881–1886; Ernst Kornemann, "Tabulae publicae," *ibid.*, 1957–1962; Leopold Wenger, *Die Quellen des römischen Rechts* (Vienna, 1953), pp. 74–78. Viktor Emil Gardthausen, *Griechische Paleographie*, 2d ed., I (Leipzig, 1911), shows on p. 129 a *codex ansatus*, one equipped with a hook that could be used to carry it or to hang it up. See also David Diringer, *The Hand-Produced Book* (New York, 1953), pp. 29–33, 35–36; on p. 32 a "page" of a codex in the British Museum and a reconstruction of a Herculaneum codex are reproduced.

them up in two neat piles, ready to be "disposed of" by fire.[3] Wooden records also came in handy when, in 52 B.C., a mob escorted the corpse of the rabble-rouser Clodius to the Senate Building and cremated it there, using benches, seats, tables, and records for the purpose.[4]

Even if not purposely used as fuel, wood tablets could not be expected to last; hence only a few examples of them have come down to us. The most important specimens are wax tablets found in the ancient gold mines of Transylvania and in Pompei.[5] The latter accumulation, receipts that the auctioneer L. Caecilius Jucundus had obtained from his clients and that, in turn, he had received from the municipality of Pompei, had been kept in a wooden chest which the owner apparently left behind as less important than other parts of his archives when Mount Vesuvius erupted. He must have had a sense of order, for frequently the contents of the various triptychs are indicated in ink on the rim so that a wanted item could easily be extracted. Quite recently, another collection of wax tablets (ca. A.D. 37–55) was discovered in Pompei. Apparently constituting the archives of C. Sulpicius Cynnamus, who owned storage magazines for grain and lent money to the producers, these tablets were found to be particularly well preserved because they had been embedded in swampy tidelands. They pose the problem of drying them out slowly and carefully in order to keep the wood from cracking.[6] Mention might also be made of the famous Albertini tablets, forty-five business documents of a much later period when North Africa was ruled by the Vandals.

---

3. Ludwig Curtius, *Das antike Rom*, ed. Ernest Nash, 3d ed. (Vienna, 1957), p. 35 and illustration no. 20.

4. Kornemann, "Tabulae publicae," 1961.

5. The Transylvania and Pompei tablets have been published by Theodor Mommsen and Karl Zangemeister respectively in *Corpus Inscriptionum Latinarum*, III (1873), 921–959, and IV (1898), supplement 1. See also Theodor Mommsen, "Die pompeianischen Quittungstafeln des L. Caecilius Jucundus," *Hermes*, XII (1877), 88–141, and the literature referred to by Wenger, *Die Quellen*, p. 76.

6. Accademia Nazionale dei Lincei, Classe di Science Morali, etc., *Rendiconti*, XIV (1960), 435–436; Olga Elia, "Il portico dei triclini del Pagus Maritimus di Pompei," *Bolletino d'arte*, XLVI (1961), 202, 211.

These are diptychs or triptychs that were written on directly with ink, and in a sense most of them are palimpsests, that is, they were reused once or even several times.[7]

As in Greece, a large whitened board, called an *album*, was used by the magistrates for the publication of laws and important issuances that had to be brought to the attention of the people by displaying them near the seats of the officials concerned. Later on such documents were incised on bronze tablets. These tablets as well as the whitened boards were but reproductions of the originals in the archives or, even more likely, reproductions of ad hoc copies, because the originals would hardly have been entrusted to the painter or engraver. In imperial days whole rosters of veterans who had been granted certain privileges were recorded on bronze tablets. Upon request, individual veterans could obtain copies of the text, with only their names inserted, in the form of "military diplomas," actually diptychs with an exterior and interior text, the latter secured by a wire device and the seals of witnesses.[8]

Whether the Etruscans also wrote on wood we do not know. The only extensive piece of Etruscan writing that has been found so far is a linen document that was cut in strips by an Egyptian embalmer to serve as a "wrapper."[9] Some linen was also used in Rome, for Livy refers to *libri lintei*, in which, according to the historian C. Licinius Macer, the names of Roman magistrates were recorded. These linen books, kept in the temple of the Juno Moneta on the northern summit of the Capitol, were possibly the earliest archival accumulation in the city.

7. Christian Courtois and others, *Tablettes Albertini: Actes privés de l'époque Vandale* (Paris, 1952), pp. 7–12. For a reference to other documents of the same physical type, see *ibid.*, p. 9, n. 2.

8. An example of a bronze diptych may be seen on plates III and IV accompanying Wilhelm Kubitscheck, "Ein Soldatendiplom des Kaisers Vespasian," *Jahreshefte des Österreichischen Archäologischen Institutes in Wien*, XVII (1914), 148–193. See also Wenger, *Die Quellen*, pp. 57–58.

9. Massimo Pallotino, *The Etruscans* (Harmondsworth, Middlesex, 1955), p. 242. On three gold tablets found at Pyrgi near Rome and recording in Punic and Etruscan the dedication of a temple about 500 B.C., see H. H. Scullard, *The Etruscan Cities and Rome* (London and Ithaca, N.Y., 1967), pp. 102–104.

Private archives-keeping preceded concern about the preservation of public records. From relatively early times on, Romans entered in their *adversaria* (daybooks) information on their business transactions and at the end of each month they prepared a summary in the *tabulae* or *codex accepti et expensi* (register of receipts and expenditures). They had to present these summaries when the census was taken, and the need for preserving them carefully in a house archives (*tablinum*) was therefore quite obvious. In the absence of public archival institutions, an outgoing magistrate was quite likely to place in his *tablinum* the records of his term of office, possibly for the benefit of a son who might be planning a career in the public service.[10]

Included in the records an official might take with him were the daybooks he kept as the incumbent of a public office, an informal daily record of his transactions and of those in which he played a part. These daybooks, called *commentarii*[11] in Rome, were the equivalent of the *hypomnêmatismoi* we encountered in the East. There is no reason, however, to assume that the latter served as a model for the Roman *commentarii*. In fact, it is possible, though not probable, that in Rome daybooks were already kept by the kings. Those of consuls and other magistrates are frequently mentioned in our sources.

Since the magistrates took the records of their term of office into their private *tablina*, public archival institutions were slow in developing. The most important we know of was not an institution exclusively charged with archives-keeping but the state treasury, the Aerarium, whose origin is supposed to date to the first days of the Republic. According to Plutarch, it was established through a law of the first consul, P. Valerius Poplicola, and controlled by the quaestors.[12] As assistants to the con-

10. Theodor Mommsen, *Römisches Strafrecht* (Leipzig, 1899), p. 513, n. 3, and his *Römisches Staatsrecht*, 3d ed. (Leipzig, 1887–1888), I, 5, n. 2, where he refers to Cicero's urging that those who have retired from office turn over their papers to the censors.

11. A. von Premerstein, "Commentarii," *RE*, IV (1901), 726–759, and "A commentariis," *ibid.*, 759–768; Giorgio Cencetti, "Gli archivi dell'antica Roma nell'età repubblicana," *Archivi*, ser. 2, VII (1940), 9–12; Wenger, *Die Quellen*, pp. 417–418.

12. *Lex de quaestoribus aerarii.* See Mommsen, *Staatsrecht*, II, 525, n. 2; Dziatzko,

suls, these officials combined judicial functions with the administration of the state treasury, where public funds, precious metals, insignia, and treasures of all kinds were stored. It was only logical for quaestorial documents pertaining to receipts and expenditures to be kept in the treasury, where later other important series of records were to join them. Dedicated to the god Saturn, to whom tradition ascribed the origin of the art of reckoning and of all external order,[13] the Aerarium was located in a room east of the flight of steps leading to the Saturn temple (figure 35). Access was from the *Clivus Capitolinus.*[14] Although the Aerarium served as both a treasury house and a record depository and although storage space, therefore, must have been very limited, it served its dual purpose until 79 B.C., when the Tabularium was built to become Rome's state archives.

From then on, although the administrative relationship between Aerarium and Tabularium was not discontinued and although the latter was still a division of the treasury, the Tabularium was in effect a quasi-central archives of the Republic into which most, though not all, of the agency archives of that period were gathered together. It continued with a limited competence during the Empire when, of course, the more important documentation was to be found on the Palatine, the seat of the emperors.

At first the archives function of the Aerarium was fairly narrowly circumscribed. It had, of course, the documents generated by the fiscal responsibilities of the quaestors or, more precisely, after the number of these magistrates had been increased from two to four in 21 B.C., of the two *quaestores urbani,* the urban quaestors, who remained in the city while the other two accompanied the consuls on their campaigns.[15] The

"Archive," p. 562; H. Volkmann, "Valerii Poplicolae," *RE*, ser. 2, vol. XV (1955), 183.

    13. Dziatzko, "Archive," p. 559.

    14. On the temple of Saturn, see Ernest Nash, *Bildlexikon zur Topographie des antiken Rom*, II (Tübingen, 1962), 294–298.

    15. Mommsen, *Staatsrecht*, II, 523–673; H. F. Jolowicz, *Historical Introduction to the*

quaestorial records must have included the records of receipts and expenditures, those pertaining to negotiations with the tax farmers, and the *commentarii* of the quaestors. In addition—and this may have been its most important archival function— the Aerarium became the repository for certain documents of the Senate.

As will be recalled, the Senate was not a legislative but a consultative body to which the magistrates endowed with the *jus agendi cum patribus* (the right to transact business with the Senate) turned for advice. This advice they obtained in the form of a resolution (*sententia*), and although Senate resolutions did not have the force of law, they were policy decisions of the first magnitude that no magistrate could disregard. Because of their quasi-legal and binding character, their safe and un-adulterated preservation was a matter of the greatest importance. Since the Senate itself had no secretarial office for handling its business, the magistrate submitting a question to the Senate and obtaining its advice had the duty of filing the resolution in the Aerarium; and no Senate resolution was considered valid until the process of filing, called the *delatio ad aerarium*, had been completed.[16]

In the Aerarium Senate resolutions were assembled in the *liber sententiarum in senatu dictarum*. Whether this series consisted of the actual *tabulae* on which the magistrates had recorded the Senate resolutions or whether the Aerarium scribes entered the texts into codices of their own, we are not certain.[17] The latter may have been the case, since probably the originals submitted left much to be desired. If there was a verbatim registration of the resolutions in the codices of the Aerarium, the originals

---

Study of Roman Law (Cambridge, Eng., 1952), pp. 37–38, 47–48; Heinrich Siber, *Römi-sches Verfassungerecht in geschichtlicher Entwicklung* (Lahr, 1952), pp. 95–99.

16. A minimum of ten days, however, had to elapse between a Senate resolution carrying a death sentence and its filing in the Aerarium (Mommsen, *Strafrecht*, p. 912).

17. On this question, see Cencetti, "Gli archivi," pp. 16–18, and particularly p. 17. n. 37. See also O'Brien Moore, "Senatus consultum," *RE*, supplement 6 (1935), 800–812, and Fritz Freiherr von Schwind, *Zur Frage der Publikation im römischen Recht* (Munich, 1940), pp. 56–58. A Senate resolution of 44 B.C. concerning the Jews had to be readopted after Caesar's death because it had not been properly registered.

might have been kept as a separate series to be referred to in case of need. The *delatio* procedure was certainly by no means safe, for Senate resolutions could be tampered with because their wording did not have to be approved by the Senate. The quaestors, therefore, had the right to require proof of the respective magistrates and even the testimony of witnesses. Thus, as quaestor, Cato of Utica (95–46 B.C.) refused to accept a Senate resolution into the Aerarium until both consuls had testified to its genuineness.[18] Not all of Cato's successors were as conscientious as he, nor could they afford to be so during the times of trouble that marked the end of the Republic. Cicero tells us that Caesar concocted Senate resolutions at his home, adding as witnesses the names of senators he picked at random,[19] and after Caesar's assassination Antonius followed his example when Senate resolutions never enacted were deposited in the Aerarium.[20] In all probability there was a separate codex or possibly more than one for the Senate resolutions of each year, for Cicero refers to the book that contained the Senate resolutions adopted during the consulship of Cn. Cornelius L. Mummius.[21]

The discussions of the Senate were not recorded, although the presiding officer might have informal notes taken in order to include them in his *commentarii* for preservation in his private archives (*tablinum*). Not until Caesar's first consulate was the practice of officially recording the transactions of the Senate begun. Augustus, however, discontinued it, and in its place a younger member of the Senate, with the title of *curator actorum senatus* (curator of the acts of the Senate), was charged with preparing minutes of the meetings for the emperor, who thus knew who had said what in the Senate. These minutes were probably preserved in the imperial archives on the Palatine.[22]

18. Wilhelm Kubitschek, "Acta," *RE*, I (1894), 289.

19. Mommsen, *Staatsrecht*, III, 1013, n. 3.

20. Hermann Peter, *Die geschichtliche Litteratur über die römische Kaiserzeit*, I (Leipzig, 1897), 238.

21. Cencetti, "Gli archivi," p. 17, n. 38.

22. Mommsen, *Staatsrecht*, III, 1017–1021.

Inasmuch as the legislative power rested with the people rather than with the Senate, the most important documentation pertaining to the enactment of laws originated in connection with the voting process in the *comitia*.[23] The proposing magistrate would first have his bill discussed in the Senate, however, and, in accordance with the *lex Licinia Junia* of 62 B.C., would deposit a copy in the Aerarium, a requirement designed to prevent any unauthorized changes in the text of the bill. He would also promulgate it so that it might be discussed in informal gatherings during the *trinundinum*, a period of three times eight days. Thereupon the vote would be taken in the *comitia*, and, if approved, the law would be proclaimed through oral *renuntiatio* by the herald and possibly, though not necessarily, publicized on the announcement board, the *album*. The laws enacted, if not the documents pertaining to their passage, would logically go to the Aerarium, where the texts of the respective bills were already kept.

As long as the struggle between patricians and plebeians practically divided the people into two separate orders, it was only natural for the plebs and its magistrates to be in need of an archival establishment of their own, "sort of an archives of the opposition, as we would say nowadays."[24] It was located in the temple of Ceres, Liber, and Libera, probably situated on the *Forum Boarium*, where remnants of it have been discovered below the present church of Santa Maria in Cosmedin.[25] The archives, administered by the two aediles, assistants to the tribunes, held the records of the plebiscites voted by the plebs. In addition to the plebiscites, and as a matter of precaution, Senate resolutions that formerly "were wont to be suppressed or

23. Cencetti, "Gli archivi," pp. 20–23, and particularly n. 56. See also further sources referred to by the author, particularly Mommsen, "Sui modi usati da'Romani per conservare e pubblicare le leggi ed i senatus consulti," *Gesammelte Schriften*, III (Berlin, 1907), 290–313, and his *Staatsrecht*, III, 369–419.

24. Michelangelo Puma, *La conservazione dei documenti giuridici nell'antica Roma* (Palermo, 1934), p. 36. Mistakenly, Ernst Stein suggests in "Beiträge zur ältesten römischen Geschichte," *Wiener Studien*, XXXVII (1915), 353–356, that the archives of the plebeian aediles was the oldest archives in Rome.

25. Nash, *Bildlexikon*, I, 227–229.

falsified at the pleasure of the consuls"[26] had to be deposited in the Ceres archives. This was especially true of resolutions that had a bearing on the interests of the plebs, as, for instance, those confirming the plebiscites. In 367 B.C., the plebeian aediles were joined by the curule aediles who "as true magistrates of the whole people" were elected in the *comitia tributa*, and the four magistrates acted together as a college (*collegium*).[27] When, in 286 B.C., the *lex Hortensia* ended the struggle between patricians and plebeians by ruling that enactments of the plebs would have the validity of laws passed by the entire people, Senate resolutions were no longer needed for the confirmation of plebiscites, and therewith disappeared likewise the need for an "archives of the opposition."[28] Logically, therefore, the Ceres archives was taken over by the Aerarium, an assumption confirmed by the fact that until the times of Augustus the aediles participated in the administration of the Aerarium. On what basis the work was divided between them and the quaestors, we cannot determine.

A body of records of considerable importance originated with the censors.[29] It stemmed partly from the registration of the entire people, a process in which the heads of families had to submit their financial records for purposes of assessment. These records were kept in the temple of the Nymphs (*Aedes Nympharum*) on the Campus Martius, close to the public building in which the censors had their office. A separate review of the knights (*equites*) was held in the *Atrium Libertatis* near the Forum and produced another accumulation of records. Censorial records were of a particularly sensitive nature, because they included the notes of censure that the censors might see fit to enter against a man's name. Equally sensitive were the records that resulted from revising the list of members of the Senate, another duty of the censors. Finally, their fiscal and housekeeping functions, such as assessing the taxes, farming them

26. *Livy* iii.lv.13, as cited by Kubitschek, "Acta," p. 287.
27. Jolowicz, *Roman Law*, p. 48.
28. Puma, *La conservazione*, p. 38.
29. Mommsen, *Staatsrecht*, II, 359–424; Cencetti, "Gli archivi," pp. 24–28; Puma, *La conservazione*, p. 35.

out to tax collectors, contracting for the construction of public buildings and roads, and keeping an inventory of state-owned land, must have produced a great quantity of records whose importance transcended the term of service of the censors. And since they had to relinquish their office after the census had been taken (normally every four or five years) or at the most eighteen months after they had been elected, the records of the censors were taken over by the Aerarium so that they would be available to other magistrates of the Republic.[30]

The records of the censors, actually their current records, were in the normal course of events transferred to the custody of the quaestors. Other agencies kept their archives indefinitely. Special provision seems to have been made for the long-term preservation of international treaties, including treaties with federated states. Apart from their being publicized on bronze tablets displayed in the vicinity of the Jupiter temple on the Capitol and at the Deus Fidius temple on the Quirinal, the originals were kept in the temple of the Fides Populi Romani, which thus could be considered a foreign relations archives of the state.[31]

The archives of the College of Pontiffs also maintained its separate position and its secret character for a long time. The pontiffs were in possession of the formulas that a citizen had to use in any of his legal business; they were familiar with the calendar and hence with the days on which a lawsuit could be instituted; and they had the records of the inquiries addressed to them and of the responses given, a collection of precedents of immense value that made the college a powerful force in the

30. I cannot agree with John E. A. Crake, "Archival Material in Livy, 218–167 B.C.," Ph.D. diss., Johns Hopkins University, 1939, p. 30, who prefers to think that the census records remained in the office of the censors. He concedes, however, that their financial records had to be transferred to the Aerarium (*ibid.*, p. 35).

31. Mommsen, *Gesammelte Schriften*, III, 306–313; Puma, *La conservazione*, p. 65; Wenger, *Die Quellen*, pp. 67–70. Crake, "Archival Material in Livy," p. 6, concludes from Suetonius' *Vespasian* viii, 5, that, once the Aerarium had begun to function as a state archives, the original treaties were preserved there. The passage refers to the destruction of 3,000 bronze tablets that perished in a fire on the Capitoline Hill and to Vespasian's attempt to have them replaced by copies obtained from other places.

development and application of Roman law. "There was at their exclusive disposal the entire tremendous legal tradition of the college, the treasure of century-old experiences."[32] Since originally the college was composed exclusively of patricians, its role remained unpopular until the lex Ogulnia of 300 B.C. ruled that four of the eight pontifices had to be plebeians. From then on any citizen could become a member of the pontifical college and engage there in legal studies, use the archives, and, in his capacity of pontifex, advise his plebeian equals.[33] The secret character of the pontificial archives, as far as temporal law was concerned, came to an end when in 304 B.C. its contents were published by Appius Claudius and Gneus Flavius and when about 250 B.C. the first plebeian Pontifex Maximus started the practice of giving responses in public.[34] In all questions of sacred law, however, the power and pre-rogatives of the College of Pontiffs remained unchanged.

The *commentarii* of the College of Pontiffs are specifically mentioned among the public and private records that perished when Rome was burned by the Gauls (387/6 B.C.).[35] That the quantity of records on hand was greatly reduced by that conflagration can be assumed, and this may help to explain why the Aerarium next to the Saturn temple could serve as the main archival depository of the state as long as it did. A fire on the Capitoline Hill in 83 B.C., which made it necessary to rebuild the temple of Jupiter and might have affected the Aerarium, may have led to the decision to provide a separate state archives building. One man, Q. Lutatius Catulus (consul in 78 B.C. and later Pontifex Maximus) was in charge of both the

32. Wenger, *Die Quellen*, p. 476, based mainly on Paul Jörs, *Römische Rechtswissenschaft zur Zeit der Republik. I. Bis auf die Zeit der Catonen* (Berlin, 1888), p. 57.

33. Wenger, *Die Quellen*, p. 478.

34. Jörs, *Römische Rechtswissenschaft*, I, 58; Wenger, *Die Quellen*, pp. 477–481. According to Cicero *De oratore* ii.xii.52, the Pontifex Maximus recorded and publicized on an *album* the principal events of the year, "so that the people might know." Pontifex Maximus P. Mucius Scaevola published the entire collection known as the *Annales Maximi* late in the second century (see Crake, "Archival Material in Livy," p. 9).

35. Puma, *La conservazione*, p. 21. Livy vi.i.2, says that most documents were destroyed "even if some of them were in the daybooks of the pontiffs and in other public and private archives (*monumentis*)."

Figure 36. Rome's Tabularium seen from the Forum.

restoration of the Jupiter temple and the construction of the archives building.[36] He approached his double task in an imaginative, almost grandiose, fashion. What now appears to us as the one Capitoline Hill then consisted of two elevations or summits: a northern one with the temple of Jupiter, the Capitol in the strict sense of the word, and a southern one, the *arx* (citadel), with the temple of the Juno Moneta, both buildings facing the Forum (figure 34). They were separated by a depression, part of which was called *inter duos lucos* (between the two groves).[37]

It must have seemed important and desirable to facilitate communication between the two temples and the two elevations; hence, Q. Lutatius Catulus or the architect who advised him planned for the state archives, the Tabularium, a building that would connect the two separate hills and at the same time would give an imposing terminal point to the Forum.[38] The building (figure 36) certainly served these purposes very well. A substructure of twenty-five layers of stone supported two rows of arcades. Only the lower one of these has been preserved and of its original eleven arches three have been opened up. Behind the lower arcade, a corridor, five meters wide and ten meters high and not connected with the interior, extends the entire length of the building (figure 37). Now open at both ends again, it was designed to serve as a passage between the two formerly separate summits of the present Capitoline. During the Middle Ages the building was used as a prison

36. For details on Q. Lutatius Catulus' career, see T. Robert S. Broughton, *The Magistrates of the Roman Republic*, II (New York, 1952), 583. Caesar "attempted to rob Catulus of the credit for restoring the Temple of Jupiter in the Capitol and give it to Pompey" (*ibid.*, p. 173).

37. On the history of the Capitol in ancient times, see Herbert Siebenhüner, *Das Kapitol in Rom: Idee und Gestalt* (Munich, 1954), p. 17 and plate 1.

38. Nash, *Bildlexikon*, II, 402, lists the literature pertaining to the Tabularium and gives, on pages 402–408, excellent pictures of the building and of certain parts of it. The most detailed description is found in Richard Delbrück, *Hellenistische Bauten in Latium*, I (Strassbourg, 1907), 23–46. An official publication on the building, expected after two more arches had been opened in preparation for the 1942 World's Fair, has not yet been published. Crake, "Archival Material in Livy," p. 25, rightly thinks that the Tabularium was used for the records only.

Figure 37. The lower row of arcades of the Tabularium.

and as a storage place for salt. Michelangelo later destroyed the upper and western part and built the present Palazzo del Senatore on the ancient structure.[39] Delbrück's reconstruction gives an idea of what the Tabularium may have looked like in the days of the Roman Empire (figure 38).

One entrance to the building is on its southwest side from the *Clivus Capitolinus*. There is also a magnificent staircase of sixty-six steps (figure 39) that leads from the Forum to the first floor of the Tabularium, apparently intended to facilitate reference service should records be needed by the Senate sitting in the *Curia Senatus* on the Forum, only a short distance to the east. Entrance to the staircase was later blocked by the temple of Vespasian, since at that time intercourse between the Senate and the Tabularium was no longer deemed important.

The plan of the building as conceived by Catulus and his brilliant architect was L-shaped, since it had to take into consideration the precinct of the god Veiovis that stood at what

Figure 38. Reconstruction of the Tabularium.

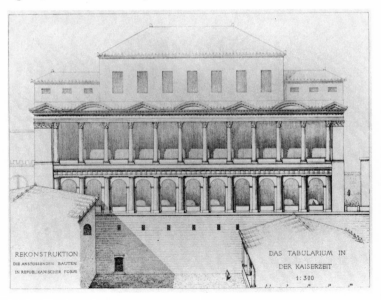

39. Samuel Ball Platner, *A Topographical Dictionary of Ancient Rome*, completed and rev. by Thomas Ashby (London, 1929), p. 507.

*Figure 39. Staircase leading from the Forum into the interior of the
Tabularium.*

would have been its northwest corner.[40] In selecting materials for the construction of the building, its purpose was clearly borne in mind, for, while on the inside Anio Tufa, a porous rock, was used, the substructure was built of Gabine blocks (*sperone*). This stone was doubtless selected in order to have a fireproof material in a hall of records.[41]

Unfortunately, we cannot tell how the interior of the building was divided up for use as an archival depository. One of the writers on the Tabularium thinks that, because for archival storage large rooms easily to be secured were needed and because such rooms were not to be found in what remains of the building, the Tabularium proper must have been on the second floor which no longer exists.[42] We know even less about the equipment that was provided for storing records. Shelves rather than niches in the walls must have been most appropriate for the purpose, since down to imperial days archival holdings consisted of wood tablets and of codices composed of such tablets. Codices equipped with a metal handle (*ansa*) were possibly suspended on wires or poles.[43]

Strangely enough, the archives building in its prominent location is not mentioned by ancient authors, and its attribution to Consul Q. Lutatius Catulus (ca. 121 to ca. 60 B.C.) is based solely on two inscriptions. One of them, found on the premises (figure 40) reads:

[Q. LU]TATIUS Q.F. Q.[N.]
[CATULUS COS. DE S]EN. SENT. FACIUNDU[M]
[COERAVIT] EIDEMQUE PRO[BAVIT]

Quintus Lutatius, son of Quintus, grandson of Quintus, Catulus, Consul, has been in charge of constructing [the

40. Marion Elizabeth Blake, *Ancient Roman Construction in Italy from the Prehistoric Period to Augustus* (Washington, 1947), p. 143.

41. Tenney Frank, *Roman Buildings of the Republic: An Attempt to Date Them from Their Materials* (Rome, 1924), p. 50.

42. Delbrück, *Hellenistische Bauten*, I, 25. Giuseppe Lugli, *Roma antica: Il centro municipale* (Rome, 1946), pp. 44–46, states his belief that the archives were on the lower floors and the offices on those above.

43. See note 2 above.

Figure 40. Cornerstone-type inscription attributing the Tabularium to Q. Lutatius Catulus.

Tabularium] in accordance with a resolution of the Senate and secured its approval.[44]

Since Catulus played a distinguished role in Roman politics—it was he who hailed Cicero as the father of the fatherland—and was a historian in his own right,[45] it is indeed probable that he took considerable personal interest in the "redevelopment" of the Capitol area and in the construction of the Tabularium as part of the task.

While we know practically nothing about the techniques of records storage in the building, we are quite well informed about the composition of the archives staff and its performance and reputation. Before as well as after its transfer to the Tabularium, the state archives was administered by the quaestors.[46] They were elected in the *comitia tributa*, and since the quaestorship was the first step of the Roman *cursus honorum* (career of office) and since the minimum age required for this office was twenty-eight (later thirty) years, relatively young and inexperienced men were put in charge of the treasury as well as the state archives; furthermore, they served for one year only. This almost haphazard arrangement was not changed until the days of Augustus, and it goes a long way toward explaining the unsatisfactory conditions that existed in the state archives. Since the quaestors could not be expected to familiarize themselves with the records, they had to depend entirely on their subordinates.[47]

The subordinate employees of the quaestors belonged to the

44. "Q. Lutatius Q.f. Q.n. substructionem et tabularium de s.s. faciundum coeravit et eidem probavit." The inscriptions are found in *Corpus Inscriptionum Latinarum*, VI (1882), 1314 and 1315. See also Platner, *Topographical Dictionary*, p. 507.

45. See the article on him in *RE*, XIII (1927), 2082–2094.

46. On the functions of the quaestors, see Mommsen, *Staatsrecht*, II, 523–573, and III, 1004–1021.

47. On the various groups of subordinate personnel (*apparitores, scribae, viatores servi publici*) see Mommsen, *Staatsrecht*, I, 320–371. According to Mommsen, *ibid.*, p. 351, there were twenty-seven quaestorial scribes or secretaries before Sulla, thereafter thirty-six. Each of the eleven quaestors normally assigned to the provinces took two secretaries with him so that fourteen remained behind in the capital. On p. 354, Mommsen calls them *durchaus Rechnungsführer und Concepienten* (definitely employees who keep accounts and draft issuances).

group of the *apparitores* (public servants), free Roman citizens who were paid out of public funds. Strictly speaking, they were appointed for the term of service of the elected official to whom they were attached, that is, mostly for one year. Since an *apparitor* could be reappointed, however, he served practically for life, and if he resigned he could present a successor, a situation that led to the sale of jobs and to the acquisition of corporate rights by the *apparitores*. Their corporations (*decuriae*) could own property and had considerable status.

Among the *apparitores*, the scribes of the quaestors and those of the curulian aediles were the most highly regarded. There were attached to the office of the quaestors three *decuriae* of scribes, while the curulian aediles had one *decuria* only; it participated in the administration of the state archives but had nothing to do with the treasury. It should be noted that the title scribe designated an official capable of performing high-level secretarial duties, while the term *librarius*, from which our word librarian stems, meant a person engaged in mere copying.

We do not know how the three corporations of quaestorial scribes divided among them the work in the treasury and in the state archives. Of one illustrious quaestorial scribe we know. After Horace had fought for the losing cause of Brutus, he returned to Italy in 41 B.C. and, with what was left of his father's estate, bought himself a job as *scriba quaestorius*. He abandoned it after about a year, when Maecenas began to provide for him, but even thereafter his former colleagues considered him an emeritus member of their group and asked him to participate in "fresh and important business of common interest."[48] Assuming that his poetical penchant disqualified Horace for work with figures, one would like to think that he was employed in the state archives rather than the treasury and can thus be claimed as a distinguished, although short-term, ancestor of the archival profession.

Registration of the Senate resolutions was most certainly a

---

48. E. Stemplinger, "Q. Horatius Flaccus," *RE*, VIII (1913), 2340, on the basis of Suetonius' *Horace* and of the poet's *Satires* ii.6.36.

duty of the scribes, as was the servicing of records to those who wanted to make certified copies of them. Since both the quaestors and the aediles were young people and changed every year, the scribes must have wielded considerable power. With their legal experience, they considered themselves as belonging to the order of the knights. Men in that position could not be expected to do the menial tasks of archival housekeeping. They left these to public slaves (*servi publici* or simply *publici*), who served in both the archives and the treasury. In addition, *viatores quaestorii* (quaestorial summoners) were available as messengers.

The holdings of the Tabularium were open for research by qualified persons. Cato the Younger had prepared for himself, for a fee of five talents, a tabulation of the public revenue and expenditures from the days of Sulla down to his own quaestorship; and under the Empire, Tacitus, Suetonius, and other writers used the records.[49] Permission to use and make copies from the official records was termed *potestas inspiciendi describendique* (authority to inspect and copy), and it was given by the *sex primi*, who headed the three *decuriae* of quaestorial scribes. It seems that the right to copy was carefully regulated, for a certain L. Alenus was sued in court because "he had forged a permit of the *sex primi* for the purpose of copying official records."[50] Nevertheless, it appears that security conditions at the state archives left much to be desired. Cicero's complaint is well known: "We have no custody of the laws and therefore they are whatever the *apparitores* want them to be; we have to ask the copyists for them, but we have no memory confided to the public records."[51]

---

49. On Livy's use of the records in the Aerarium, see Crake, "Archival Material in Livy," pp. 365, 372, 388.

50. This is the interpretation that Peter, *Die geschichtliche Litteratur*, p. 239, has placed upon a statement in Cicero's *De natura deorum* iii.xxx.74.

51. *De legibus* iii.xx.46, frequently referred to in the pertinent literature. According to Mommsen, *Staatsrecht*, I, 349, n. 2, Cicero uses the derogatory term copyist (*librarius*) intentionally, probably to indicate that the secretaries did not stoop to actually helping the clients of the State Archives.

Cicero himself, however, was not above reproach. While he accused his inveterate enemy Clodius of having set fire to the censorial archives in the *Atrium Libertatis* to extinguish the record of his public censure, he himself was said to have gone to the Capitol during Clodius' absence from the city and there to have destroyed, under a specious pretext, the wood tablets of the tribunes in which the records of their administration were enclosed.[52]

From what has become known of the functions of the various legislative bodies and the magistrates of republican Rome, the composition of the holdings of the state archives can be inferred with considerable certainty down to the series, to use a modern term. Giorgio Cencetti specifies eighteen such series that were transferred to the state archives and an additional four that probably were deposited there. By provenance, they would fall into the following "record groups":

1. Records of the *comitia*.
2. Records of the Senate.
3. *Commentarii* of the consuls.
4. Records of the censors.
5. Records of the praetors.
6. Records of the urban quaestors.
7. Records, particularly fiscal records, of the provincial governors.[53]

Cencetti cautiously suggests that in organizing the archives their provenance might have been observed. It is almost impossible not to accept his hypothesis. Apart from literary statements that point in this direction, one has only to think of the gradual absorption of agency archives into the Aerarium and of the regular accessions of the records of the censors, and one will agree that it is highly improbable that "the series were placed

52. Plutarch, *Cicero* xxxiv.
53. I am following the careful listing by Cencetti, "Gli archivi," pp. 34–38. On p. 38, n. 112, he refers to earlier summaries of the contents of the Archives.

in simple chronological order and that the distinction between the various archives groups became lost."[54]

Among the record groups that we suppose were in the Tabularium, we have mentioned the accounts rendered by the provincial governors upon their return to the city. What happened, however, to the *commentarii* that they and their quaestors kept while they were in charge? Could it be that even under the Republic archival repositories were established in the provinces? It seems unlikely. In 59 B.C., the *lex Julia de repetundis* prescribed that provincial magistrates must leave copies of their accounts in the two principal cities of the province but made no mention of provincial *tabularia* of the kind that developed under the Empire. Until then, provincial magistrates may have adhered to the practice of their ancestors, taking their records to Rome and keeping them in their house archives (*tablina*).

The house archives as an institution played an important role, since in Republican Rome there was no procedure for the official registration and validation of business transactions. Not only business documents and official records of an outgoing official were kept there, for we know that Cato the Elder had a collection of his speeches in the house archives and was able to refer to them. To some extent, temples may have served as safe places in which to deposit important documents. Both Julius Caesar and Augustus placed their wills in the custody of the Vestal Virgins.[55] Undoubtedly the temples had to have safe places in which to keep their valuables and the *commentarii* of the priests and priestesses.[56]

Appraised from the point of view of modern archives administration, Rome's achievements during the republican era were by no means inconspicuous. For the first time in the history of mankind, a monumental and fire resistive structure for

---

54. *Ibid.*, p. 39.

55. Dziatzko, "Archive," p. 563; and Eugenio Casanova, *Archivistica*, 2d ed. (Siena, 1928), p. 297.

56. Herbert Hunger and others, *Geschichte der Textüberlieferung der antiken und mittelalterlichen Literatur*, I (Zürich, 1961), 316.

housing the state's archives was erected; there was a definite trend toward absorbing into the state archives the records of various agencies and institutions of the government and thus developing the Tabularium into a general archives of the Republic; and there was provision, though obviously not satisfactory, for servicing records to magistrates and individuals. The shortcomings of archival arrangements in republican times stem undoubtedly from the fact that Rome did not have a civil service that would have provided continuous systematic care and complete protection for its archives. When a regular civil service came into existence under the Empire, the output of official records on the central as well as on the provincial level grew to enormous proportions. It may well be doubted, however, whether methods of preserving records and putting them to use were superior to those of the Republic.

[7] Imperial Rome

Rome in the days of the Republic had clung with great
tenacity to the wood tablet, its surface either whitened or
covered with wax, or left untouched and written upon with ink,
as the preferred writing material. As a result of Rome's penetra-
tion into the eastern Mediterranean and particularly after the
conquest of Egypt, papyrus became available in quantity and
must soon have proved superior to the tablet with its limited
writing surface.[1] For administrative and business purposes it
was a far more convenient medium. In fact, one can hardly
imagine how Rome would have been able to rule its vast
empire had its government continued to rely on the wood
tablet as a means of communicating with the administrative
and military authorities in the provinces. The enthusiastic
praise papyrus received from the literary Cassiodorus (ca.
A.D. 487–580), high official of the Ostrogothic Kingdom in
Italy under Theodoric, could have been applied with equal
force to its value for official purposes:

Then was papyrus invented, and therewith was eloquence made
possible. Papyrus, so smooth and continuous, the snowy entrails
of a green herb; papyrus which can be spread out to such a vast
extent, and yet be folded up into so little space; papyrus, on whose
white expanse the black characters look beautiful; papyrus which
keeps the sweet harvest of the mind and restores it to the reader

---

1. The most complete information on the writing materials used during this period
is found in Leo Santifaller, *Beiträge zur Geschichte der Beschreibstoffe im Mittelalter*. I.
Untersuchungen (Graz and Cologne, 1953). See also Hans Foerster, *Abriss der lateinischen
Paläographie*, 2d ed. (Stuttgart, 1963), pp. 37–68; Leopold Wenger, *Die Quellen des
römischen Rechts* (Vienna, 1953), pp. 54–101; David Diringer, *The Hand-Produced Book*
(New York, 1953), pp. 151–153, 161–166, 190–205; Franz Wieacker, *Textstufen
klassischer Juristen* (Göttingen, 1960), pp. 93–119. Leo Santifaller, "Über späte Papyrusrollen und frühe Pergamentrollen," in Clemens Bauer and others, eds., *Speculum
Historiale* (Munich, 1965), pp. 117–133, gives examples of late papyrus rolls since the
beginning of the third century and of early parchment rolls. Neither Greek and Latin
formal documents on papyrus nor Latin parchment documents appear in Santifaller's
list, although Greek documents on parchment are included.

whenever he chooses to consult it; papyrus which is the faithful witness of all human actions, eloquent of the past, a sworn foe of oblivion.[2]

Papyrus had indeed become "folded up" to form papyrus books or codices, easier to handle and to read than the customary papyrus rolls. For use in book form, however, it was soon to be superseded by parchment, or, more specifically, "in the third century, and to a less extent in the fourth, the roll was in an overwhelming majority for pagan works, while the codex had a decided and growing majority for Christian works."[3] As time went on, the greater durability of parchment became obvious and the papyrus book disappeared. Yet what recommended parchment for use in book production, its permanence, was offset by its scarcity. It could not possibly satisfy the needs of a busily scribbling bureaucracy—to meet them, the government maintained a papyrus warehouse, the *horrea chartaria*—; hence, papyrus remained in use down to the early Middle Ages until the last remnants of Rome's bureaucratic system had vanished. Papyrus, too, was a relatively expensive writing material, which explains why the wood tablet in its various forms survived. The tablet remained particularly handy as a cheap medium on which to make notes and to take down court proceedings, and it even served for the recording of business transactions, as evidenced by the so-called Albertini Tablets.[4]

The transition from the wooden tablet to papyrus was but a minor aspect of the profound metamorphosis the Roman body politic was to undergo after the collapse of the Republic. This transformation had two characteristics of fundamental importance and far-reaching effect. One of them was the progressive centralization of administrative, judicial, and ultimately

2. Cassiodorus' "Variae," in *Monumenta Germaniae Historica, Auctores Antiquissimi*, XII (Berlin, 1894), 352, here given in the English translation of Thomas Hodgkin, ed., *The Letters of Cassiodorus* (London, 1886), except that the word "papyrus" has been substituted for "paper" as the proper translation of the Latin *carta*.

3. Sir Frederic G. Kenyon, *Books and Readers in Ancient Greece and Rome*, 2d ed. (Oxford, 1951), p. 98.

4. See p. 163 above.

legislative authority in the person of the emperor. The other was the evolution of a bureaucratic machinery that served the emperor in the exercise of his prerogatives, for the Roman Empire became "before all things a bureaucratic state," and "without its civil servants the whole complicated machine of government which held the vast empire together would have collapsed."[5] To be sure, bureaucracy accompanied the empire on its road to decline and ultimate disruption, but if anything it helped it to survive for centuries. Bureaucracy was by no means the cause or even a cause of the Empire's demise. On the contrary, with all its weaknesses it enabled the Empire to function as one of the great political structures the history of the West has seen, a valiant attempt to govern and to protect against foreign enemies the vast areas of the Near East, North Africa, and much of Europe with the help of a centralized administrative and military machinery. It was truly an impressive experiment in worldwide government, an experiment that the great empire builders of the Near East had never attempted.

The process of transformation we have referred to divides itself into two parts, a generally accepted periodization. The first part begins with the coming into power of Augustus and extends roughly until the end of the third century A.D. This was the period of the Principate, and it saw the slow evolution and institutionalization of imperial administrative arrangements. It was followed by the period of the Dominate or Autocracy, ushered in by the great reforms of Diocletian that profoundly changed the structure as well as the system of government of the Empire.

This chapter surveys archival developments under both the Principate and the Dominate down to and including the codification of Roman law, although, when that was undertaken under Emperor Justinian, the unity of the Empire had broken down and practically all of its Western half was under the rule of Germanic kings. Leopold Wenger, in his monumental work on the sources of Roman law, has stated: "To the

5. A. H. M. Jones, *History of the Later Roman Empire, 284–602*, II (Oxford, 1964), 563.

jurisprudent the Corpus Juris Justiniani furnishes the decisive caesura between the history of Roman law and the history of Byzantine law."[6] The archival historian fully accepts this dictum of a great jurisprudent, because the archival institutions of the later Roman Empire come to life for him in the great law codes of the fifth and sixth centuries. Thus Justinian's codification will serve as the divide between Roman and Byzantine archives administration. Because the Diocletian reforms had far-reaching effects on administrative organization and procedures, and consequently on the management and preservation of records, this chapter will be divided into two sections, the first on archives administration under the Principate and the second on developments during the period of the Dominate.

1. *The Period of the Principate*

Under the unwritten constitution of the Principate, the emperor's rule was based on his assuming the functions exercised by certain officials of the Republic. The most important among them were the proconsular imperium; the tribunate, which gave him the right to convene the Senate, to preside over its sessions, to cancel its resolutions, and to veto the decisions of senatorial officers; the office of the censor, through which he controlled the composition of the Senate; the office of aedile, which enabled him to police Rome; and that of the Pontifex Maximus, the head of the state religion. This process of concentrating all power in the emperor's hands was completed when the *lex de imperio Vespasiani* or *lex regia* (A.D. 69) conferred upon the emperor the sovereignty of the people. In the course of time, the emperor's god-like position became more and more pronounced, until the terms imperial and sacred could be used interchangeably.

As the Senate was being deprived of its preeminent status, and as the center of political gravity shifted from "Capitol Hill"

6. Wenger, *Die Quellen*, pp. 679–680.

to the "Executive Mansion," the imperial palace on the Palatine, the Tabularium lost its character as a quasi-central archives of the Roman body politic, for the emperor as the permanent holder of the most important state offices retained the pertinent records. Furthermore, the resolutions of the Senate (*senatus consulta*), expression of its legislative will and a key record series in the Tabularium, now became nothing but confirmations of the imperial initiative, inasmuch as the imperial bills, the *orationes in senatu habitae*, were always enacted by the Senate. As a consequence that august body became a mere publication office for imperial decrees.[7]

During his first consulate in 59 B.C. Julius Caesar, possibly with the intent to reduce the power of the Senate,[8] had decreed that its deliberations be recorded and published. Under Augustus the publication of Senate deliberations was discontinued. Provision was made, however, for having the transactions recorded by the *curator actorum senatus*, later called the *ab actis senatus*, obviously in order to guard against the tampering with the texts of Senate resolutions that had gone on before.[9] Rather full minutes were taken during the sessions, judging by those recording the publication of the Theodosian Code in A.D. 438, the only set of Senate minutes that has survived. Even the many and repeated senatorial outbursts of studious enthusiasm were entered, showing the servility of the once powerful assembly, such as: "'Augustus of Augustuses, the greatest of Augustuses.' Repeated eight times," or "'God gave You to us! God save You for us!' Repeated twenty-seven times."[10]

Even after the publication of the Senate deliberations had stopped, its resolutions were still included in the *populi diurna acta*, an official gazette that from the days of Julius Caesar down

7. *Cambridge Ancient History*, XII (1939), 375; Ernst Stein, *Geschichte des spätrömischen Reiches*, I (Vienna, 1928), 51.

8. Hermann Peter, *Die geschichtliche Litteratur über die römische Kaiserzeit*, I (Leipzig, 1897), 206.

9. See p. 168 above.

10. *The Theodosian Code and Novels and the Sirmondian Constitutions*, trans. Clyde Pharr (Princeton, 1952), pp. 3–7.

to the third century also contained news about important matters of state and about the imperial family. Apparently of the tabloid character, the *acta* were of small value as a source for the Roman historian, and Seneca said of them contemptuously: "Nulla sine divortio acta sunt" (There is not a single issue of the *acta* that does not have a divorce case).[11]

In spite of the diminution of the powers of the Senate, the Tabularium continued to function as a senatorial archives down to the middle of the third century. A number of administrative changes, however, took place under the Principate.[12] Long before that, good management should have called for separating the archives and treasury functions of the Aerarium and for entrusting the treasury to officers of proven experience rather than to young men in the early stages of their career. This was finally done in 23 B.C., when two former praetors elected by the Senate took charge of the treasury with the title of *praefecti aerarii Saturni*. Nero in A.D. 56 assumed the right to appoint these prefects.[13]

Relieved of responsibility for the state treasury, the urban quaestors were now limited to what had been the archives section of the Aerarium. They no longer shared that responsibility with the aediles, whom Augustus had deprived of their archival duties because they had left their performance entirely to their servants. Although the quaestors now had sole control of the Tabularium, conditions were so unsatisfactory that in A.D. 16 Tiberius appointed three *curatores tabularum publicarum* to procure missing documents and to repair those that had become damaged. In A.D. 46 this job still remained to be finished.

Although it appears that the first emperors concerned themselves with the administration of the Tabularium, the records

11. Peter, *Die geschichtliche Litteratur*, I, 215, n. 3, on the basis of Seneca *De beneficiis* iii.xvi.2.

12. Giorgio Cencetti, "Tabularium principis," in A. Giuffrè, ed., *Studi . . . in onore di Cesare Manaresi*, I (Milan, 1953), 135. Tacitus *Annales* xiii.xxix gives a short administrative history of the Aerarium.

13. Theodor Mommsen, *Römisches Staatsrecht*, II (Leipzig, 1887–1888), 559–560.

they kept became the principal archival holdings of the state.[14] There is every reason to doubt the existence on the Palatine of a central archives of the imperial government, comparable to the Tabularium on Capitol Hill. As the various departments of the imperial chancery took shape, one of them, the office *a memoria*, may have been housed on the Palatine in or near the palace. The others, however, were located in the city and kept their records at their respective places of business.[15] Nevertheless, the records of the various departments were spoken of as the *tabularium Caesaris*, as if they constituted an organic whole.

If then we must deal with a number of archival repositories during the period under discussion, we have to determine the key points at which records were generated. The one of greatest importance was the person of the emperor with his immediate entourage; a personal or secret archives of the emperors is frequently referred to in the literature. Since from time immemorial it had been the practice of Roman magistrates to retain the records of their term of office, it was only natural for Caesar to keep his papers and for his successors to follow established custom. This required the setting up of some kind of archival repository on the Palatine. It was from such a repository, identified as the inner sanctum (*sacrarium*), that Livia produced codicils to Augustus' will;[16] after Nero's death the draft of a public address to the people was found in his record chest (*scrinium*); and Caligula's secret papers contained two lists of

14. Cencetti's essay on the *tabularium principis* deals admirably with the subject. It supersedes M. Memelsdorff, *De archivis imperatorum romanorum qualia fuerint usque ad Diocletiani aetatem*, Ph.D. diss., University of Halle, 1890. See also Michelangelo Puma, *La conservazione dei documenti giuridici nell' antica Roma* (Palermo, 1934). According to Peter, *Die geschichtliche Litteratur*, I, 232, there existed on the Palatine a single imperial archives to which the different central establishments transferred their records. Cencetti, "Tabularium principis," p. 158, considers this a "perplexing" assumption.

15. Friedrich Preisigke, *Die Inschrift von Skaptoparene in ihrer Beziehung zur kaiserlichen Kanzlei in Rom* (Strassbourg, 1917), p. 55.

16. Reporting on the discovery of "The House of Augustus," *Illustrated London News*, September 20, 1969, Gianfilippo Carettoni mentions two rooms with niches that "recall the design of ancient libraries." Such niches were also used for storing record material. Did Augustus keep his most important personal papers in these niches? And was it possibly from one of the two rooms that Livia produced the codicils to Augustus' will?

Romans whom he had earmarked to suffer the death penalty. We also know from Suetonius that the papers of Tiberius, his *acta* and *commentarii*, were the only reading of Domitian, so they, too, seem to have been on hand in the secret archives. Upon the death of an emperor, his successor had the right to use, or dispose of, his predecessor's files as he saw fit. Since it could be assumed that they contained correspondence likely to hurt the writer in the eyes of the new emperor, it was considered a sign of magnanimity if, upon succeeding to the throne, he destroyed the papers he inherited.[17]

It can be assumed that the secret archives (*secretarium*) was located in some room of the imperial palace on the Palatine and that, although it was not part of the bedchamber (*cubicularium*), it was in the custody of the most trustworthy of the emperor's secretaries or bedchamber personnel. Its keepers were variously designated as *notarius secretorum* (notary in charge of secret documents), *chartularius cubicularii* (archivist of the bedchamber), or *tabularius* (archivist of the emperor).[18]

Closely related to the emperor's personal papers were the records originating from his consultation with his intimate advisers, the "friends of the Princeps," who had replaced the Senate as what we would call a policy-formulating group. During the next three centuries this body developed into a formal organization called the Consistorium, with its own secretarial staff and with its composition and functions more clearly delineated.[19]

Below the policy level central agencies charged with the administration of the emperor's prerogatives were slow in developing. During the first and second centuries offices principally concerned with the judicial, financial, and administrative functions began to take shape.[20] In the administration of

17. Peter, *Die geschichtliche Litteratur*, I, 227–229.

18. Cencetti, "Tabularium principis," p. 138.

19. See John A. Crook, *Consilium Principis: Imperial Councils and Counsellors from Augustus to Diocletian* (Cambridge, Eng., 1955).

20. Otto Hirschfeld, *Die kaiserlichen Verwaltungsbeamten bis auf Diocletian*, 2d rev. ed. (Berlin, 1905), deals with all facets of this process. See also, to cite some of the many

justice—still a personal function of the emperor in his audience
hall on the Palatine with its tribunal apse[21]—the Praetorian
Prefect participated concurrently. He was in fact responsible
for all business that the emperor had not reserved for himself or
his immediate staff. In charge of army supplies and of the
command of troops garrisoned in Italy, the Praetorian Prefect
also assumed considerable importance in the area of finance
when, toward the end of the Principate and as a result of the
complete breakdown of the currency, it became necessary to
resort to taxation in kind (*annona*) and to make the prefect
responsible for apportioning and raising this tax. He thus
became an important minister of finance, joining in that
capacity the *rationalis*, chief of the imperial treasury of receipt
for ordinary revenue (later to be called the *comes sacrarum
largitionum*), and the *magister rei privatae*, who administered the
income derived from confiscations and property inherited by
the emperor.

There was, of course, no clear separation of functions between
the emerging central agencies, and much business remained in the
hands of personnel directly responsible to the emperor—
originally all freedmen.[22] Under Claudius they began to be
organized into offices, and under Hadrian freedmen began to be
replaced by knights assigned to offices that were designated on
the basis of their functions. Together they constituted the
imperial chancery or executive office. After the beginning of the
fourth century, when under Diocletian the imperial court no
longer had a fixed residence and moved from place to place,
these offices were called *scrinia* (shrines), a *scrinium* being a

pertinent studies, Harold Mattingly, *The Imperial Civil Service of Rome* (Cambridge,
Eng., 1910); H. Stuart Jones, "Administration," in Cyril Bailey, ed., *The Legacy of
Rome* (Oxford, 1923), pp. 91–139; A. H. M. Jones, *Studies in Roman Government and
Law* (Oxford, 1960).

21. Crook, *Consilium Principis*, p. 107. An inscription at the temple of Dmeir
between Damascus and Palmyra is a copy from Caracalla's *commentarii* of proceedings
that took place in Antioch on May 27, 212. See *ibid.*, p. 83, and P. Roussel and F. D.
Visscher, "Les inscriptions du temple de Dmeir," *Syria*, XXIII (1942–1943), 173–194.

22. Harold Mattingly, *Roman Imperial Civilization* (Garden City, N.Y., 1959), pp.
135–141; Jones, "Administration," p. 119.

cylindrical chest usually made of thin curved wood and serving to keep documentary material, such as books and manuscripts of all kinds.[23] In this case a piece of equipment gave its name to the office that used it, just as later the English Exchequer was to receive its name from its chessboard-like counting table. Similarly, bureau, a table covered with a coarse woolen cloth called *burel*, was in France to stand for government agency or office.

Though not yet called *scrinia*, the components of the imperial chancery or executive office began to take form under the early emperors.[24] We find an office *ab epistulis* in charge of official correspondence, subdivided in the days of Emperor Hadrian into departments for Latin and Greek letters; an office *a libellis*, the office for petitions; and the office *a memoria*, which seems to have been added by Hadrian and was later to become the main office for expediting all business of the imperial chancery. The learned Claudius appointed an official *a studiis* as an adviser on general administrative and judicial matters, with responsibility for furnishing the pertinent reference material. Under Hadrian, L. Julius Vestinus, former head of the Alexandria Museum and chief librarian and personal secretary of the emperor for Greek correspondence, held the position of the *a studiis*.[25]

Before the *a memoria* office rose to a position of preeminence among the other *scrinia*, as it did in the post-Diocletian period, the various offices seem to have kept their own records. The records consisted of fair copies of the incoming correspondence;

---

23. Theodor Mommsen, "Constitutiones corporis munimenta," *Zeitschrift der Savigny-Stiftung für Rechtsgeschichte, Romanistische Abteilung*, XI (1890), 146. He shows on pp. 147 and 148 two sculptures on which *scrinia* are represented. On the *scrinia* as fully developed offices, see below.

24. If one wishes to understand the *modus operandi* of the imperial chancery and especially its office *a libellis*, Friedrich Preisigke's *Die Inschrift von Skaptoparene* remains invaluable. In this essay, Preisigke, a high official in the German Postal Service who was also one of Europe's most distinguished papyrologists, has analyzed the processing of a petition of the village of Skaptoparene in A.D. 238 with the realism and insight of the experienced administrator.

25. Hirschfeld, *Die kaiserlichen Verwaltungsbeamten*, pp. 332–333.

the originals of complaints received, which carried the decisions rendered by the emperor; approved drafts of imperial mandates and other issuances; the imperial *constitutiones* (laws), in all probability the originals; the minutes of judicial proceedings before the emperor; or, "in short, something absolutely analogous in substance, if not in its external form, and in quantity to the records that are preserved in today's state archives." [26] To these should be added the cadastres in the form of metal tablets that gave complete information about all real estate matters, such as survey documents and evidential material pertaining to the division of property and the determination of boundaries. Though also available in the provincial *tabularia*, the copies in the imperial archives had to be consulted in contested cases. [27] Finally, there were the records that the provincial governors had to turn in at the end of their terms of office. [28]

We know nothing about the archives of the Praetorian Prefect and little about those of the financial agencies. The archives of the *rationalis* probably included, for the use of the minister's staff, a copy of the census, or at least a summary thereof, while another copy was available in the province where the census was taken. [29] The *tabularium castrense*, as the accounting office for the imperial household, must have been in charge of the pertinent records.

What little information we have does not enable us to envisage the *modus operandi* of the various depositories. We can only guess that series were not intermingled but were kept separate. [30] This, we have seen, was done in the Tabularium, and thus it is likely that the same system was followed in the imperial repositories. The system was "in substance, then, something not very different from modern archives in regard

26. Cencetti, "Tabularium principis," p. 162.
27. Hirschfeld, *Die kaiserlichen Verwaltungsbeamten*, p. 63, n. 2; C. Dziatzko, "Archive," *RE*, II (1896), 562; Cencetti, "Tabularium principis," p. 144; and Wenger, *Die Quellen*, p. 439.
28. See, however, n. 42 below.
29. Cencetti, "Tabularium principis," pp. 144–145.
30. *Ibid.*, pp. 155–156.

to the organization of the records in organic series; a rather interesting similarity, although only conceptual." [31]

Record documents were pasted together to form a roll (*rotulus*). This was done by covering with paste the left margin of the item to be added and placing it under the right margin of the last document on the roll. A *titulus*, attached to one end of the roll, helped to identify the record unit. Rolls were stored on shelf-like structures,[32] although chests (*scrinia*) may also have been used. *Scrinia* served as the standard equipment when later the imperial court became a government on wheels. To facilitate searches, there were probably inventories or lists [33] of the type of the *diastrômata* found in Roman Egypt. Servicing and searching the records was the job of an official called *regendarius*.

Among the various archival establishments, that of the imperial chancery, spoken of as the *tabularium Caesaris*, must have been well known; in cases of litigation, officials as well as ordinary citizens would seek to obtain documentary evidence from it. Not trusting documents that the province of Bithynia had submitted in a law suit—an edict supposedly issued by Emperor Augustus and certain letters of Vespasian, Titus, and Domitian—Pliny the Younger, the governor of the province, asked Emperor Trajan about A.D. 112 for the true and authentic documents, which he believed to be in the imperial archives. He was told by Trajan that nothing could be found in "the daybooks of the emperors who were before me." [34]

More successful was the city of Smyrna when, in A.D. 139, it sent to Rome an emissary to obtain a certified copy of an edict of Emperor Hadrian relating to a municipal festival. According to the proceedings before the Emperor Antoninus Pius, Acutianus, the city's emissary, asked the emperor for a

---

31. *Ibid.*, p. 157.

32. Preisigke, *Die Inschrift von Skaptoparene*, p. 72, referring to Theodor Birt, *Die Buchrolle in der Kunst* (Leipzig, 1907), p. 247.

33. Such a list is found in Abate Gaetano Marini, ed., *I papyri diplomatici* (Rome, 1803), no. 138, on p. 205.

34. Peter, *Die geschichtliche Litteratur*, I, 240; Hirschfeld, *Die kaiserlichen Verwaltungsbeamten*, p. 325, n. 1.

copy of the edict of his divine father as entered in his daybooks. Through a rescript of April 8, signed by the emperor with the word *rescripsi*, Acutianus received permission to copy Hadrian's edict, provided it had been issued. Acutianus obtained for himself a copy of Antoninus Pius' rescript, had it corroborated by seven witnesses, and submitted it to the custodian of the imperial daybooks, the *commentariensis*, who in turn instructed two of his office slaves to issue a copy of Hadrian's decree: "Stasime, Daphni, edite ex forma sententiam vel constitutionem." This copy Acutianus took to Smyrna, where the entire transaction was recorded on stone. From the account it appears that in A.D. 139 the records of Hadrian's regime were available for consultation by third parties and that such consultation was regulated by a careful although somewhat cumbersome routine.[35]

The fate of the holdings of the *tabularium Caesaris* and of other accumulations is not known. Were all or part of them shipped to Constantinople when it became the residence of the emperors? If they were, they may have perished there, for in a letter of A.D. 599 Pope Gregory I wrote that the record repository (*cartofilacium*) of Emperor Justinian was destroyed by fire so that "practically no documents of his times have been preserved."[36] The difficulties encountered in the compilation of the law code of Emperor Theodosius by a commission appointed in A.D. 435 make it quite certain that, even before the days of Justinian, the Constantinople archives were so inadequate that searches in the provincial archives became necessary for that purpose.[37]

Archives administration in the provinces had indeed made

35. Peter, *Die geschichtliche Litteratur*, I, 237; Hirschfeld, *Die kaiserlichen Verwaltungsbeamten*, p. 327, n. 2; Ulrich Wilcken, "Zu den Kaiserreskripten," *Hermes*, LV (1920), 16–17; Wenger, *Die Quellen*, p. 427, n. 31, and p. 429, n. 43. According to Preisigke, *Die Inschrift von Skaptoparene*, p. 53, the draft of a document is called a *forma*. This means that Stasimus and Daphnis are instructed to give Acutianus a copy of the decree on the basis of the draft which is on the papyrus roll.

36. *Gregorii I Papae Registrum Epistolarum*, Pt. II, Ludovicus M. Hartmann, ed., *Monumenta Germaniae Historica, Epistolae*, II (Berlin, 1899), 225.

37. See pp. 209–210 below.

great strides under the Principate. In Republican times Rome had not succeeded in establishing a satisfactory system for the administration of its provinces, ruling them with the help of "the unpaid aristocrat"[38] who was usually bent on crude exploitation of the subjects. Augustus and his successors introduced much-needed reforms, in the course of which a dual archival setup originated. In each province there was a *tabularium Caesaris*, partly a financial agency charged with the administration of the imperial domains and with the levying of direct and indirect taxes, and partly an archival agency for the preservation of the census lists compiled in special districts or in the municipalities.[39] Notices of birth had to be filed in these provincial imperial *tabularia*, and upon request certified copies of them were made available. The *tabularia* were staffed with imperial freedmen with the title *tabularius* and with *adiutores* (assistants), some of whom were slaves. We can identify the provinces in which imperial provincial archives were functioning.[40] Dio Cassius tells us that Caligula used the census archives of Gaul to select the persons he wanted to put to death so that he might "inherit" their possessions.[41]

The imperial provincial archives must be distinguished from the provincial gubernatorial archives. Theodor Mommsen referred to a bronze tablet containing the decision in A.D. 68 of L. Helvetius Agrippa, proconsul of Sardinia, in a boundary conflict between two communities of the island.[42] In violation of a ruling of a predecessor of the proconsul, one of the parties had appropriated territory to which, according to this ruling, it was not entitled. Although subsequent officials decided in

---

38. Jones, "Administration," p. 107.

39. Hirschfeld, *Die kaiserlichen Verwaltungsbeamten*, pp. 60–61. The head of the census office in Rome may have been associated with the imperial archives. *Ibid.*, pp. 65, 68.

40. *Ibid.*, p. 60, n. 3.

41. *Ibid.*, pp. 61–62, referring to Dio Cassius lix.xxii.

42. Theodor Mommsen, "Decret des Proconsuls von Sardinien L. Helvetius Agrippa J. 68 n. Chr.," *Gesammelte Schriften*, V (1908), 325–351. Mommsen believed originally that Agrippa's records had been transferred to Rome and were consulted there. In his *Staatsrecht*, I, 349, n. 2, he points out that probably this was done in Karalis, the seat of the proconsul. See also Cencetti, "Tabularium principis," p. 135, n. 7.

favor of the injured community, the matter dragged on until L. Helvetius Agrippa issued a final ruling against the defendants. At the request of the winning party, the quaestorial secretary (*scriba quaestorius*) produced from the proconsular archives the *codex ansatus*, a polyptychon of the hinged type, with the final ruling, contained in the codex on tablets VIII through X. It was then incised on a bronze tablet which was affixed to the city hall or displayed on the contested land.[43]

The records pertaining to the Sardinian lawsuit contain no official documents other than the proconsular decrees. It was the practice of Roman magistrates, however, whether sitting in a judicial or administrative capacity, to have a full record of the proceedings prepared for future reference, and such proceedings are missing in the Sardinian case. Because of this, Artur Steinwenter has concluded and has attempted to prove that the minutes of proceedings before the provincial governor, particularly those of judicial proceedings, did not become part of the regular gubernatorial archives but were preserved in separate proceeding or minute archives (*Protokollarchive*).[44] There does not seem to be enough evidence to support this thesis. Should not one rather think of the proceedings being kept as appendices to the main records or, at best, as a division of the regular provincial archives?

That a verbatim record of court proceedings was prepared and preserved is confirmed by the proceedings against early Christian martyrs. The so-called martyr records—about a dozen genuine ones have survived—are nothing but copies of the minutes of their trials before the competent Roman officials. These minutes were in the custody of the judge's *commentariensis*, the keeper of his daybooks. He could turn a profit by making them accessible to the Christians, who were eager to obtain copies of them for the purpose of fortifying their brethren in the faith or arousing the sympathies of the heathen. In one case they

43. Wenger, *Die Quellen*, p. 415, n. 110.
44. Artur Steinwenter, *Beiträge zum öffentlichen Urkundenwesen der Römer* (Graz, 1915), pp. 11–16; Wenger, *Die Quellen*, p. 424, n. 192.

had to pay 200 denarii for permission to transcribe the proceedings.[45] Naturally the authorities did not want to see the proceedings exploited for "publicity" purposes and might have seized the copies they discovered in the hands of the faithful and destroyed them; or they might have burned the originals to prevent the Christians from obtaining access to them.[46] When the Church was officially recognized by the state, it turned against the traitors who, during the last persecution, had handed over to the authorities the Holy Scriptures, the sacred vessels, or the names of the brethren. To prove such accusations, the Church produced the public records that revealed the facts.[47]

Like the civilian authorities of the provinces, the commands of the legions that were stationed there made provision for the administration and preservation of their records. In fact, the term *tabularium* designates, as it does on the civilian side, the combined agency responsible for financial matters as well as for the records of the unit. The *tabularium* was headed by an official called *a tabulario castrensi*, while the *actarius* or *actuarius* was mainly responsible for expediting military orders and other issuances. The commanding general—for example, Alexander the Great[48]—kept his papers with him while on a campaign. In a stable encampment, however, there seem to have been fairly standardized arrangements for the housing of offices and records. The *praetorium*, located at the far end of the parade

---

45. R. P. Dom H. Leclercq, *Les martyrs*, 3d ed., I (Paris, 1906), xxi–xxii. See also Wenger, *Die Quellen*, pp. 420–422, and Hans Niedermeyer, *Über antike Protokoll-Literatur*, (Göttingen, 1918). Throughout history, social, political, and religious movements have been eager to preserve the record of their persecutions. In colonial Maryland, for instance, the Meeting for Sufferings, one of the most important committees of the Quaker Yearly Meetings, kept a careful record of all fines and imprisonments or other hardships inflicted on Friends. The committee was even made responsible for all the records deposited with the Yearly Meeting. See Phebe R. Jacobsen, *Quaker Records in Maryland* (Annapolis, 1966), p. 7.

46. Rudolf von Heckel, "Das päpstliche und sicilianische Registerwesen in vergleichender Darstellung mit besonderer Berücksichtigung der Ursprünge," *Archiv für Urkundenforschung*, I (1908), 413, n. 4.

47. Leclercq, *Les martyrs*, p. xx.

48. See p. 127 above.

grounds, normally consisted of an uneven number of rooms, frequently five, two of which seem to have been used as an office of the *actuarius* and his *librarii* (that is, copyists) and a storage room for the *tabularium*.⁴⁹ Below the center room, which was occupied by the *sacellum*, the sacred place for the insignia of the unit, there was a vault called the *aerarium*, where money and possibly some of the records were kept.

The famous excavations at Dura-Europos, a military post founded by the Seleucids that dominated the Euphrates River and guarded the road from Palmyra to Ctesiphon, have for the first time brought to light the remnants of a body of military records, found where the records had been created, while in Egypt we have but single specimens of such records, and most of the time we do not even know where they came from.⁵⁰ In Dura records were kept in two places. Those of the legions stationed there were stored in certain rooms of the *praetorium* next to the *sacellum* that were occupied by one *librarius* and four *adiutores*. Unfortunately these rooms were found empty. Records of the auxiliary troops, however, were discovered in the temple of Azzanathkona, which was separated from the *praetorium* by a small alley. The papyri and parchments were chiefly found in the northwest corner, and may have been stored on shelves, for holes in the wall seem to indicate that shelving had been installed for the purpose.⁵¹ The records, dating from the first half of the third century, are described as follows:

There is a calendar of official military festivals, a contract of sale and fragments of other legal documents, a record of horses purchased for the army with dates of purchase and the prices paid, two daily registers of the *Cohors* XX *Palmyrenorum*, a letter of Marius Maximus concerning the entertainment of Goces, the Parthian legate at

49. Herbert Lorenz, *Untersuchungen zum Praetorium: Katalog der Prätorien und Entwicklungsgeschichte ihrer Typen*, Ph.D. diss., University of Halle (Halle, 1936), p. 86.

50. M. I. Rostovtzeff, "Das Militärarchiv von Dura," in Walter Otto and Leopold Wenger, eds., *Papyri und Altertumskunde* (Munich, 1934), p. 378.

51. M. I. Rostovtzeff, *The Excavations at Dura-Europos . . . Preliminary Report of Fifth Season of Work, October 1931—March 1932* (New Haven, 1934), p. 166.

various places on his journey through Roman territory, part of another letter of Marius Maximus concerning the purchase of a horse for a soldier, and several lists of soldiers with particulars regarding their date of enlistment etc.[52]

Why were these records kept in the temple and not in the *praetorium*? The excavators have surmised that the temple served as a military headquarters before the *praetorium* was built, and that even after that the auxiliary troops continued to use it for storing their records.

Although only of the first half of the fourth century, the archives of Flavius Abinnaeus might be mentioned here as a good example of a mixed military and private archives. This officer, commandant of Dionysias in the Egyptian Fayyûm, was in charge of an *ala* (wing) that was not a fighting outfit but a unit that assisted the civilian administration in recruiting and levying the *annona*. When Abinnaeus left the service, he took with him some of his official as well as his private papers. It is reasonable to assume that Abinnaeus' papers, including the deeds of his wife, composed a single accumulation of records which was discovered by native diggers in 1891–1892 and sold together with other documents of the same provenance.[53]

Descending to the lowest level of government, we should remember that the Roman Empire was a conglomeration of cities with their surroundings, each of them under its city council.[54] The council (*curia*) was a large body usually composed of one hundred members, chaired by the *duoviri iure dicundo*. These two officials and additional members of the council constituted an executive committee of ten, the *decem primi*. In charge of the collection of taxes and of the *annona*, they were jointly responsible for the amounts apportioned to the municipality, the *munus curiae*, and for other services to be rendered. Since this liability could become ruinous to the incumbents,

52. *Ibid.*, p. 295.
53. *The Abinnaeus Archive: Papers of a Roman Officer in the Reign of Constantius II*, collected and reedited by H. I. Bell and others (Oxford, 1962), p. 4.
54. Jones, *Later Roman Empire*, II, 712.

many tried to evade serving on the *curia*, while the state did everything possible to prevent eligible citizens from fleeing, as many of them did for self-preservation.

City records originated at two points. Municipal officers kept daybooks or *commentarii* and customarily took them home with them when they relinquished their offices, because formally they were not records of the curia.[55] The *curia*, with the help of its municipal office, kept separate records of its proceedings. An inscription of A.D. 114 that was discovered in Caere, now Cerveteri, in Etruria gives us an idea of how they were entered in the council's *commentarii*. The text of the inscription is identified as a certified copy from the minutes of the council produced by the municipal scribe from the city archives, from which a copy was prepared in the front hall of the temple of Mars, where that archives was located. Reference is by pages and chapters of the *commentarium cottidianum municipi caeritum*.[56] Municipal proceedings of Oxyrhynchus in Egypt at the end of the third and fourth centuries show in an amusing fashion how time-honored subterfuges were used by council members unwilling to accept office.[57]

Proceedings of the city council were taken down in shorthand on wax tablets and later copied on papyrus, as illustrated by the following incident. During the Donatist trials in Africa at the time of St. Augustine, a former *duovir* was asked to submit records from eleven years earlier. When he confessed that he no longer had them, the secretary intervened and said: "The magistrate took all his records to his home after he had completed his year. I shall see whether they can be found in the wax tablets," which apparently the secretary had kept as a "security copy."[58]

55. Wenger, *Die Quellen*, p. 419.

56. Giorgio Cencetti, "Gli archivi dell' antica Roma nell' età repubblicana," *Archivi*, ser. 2, VII (1940), 10, n. 12; Wilhelm Kubitschek, "Acta," *RE*, I (1894), 298; and Wenger, *Die Quellen*, pp. 390–391.

57. Wenger, *Die Quellen*, pp. 391–392.

58. Von Heckel, "Das päpstliche und sicilianische Registerwesen," p. 399, n. 4; Wenger, *Die Quellen*, p. 424.

Municipal record-making and record-keeping received particular importance when a law of A.D. 366 conferred upon municipal officers the right to prepare records of legal transactions that took place before them, the *ius actorum conficiendorum*. This is part of the story of archives administration during the late Roman Empire.

2. The Period of the Dominate

The reforms of Diocletian profoundly changed the structure as well as the system of the imperial government. From the sacred person of the emperor the will of the master now descended through a seemingly perfect hierarchy down to the lowest level of governmental organization. Civilian and military authority were being separated, and there came into existence a thoroughly organized bureaucracy that has bequeathed to us much of its terminology. When we speak of office (*officium*), diocese (*diocesis*), fisc (*fiscus*), or minister, we are using terms of the Roman administration of the late Empire. In addition, its procedures had much in common with, and actually anticipate, practices that had to be rediscovered in the age of the early modern state.

Although this bureaucracy of the late Empire helped to make and keep the vast empire a viable unit, its vices stand out clearly. Excessive centralization; a system of espionage under which the subordinates were responsible for, and had to report on, the behavior of the head of the office; the constant swelling of the ranks of the officials employed; and the sale of jobs were some of the unhappy characteristics of this bureaucratized administration. To obtain judicial action the citizen had to pay a fee (*sportula*) and even had to furnish the papyrus for the necessary paperwork.[59] Officeholding became a lucrative occupation and, since the number of statutory positions was fixed and waiting periods were long, wise parents had their sons entered on the civil service lists as supernumeraries while still infants. A. H. M.

59. A. H. M. Jones, *Studies in Roman Government and Law* (Oxford, 1960), p. 171.

Jones mentions the case of a doctor, Marcellus, whose sons had been enrolled as soon as they had been weaned.[60] Even among those actually serving, morale must have been lax and absenteeism rampant, for we know of regulations prescribing mild penalties for officials who have been absent from their office for one or more years.[61] Small wonder that while paperwork steadily increased, its handling and control left much to be desired, and that emperors, though they worked hard, were unable to examine all the documents that they had to sign. Valentinian III (A.D. 425–454) discovered, for instance, "that he had been granting pardons to murderers without his own knowledge" or that of his minister of justice, and "emperors were not infrequently obliged to announce in their laws that rescripts contrary to their provision, even if they bore their own signature, were invalid."[62]

As behooves a bureaucratically organized government, the pattern of the military and civilian administrative arrangements in both the Eastern and Western Empires was detailed in an official handbook. This is the famous *notitia dignitatum*, compiled some time after A.D. 395 and preserved in a medieval copy.[63] It specifies military commands and civilian agencies and indicates the insignia that identify them. The *notitia* is an unsurpassed source of information that helps us to determine the places at which records were made and kept.

This observation holds true in regard to that originally informal group that advised the emperor in the most important judicial and administrative matters, his companions (*comites*). Now consisting of the highest officials who, in addition to their official titles, still had the title of *comes* (our count), this group

60. Jones, *Later Roman Empire*, II, 586.

61. Jones, *Studies*, p. 170.

62. Jones, *Later Roman Empire*, I, 410.

63. *Notitia Dignitatum: Accedunt Notitia Urbis Constantinopolitanae et Laterculi Provinciarum*, ed. Otto Seeck (Berlin, 1876). Another copy was published by the French Bibliothèque Nationale, Département des Manuscrits, under the title *Notitia Dignitatum* (Paris, n.d.). For a discussion of the genesis of the *notitia*, see E. Polaschek, "Notitia Dignitatum," *RE*, XVII (1937), 1077–1116, and Jones, *Later Roman Empire*, III, 347–380.

was designated as the Consistorium,[64] because its members had to remain standing in the presence of the emperor. Secretarial duties were performed by notaries, who formed a corporation (*schola*) and were organized in three classes. The first class, that of the *tribuni et notarii*, kept the minutes of the Consistory, none of which have survived. They also named the candidates for the positions of the *referendarii*, who served as the emperor's judicial clerks and messengers.[65] The notaries were headed by the *primicerius notariorum*, who also had the important function of keeping a roster of the incumbents of all higher offices, a civil service register called the *laterculum maius*, and probably of issuing their letters of appointment (codicils), which earned this official considerable fees. The *primicerius* is shown in the *notitia dignitatum* (figure 41) with his *laterculum maius* in the form of a modern catalog with exchangeable leaves, wrapped in a red cover.[66]

Diocletian's reforms, which provided for two emperors for the two halves of the Empire and for two caesars who were to succeed them, had the underlying aim of making the emperor as omnipresent as possible, and to implement this aim the central government became "in fact a migratory body." When it was on the move with its guards, numbering about three hundred, and an even larger number of civil servants and military staff officers, roads must have been "choked with trains of wagons piled with boxes of files (*scrinia*) and sacks of coins and bars of gold and silver."[67] In both parts of the Empire the *scrinia*, now fully developed branches of the imperial chancery or executive office, were headed by officials with the title of *magister*. They were the *magister epistularum*, the secretary for correspondence; the *magister libellorum*, the secretary for peti-

64. Ferdinand Lot, *The End of the Ancient World and the Beginnings of the Middle Ages* (New York, 1961), pp. 20, 89; Stein, *Geschichte*, I, 169; and, in general, Crook, *Consilium Principis*.

65. Jones, *Later Roman Empire*, II, 572–575.

66. Wenger, *Die Quellen*, p. 426, n. 22; *Notitia Dignitatum*, Or. XVIII and Occ. XVI in Seeck's edition and figs. 35 and 79 in that of the Bibliothèque Nationale.

67. Jones, *Later Roman Empire*, I, 367.

Figure 41. Insignia of the primicerius notariorum.

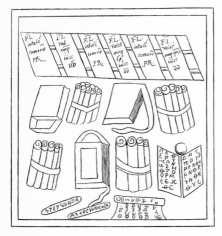

tions; and the *magister memoriae*, the secretary mainly charged with dispatching the decisions prepared by the other *scrinia*. Originally a subdivision of the office *a memoria*, the *scrinium dispositionum* seems to have made the arrangements for the emperor's travel; and, being of lesser importance, it was not headed by a *magister* but by a *primicerius* equal in rank to the *proximi*, the officials assisting the *magistri* of the other *scrinia*. In the east, a special *magister epistularum graecarum* appears.[68]

The *magistri* and their *scrinia* in both parts of the Empire are listed in the *notitia dignitatum* and shown with their insignia (figure 42). These consist of papyrus rolls, a diptychon, and codices that can be tied together with a cord. All of the *scrinia* officials were supervised by the *magister officiorum*,[69] and by the fifth century the posts of the *memoriales*, *epistulares*, and *libellenses* could be sold and were indeed coveted. "Members of the scrinia must have made a handsome income, not so much from their salaries as from fees," and from bribes "for drafting and forwarding illegal petitions and similar services."[70]

The division of labor among the *scrinia* has been the subject of much discussion, but the relative paucity of our information makes it rather difficult to determine their respective functions. It can be said with considerable certainty, however, that the *scrinium a memoria* occupied a prominent position and that as the office in charge of expediting all imperial issuances it served as the archival agency of the entire executive office. A number of facts make this more than an educated guess. A constitution of Justinian gave the office *a memoria* sixty-two statutory positions as against only thirty-four each in the *ab epistulis* and the *a libellis*, clear indication of its particularly heavy workload. The same constitution furthermore required that there must

68. For a discussion of the *scrinia*, see Otto Seeck, "Scrinium," *RE*, ser. 2, vol. II (1923), 893–904; Hirschfeld, *Die kaiserlichen Verwaltungsbeamten*, pp. 318–342; Cencetti, "Tabularium principis," pp. 140–142; Jones, *Later Roman Empire*, II, 575–578.

69. See Arthur E. R. Boak, "The Master of the Offices in the Later Roman and Byzantine Empires," in Arthur E. R. Boak and James F. Dunlap, *Two Studies in Later Roman and Byzantine Administration* (New York and London, 1924).

70. Jones, *Later Roman Empire*, II, 578.

Figure 42. Insignia of the magistri scriniorum.

always be four *antiquarii* in the *scrinium a memoria*. Were they officials particularly competent to service the older records of the entire chancery and, if so, were they expressly put in charge of those records?[71]

If there were properly functioning archival establishments in Rome and in Constantinople, their greatest opportunity for service came when emperors of the fifth and sixth centuries undertook the ambitious task of assembling a code of laws. That is why the history of the codification of Roman law, first attempted by Theodosius II (A.D. 408–450) and later brought to conclusion by Justinian, may provide us with valuable information. The question is simply : To what extent did the imperial archives furnish the material incorporated in the Codex Theodosianus and the Codex Justinianus?

Earlier compilations, the Codex Gregorianus (ca. A.D. 290–294) and the Codex Hermogenianus (ca. A.D. 295) were the products of individual jurisprudents and possibly their collaborators who used the archival resources of Rome and Constantinople.[72] In contradistinction to these private compilations, the Codex Theodosianus was an effort to produce an official collection of all the general laws promulgated since the days of Emperor Constantine. The work was to be done by a commission of sixteen expert officials appointed in A.D. 435, after plans for a more ambitious compilation had proved impracticable. Mommsen's research[73] has proved that the codifying commission could not turn to the imperial archives or to the files of the *scrinia* in order to obtain copies of the laws, except for those of the most recent period. For the east, the commission had to rely largely on the archives of individual Constantinople officials and on the collections of the famous law school of Berytus, the present Beirut.[74] In the west, the commission tapped the

71. *Codex Justinianus* xii.xix.10.

72. Paul Krüger, *Geschichte der Quellen und Litteratur des Römischen Rechts*, 2d ed. (Munich and Leipzig, 1912), p. 318, n. 12; Wenger, *Die Quellen*, p. 535.

73. Theodor Mommsen, "Das theodosische Gesetzbuch," *Zeitschrift der Savigny-Stiftung für Rechtsgeschichte, Romanistische Abteilung*, XXI (1900), 149–190.

74. Paul Collinet, *Histoire de l'Ecole de Droit de Bayrouth* (Paris, 1925), pp. 20–21.

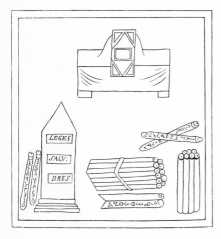

archives in the provinces, particularly those of the province of Africa, and the private collections of professors of law, juris-consults, and barristers. According to Ernst Stein, the incompleteness of the Theodosian Code is not the fault of its compilers but rather the result of the "disorganized status" (*Zerrüttung*) of the archives they had to use,[75] while A. H. M. Jones finds the inadequacy of these archival sources "amazing."[76]

In the light of what we know about the legislative process in the period before the compilation of the Theodosianus, this inadequacy of the imperial archives is indeed surprising. As part of the reforms of Diocletian, the elevated office of the *quaestor sacri palatii* had been created. Called "the mouth of the emperor," he drafted, with the assistance of *scrinia* personnel, the laws and imperial decrees, and thus he was "the organ through which the imperial will expresses itself in all matters pertaining to the law."[77] We find a quaestor of the sacred palace in each half of the empire and, accordingly, in each half of the *notitia dignitatum*.[78] His insignia (Figure 43) include: a table and on it the *liber mandatorum*, the book of basic instructions that define an official's duties;[79] a bundle of papyrus rolls and, in the case of the Western quaestor, also some loose papyri; and, finally, "some kind of coffer or cupboard, some kind of edifice in the form of a slab of stone ending in a point and raised a number of steps."[80] The stone is inscribed *leges salutares* (salutary laws) in the eastern and *leges salubres* (salubrious laws) in the western part of the *notitia dignitatum*.

There has been considerable discussion of the nature of these

75. Stein, *Geschichte*, I, 433. Mistakenly, Cencetti, "Tabularium principis," p. 155, n. 33, states that "the great law collections" are evidence of the "quality and quantity of the material preserved in the imperial archives."

76. Jones, *Later Roman Empire*, I, 474.

77. Pierre Noailles, *Les collections de Novelles de l'Empereur Justinien.* I. *Origine et formation sous Justinien* (Paris, 1912), p. 4.

78. On pp. 34 and 147 respectively of Seeck's edition of the *notitia* and figs. 30 and 74 respectively in the edition of Bibliothèque Nationale.

79. The text of the *liber mandatorum* is preserved in Justinian's Novel 17 of the year 535. See also Wenger, *Die Quellen*, p. 426.

80. Noailles, *Les collections*, I, 39.

Figure 43. Insignia of the quaestor sacri palatii.

leges salutares or *salubres*. Harry Bresslau[81] and others have been inclined to think of them as register books into which abstracts of the laws of each consular year were entered, while Pierre Noailles regards them as an actual depository in which a copy of each general law and comparable imperial issuance was to be kept—what we would call a legislative archives. He finds support for his thesis in the rendering of the *leges* in the *notitia dignitatum*, and Leopold Wenger points out that the insignia of the quaestor show papyri, a bundle of papyrus rolls, and a small edifice but not a codex, which one would expect if the official kept a register book of the laws.[82] It seems impossible to arrive at a definitive answer because, in sending his Novel 17 of the year 535 to his quaestor Tribonian, Justinian orders him to "transcribe it in the *liber legum* and to deposit it in the sacred *laterculum*," that is, the *laterculum minus* or register of staff positions that were filled upon the recommendation of the quaestor.[83] The use of the word "transcribe" makes one wonder whether the quaestor actually had a legislative archives in our sense of the term.

Apart from whether what is commonly called the *liber legum* was a book or a building, one further question remains: If, at the time the *notitia* was compiled, about A.D. 395, there was a complete record of imperial laws in the hands of the quaestor, why was it not used forty years later by the commission charged with the compilation of the Theodosian Code? Had the *liber legum* disintegrated and was the experience of the commission instrumental in having it revitalized? It seems a hypothesis worth considering, because the post-Theodosian laws that appear in the Codex Justinianus and Justinian's own laws in that code were probably culled from the imperial archives, that is, the *liber legum*, and not from the archives of officials who received

81. Harry Bresslau, "Die Commentarii der römischen Kaiser und die Registerbücher der Päpste," *Zeitschrift der Savigny-Stiftung für Rechtsgeschichte, Romanistische Abteilung*, VI (1885), 242–260.

82. Wenger, *Die Quellen*, p. 442.

83. To be distinguished from the *laterculum majus*, which the *primicerius notariorum* had to keep. See p. 207 above.

copies of them. This, however, remains to be confirmed by further research.[84]

That the provincial archives furnished much source material for the Theodosian Code has already been pointed out. In the absence of concrete data we can only assume that the existing situation did not change after the Diocletian reforms and that, on the contrary, it benefited from the progressive bureaucratization of provincial administration. These reforms discontinued the distinction between senatorial and imperial provinces in a system that even included Italy and must have made for greater uniformity of principle and practice. The number of provinces was increased from fifty to more than a hundred. They were, therefore, smaller and hence easier to administer; to provide better control over them, they were grouped into twelve circumscriptions called dioceses. These dioceses were headed by vicars (*vicarii*) of the praetorian prefects, of whom there were four, one each for the Orient, Illyria, Italy, and Gaul. Efficient though this arrangement seems, it would be "misleading to speak of an administrative hierarchy. The pyramid of emperor, praetorian prefects, vicars and provincial governments looks very neat as set out in the Notitia Dignitatum, but there was in reality no rigid chain of command."[85]

If one browses through the *notitia*, he finds in this admirable source for the administrative historian a great many offices and public servants that must have had something to do with records. The following designations appear most frequently: the *commentariensis*, the official charged with keeping the governor's daybooks; the *a cura epistularum*, who had to take care of correspondence; the *regendarius*, whose job it was to prepare abstracts (*regesta*) of documents; and the *ab actis*. In all probability, the last named was the person in charge of the custody of records, although it remains difficult to define sharply the tasks of the various officials who played a part in the creation and administration of records.

84. Noailles, *Les collections*, I, 66; Wenger, *Die Quellen*, p. 443.
85. Jones, *Later Roman Empire*, I, 374.

During the period of the persecution, provincial archival establishments had furnished Christians with source material revealing the fortitude and unshattered faith of the martyrs, and these contacts must have taught the Christians valuable lessons in administrative organization and procedure. Once recognized by the state and able to develop its own organizational structure, the Church was only too eager to coordinate it with that of the state, to adopt its principles of administration, and to copy its practices. "The Church not only transferred to the religious realm the method of preparing proceedings but quite naturally also accepted the terminology of the secular agencies in regard to the making and keeping of records."[86] This is confirmed both by the records of the dignitaries and officials of the Church and by the proceedings of the Church synods.

Occupying positions comparable to those of the praetorian prefects, vicars, and provincial governors, the patriarchs, archbishops, and bishops might be expected to adopt the business methods of their secular opposite numbers, and this they did. Thus, like other Roman officials, they kept their daybooks (*commentarii*). In the east the daybooks were still referred to as *hypomnêmata*, although both terms began to be superseded by the term *regesta* or *gesta*.[87] Like the daybooks of Roman officials, these contained copies of incoming as well as outgoing correspondence and, in addition, documents of all kinds and memoranda designed to provide a complete conspectus of the religious and secular activities and concerns of a Church official. The transfer of administrative techniques from secular to ecclesiastical governance was particularly likely to happen in those areas that became estranged from imperial rule. There, members of the senatorial class found in the Church hierarchy welcome substitutes for the posts they had held in the imperial service. "He who as the emperor's subject would have become a governor, vicar, or prefect, frequently becomes a bishop under the rule of a barbarian king."[88] Distinguished

86. Steinwenter, *Beiträge*, p. 27.
87. Von Heckel, "Das päpstliche und sicilianische Registerwesen," p. 410.
88. Stein, *Geschichte*, I, 489.

persons, although they lacked theological training, were thus converted into dignitaries of the Church without obloquy.

Just as the governors of the provinces took special care of the minutes of the proceedings that took place before them, Church dignitaries presiding over sessions of the synods saw to it that accurate minutes were entered in their *commentarii* and kept in the archives.[89] In the case of universal synods of the Church, chaired by the emperor, the minutes would be preserved in the archives of the Patriarch of Constantinople as the seat of the imperial government. Minutes were taken in shorthand by *exceptores* or *notarii* and subsequently transcribed into the *commentarii* or *gesta*. To make sure that this was done was a definite concern of the presiding dignitary, as appears from a ruling of Boniface II at the synod of Rome, A.D. 531: "What has been read, is to be entered in the church books (*annales*)."[90] This also suggests that the *commentarii* or *gesta* were kept by years.

Because of the doctrinal importance of synodical proceedings, their careful preservation was of the essence; numerous examples show how frequently the minutes of a synod and other pertinent records had to be produced in evidence at later assemblies. Whenever that happened, the *chartophylax* (custodian of records) of the respective see had to bring forth from the archives the documents that had been called for. At the synod of Carthage, A.D. 525, for instance, Bishop Boniface demanded: "I want to have produced from the archives of this church the documents we have issued and the rescripts we have received and everything that pertains to the constancy (*firmitas*) of the present business. [Thereupon] the notary Redemptiolus recited from the volume of documents (*ex volumine chartarum*)."[91] Examples of such reference use at synodal meetings could be multiplied, and if it was possible to satisfy requests speedily, as seems to have been

---

89. For the following see Von Heckel, "Das päpstliche und sicilianische Registerwesen," pp. 410–412.

90. *Ibid.*, p. 411.

91. *Ibid.*, p. 410, n. 5.

the case, the Church ar̶c̶h̶ives (referred to variously as *chartophylacium*, *archivium*, or *scrinium*) had to be a properly organized unit of Church government. In all probability the archives contained, in addition to records, hymnals and other religious texts and was situated close to the Church treasure with its holy vessels, relics, and precious priestly garments. Like the secular archives, the Church archives were quite accessible, so that during the Donatist controversy St. Augustine could state in a matter-of-fact fashion: "The necessary documents I have obtained either from the ecclesiastical or the public archives (*gesta*)."[92]

Until recently it seemed that, in regard to the care of its archives, the seat of Saint Peter could claim precedence over other episcopal sees. This claim was based on the text of an inscription in seven hexameters that Pope Damasus I (A.D. 366–384) had incised above the entrance to the basilica of San Lorenzo in Prasina, later called San Lorenzo in Damaso and now located within the Palazzo della Cancelleria.[93] In this inscription, which has come down to us in a copy in the Codex Palatinus Latinus 833 of the Vatican Library, Pope Damasus says that in this church of San Lorenzo his father advanced to the dignity of priest; that from this church he himself ascended the apostolic see; and that therefore he wanted to erect a new building for the archives (*Archibis fateor volui nova condere tecta*). Most of the writers on the history of the papal archives concluded from this statement that Damasus built or reconditioned a structure for use as an archival repository, but Paul F. Kehr questioned the relevance of this statement and felt that, at best, it could be related to a library or church archives, to be distinguished from the "papal central archives."[94] Kehr's doubts have now been confirmed in Paul Künzle's study of "The So-called 'Titulus

92. *Ibid.*, p. 413, n. 3.

93. Harry Bresslau, *Handbuch der Urkundenlehre für Deutschland und Italien*, 2d ed., I (Leipzig, 1912), 150–151.

94. In a review, *Mitteilungen des Instituts für Österreichische Geschichtsforschune*, VIII (1887), 143, of de Rossi's essay on the history of the archives and library of the Apostolic See.

Archivorum' of Pope Damasus."[95] Whoever copied the inscription misread the decisive line which simply speaks of the Pope's wish to rebuild the church that had witnessed his father's and his own careers: *Christe tibi, fateor, volui nova condere tecta* (To you, Christ, may it be known, I wanted to erect a new building).

It is surprising that the story of the Damasus archives was accepted so long by so many, because the Lateran was the seat of the Church government, and it was there that the pertinent records were created, were received, and were to be at hand. These were the records generated by the administration of the religious and secular affairs of the Church, the original records of synods held in Rome, and the registers of letters sent that undoubtedly were kept since the middle of the fourth century. Some particularly important documents were deposited in the crypt of Saint Peter's in the *confessio beati Petri apostoli*.[96]

The Lateran depository, together with the library, was controlled by the chief of the chancery, the *primicerius notariorum* and, judging by the minutes of Roman synods, must have been a well organized and well functioning unit of government at the time of the first great Lateran Synod in 649. In the course of the sessions, documents and books were constantly requisitioned *de apostolico scrinio* and produced by the *primicerius notariorum apostolicae sedis* with the words: "I have in my hands the documents referred to, which I am producing according to the orders of Your Beatitude. What is Your wish?"[97]

Though we do not have a complete ecclesiastical archives for this period, parts of such archives have come down to us in excerpts. The Avellana collection, for instance, contains, in addition to copies from the archives of the Prefects of Rome, copies from the ecclesiastical archives of Carthage and from the correspondence of Pope Hormisdas (A.D. 514–521), obtained

95. Paul Künzle, "Del cosi-detto 'titulus archivorum' di papa Damaso," *Rivista di Storia della Chiesa in Italia*, VII (1953), 1–26.

96. Bresslau, *Handbuch*, I, 151–154.

97. Giovanni Domenico Mansi, *Sacrorum conciliorum nova et amplissima collectio*, X (Florence, 1764), 998. For writings on the history of the present Vatican Archives, see the *Bibliografia dell' Archivio Vaticano*, I (1962), 72–74.

from the archives of the Holy See, the *scrinia sedis apostolicae*.⁹⁸
We also have a number of private documents on papyrus
that, though now widely dispersed, once were part of a Church
archives, that of the Archbishop of Ravenna. Drawn up in
connection with donations to the Church, the fifty-five papyri
that survive—most of them certainly written in Ravenna—
constitute the most important assemblage of papyri documents
(A.D. 445–700) that at one time belonged to the archives of a
Church institution.⁹⁹

The Ravenna papyri were created in the presence of municipal
authorities and as such illustrate what is possibly the most
noteworthy development in the field of record-making
under the late Empire. They are the product of the government's
effort to enforce the public registration of certain kinds
of legal documents, paralleled by the desire of the citizen to
have the records of his legal transactions elevated to the rank
of public documents, for:

> The private document, although superior to the red tape [*Um-
> ständlichkeit*] of the public document because of its simplicity and
> convenience, nevertheless covets the privileges granted by the state
> to documents that have already at the time of their genesis received
> the imprint of publicity [in the sense of the state or quality of being
> public].¹⁰⁰

The records of proceedings before state magistrates, records
that it was their duty to prepare and preserve for their own
purposes, enjoyed public faith, and the *duty* imposed upon these
magistrates to record their actions developed into the *right*
to create such records for private persons. This is the *jus actorum
conficiendorum*,¹⁰¹ the right to prepare minutes of proceedings

98. Otto Günther, *Avellana-Studien* (Vienna, 1896), p. 49. The collection contains
imperial and papal documents of the period A.D. 368–533, and is named after the monas-
tery Fonte Avellana, where the manuscript was found.

99. Jan-Olof Tjäder, *Die nichtliterarischen Papyri Italiens aus der Zeit 445–700*, I
(Lund, 1955), which partly supersedes the older edition of Abate Gaetano Marini.

100. Wenger, *Die Quellen*, p. 749.

101. Steinwenter, *Beiträge*, pp. 2–5, 30–32.

that take place before the magistrate, which, in the course of time, broadened into the right to conduct legal transactions and also to embody in the minutes the records of transactions already concluded. To use Harold Steinacker's definition, it is a matter of

the right of certain agencies to enter in their official records (*tabulae publicae, acta, gesta, commentarii, libelli,* etc.) minutes of private actions and declarations made before them or to enter in their records, after proper examination, completed private documents, which process from the standpoint of the party concerned is called *allegare, insinuare* [to attach, to insert]. Authorized copies of such minutes or insertion proceedings (also called *acta* or *gesta*) become documents with *publica fides* [public credibility], *instrumenta publica,* not to be confused with the *instrumenta publice confecta* [instruments drawn up in public] of the *tabelliones* [notarial scriveners], which are not public documents.[102]

Originally, state authorities only had the right to elevate private documents to the status of public documents by exercising the *jus actorum conficiendorum* or *jus gestorum.* In enabling its subjects to obtain for their legal transactions the preferred status of a public record, the state was not motivated by the desire to enhance the credibility of private transactions. Rather it was fiscal interest that prompted the government to prescribe, for certain kinds of transactions, registration in an agency's records; and it was, therefore, first applied to wills, in order to facilitate the collection of the inheritance tax, the *vicesima hereditatum.* Likewise, donations had to be registered in accordance with a constitution of Emperor Constantine of A.D. 316, if they amounted to more than two hundred, a sum first raised to three hundred and later to five hundred solidi. Except for these two types of transactions, the registration of legal documents or transactions was not prescribed, although, as the Ravenna papyri show, there was in the West at least a tendency to invest other types of business transactions with the privileged status

102. Harold Steinacker, *Die antiken Grundlagen der frühmittelalterlichen Privaturkunde* (Leipzig and Berlin, 1927), pp. 76–77.

of public documents. The legal significance of the registration process is clear: a transaction subject to being registered was not valid unless it was entered into the *gesta*.[103]

In the fourth century (A.D. 366), municipal magistrates received from the emperors Valentinian and Valens the *jus actorum conficiendorum*, which hitherto had belonged to provincial authorities only, an arrangement which must have been inconvenient for the parties concerned. The authority thus conferred resulted in the creation of an important body of municipal records, the *gesta municipalia*. The procedure for having transactions entered into the *gesta* was simple: a stenographer (*exceptor*) took down on his wax tablets the minutes of the proceedings before the competent municipal magistrate. From these minutes the official record (*scheda*) was prepared, and it was signed by the magistrate with the instruction: "Copies to be issued according to usage" (*edantur ex more*), which necessitated the payment of the established fees.[104]

In the course of time different municipal officials, acting individually or jointly, had the *jus actorum conficiendorum*, until in the second half of the fourth century the *defensor civitatis*,[105] a new officer who began to replace the former magistrates as head of the city government, became the principal authority exercising the right of registration. From Justinian's Novel 15 it appears that the provincial governors, certainly because of the fees involved, were loath to relinquish their former prerogative to the defenders. The Novel rules: "All wills, donations, and other documents of this kind shall be registered by defenders; and no governor of a province shall prohibit any instrument from being drawn up and published", and "whether the governor is in the city or not, no one shall be prohibited from filing

---

103. Steinwenter, *Beiträge*, p. 57.

104. Bruno Hirschfeld, *Die Gesta Municipalia in römischer und frühgermanischer Zeit*, Ph.D. diss., University of Marburg, 1904, is a detailed study of the institution. See also chap. XV of Frank F. Abbott and Allan C. Johnson, *Municipal Administration in the Roman Empire* (Princeton, 1926), and the relevant sections of Steinwenter, *Beiträge*, and Wenger, *Die Quellen*.

105. E. Berneker, "Defensor civitatis," *Reallexikon für Antike und Christentum*, III (1957), 649–656.

documents with the defenders in any matter whatsoever."[106]

Although protecting the right of the defenders, the emperor was critical of their morale and their care of the records created, pointing out that their records enjoyed no confidence:

> When documents are drawn up by them in the first place, they only do this for money; and then, as there are no archives in which these documents can be deposited, they are lost; and no monuments of former times are ever found in the possession of those who receive them, but when a demand is made upon their heirs or other successors, they either do not have them, or where any are found, they are not worthy of consideration or have been defaced to such an extent that they can no longer be deciphered.[107]

It appears from this statement that the defenders did not give their records to the municipal archives but kept them, a practice that resulted in either poor physical preservation or complete loss. The emperor, therefore, charged the Praetorian Prefects to see to it that in all the provinces "a public building be provided in each city in which the defenders can store their records conveniently, and to elect somebody in the province who will have custody of them, so that they will remain uncorrupted and can be quickly found by those who require them." In that manner "there will be remedied what hitherto has been neglected."[108] It is impossible to tell whether Justinian's decree had any effect.

The much debated legal aspects of the *gesta municipalia* need not concern us here. One controversial matter calls for comment, however, and that is the relationship of the *gesta* to the official registration of private business transactions in Greece and Hellenistic Egypt. Mommsen and Steinwenter deny any connection between the two processes, since the *jus actorum conficiendorum* of the cities had its origin in the right and duty of Roman agencies to record legal and administrative proceedings, a typically Roman phenomenon, although they

106. Samuel Parsons Scott, ed. and trans., *The Civil Law*, XVI (Cincinnati, 1932), 82.
107. *Ibid.*, p. 81.
108. *Ibid.*, p. 83.

admit that Greek institutions in all probability had "an indirect influence."[109] Steinacker, however, agreeing with Ulrich Wilcken, thinks it hardly a coincidence that it was Constantine with his leaning toward Greek institutions who in A.D. 316 made the registration of donations compulsory.[110] More recently, Wenger has discovered parallels between the insertion of documents in the *gesta municipalia* and the *dêmosiôsis* procedure that we encountered in Hellenistic Egypt.[111] It is certain that the *gesta* legislation could not and did not lead to the establishment of archival depositories comparable to the *bibliothêkê enktêseôn* in Egypt, possibly because only two kinds of transactions were subject to registration.

Strangely enough, the *gesta municipalia* seem to have met wider acceptance and survived longer in the Western than in the Eastern Empire, where their existence down to the days of Justinian is known to us only through legal provisions. The Ravenna papyri prove that the institution kept functioning until the second half of the eighth century and the legislation of the Germanic kingdoms of the Burgundians and West Goths shows traces of it in the *lex Romana Burgundiorum* and the *lex Romana Visigothorum*.[112] The fact that in the kingdom of the Franks "the volumes of municipal registers were preserved and could be consulted, is testified to by the chronicle of St. Wandrille of the period of Louis the Pious [A.D. 814–840]."[113] It is quite possible, however, that the documents that spell out the formalities of the registration process no longer reflected actual procedure and were nothing but stylistic routine.[114]

Certainly in Italy, as well as in other parts of the West, the Church preferred to avoid registration of donations in the *gesta municipalia*, and was indeed ready to play an increasingly

109. Steinwenter, *Beiträge*, pp. 26, 69.

110. Steinacker, *Die antiken Grundlagen*, p. 77.

111. Wenger, *Die Quellen*, pp. 749–755.

112. Hirschfeld, "Die Gesta," pp. 66–85.

113. Harold Steinacker, "Zum Zusammenhang zwischen antikem und frühmittelalterlichem Registerwesen," *Wiener Studien*, XXIV (1902), 306.

114. A. de Boüard, *Manuel de diplomatique française et pontificale*. I. *Diplomatique générale* (Paris, 1929), p. 126.

important role not only in preserving its own records but also in serving those who wished to entrust their documents to the protection of a religious sanctuary.

It is tempting to measure the archival arrangements of the Roman Empire against those of the Republic. By developing the Tabularium into a quasi-central archives of the state and housing it in a splendid and suitable building, the Republic had taken a unique step toward meeting the archival needs of a modern state. Strangely enough, this happened under a government that was in the hands of nonprofessional administrators. Perhaps the very lack of bureaucratic administration, however, made it desirable to concentrate in one place the records of amateur officials in which their equally amateurish successors took no interest.

With the transition to imperial rule, the Tabularium lost its preeminent position. The most important records then accumulated on the Palatine and in the hands of the imperial chancery and other central offices, and the concept of an archival agency serving most of the government was lost. And so progressing bureaucratization did not benefit the cause of the archives, particularly when the Empire was split into two halves and when the central government became "a migratory body." The disorganization and inadequacy of the imperial archives were shockingly revealed when the commission appointed to compile the Codex Theodosianus had to cull the texts of the laws from archives in the provinces, from the files of individual officials, and from private collections because there was no central repository to which the commission could turn.

The experience of the Theodosian commission tends to show at the same time that archival administration in the provinces had made great strides under the Empire. This development had long-range importance, because it aided the Church—once it had been recognized—in developing, within its hierarchy, archival practices similar to those of the state. As an heir to the administrative experience of imperial Rome, the Church was able to preserve some of that experience and pass it on to the emerging modern state.

In ancient Greece the institution of the public notariat as an adjunct to the public archives had given impetus to the setting up and functioning of state archival agencies, a development that, in Roman Egypt, culminated in the Property Record Office within, or on a level with, the provincial archives. This remained an isolated venture, however, until during the last centuries of the Empire completion of a limited group of private transactions by entering them into the *gesta municipalia* was ordered, and it was only under Justinian that provision was made for a municipal archives of the defender of the city. The pertinent legislation had no lasting effect.

We shall not deny the Empire its important role as a link between the archival achievements of classical antiquity and their revival in the late Middle Ages. Unless we unduly exaggerate the role of the Republican Tabularium, however, the Empire made no progress toward realizing the concept of the general archival agency which, no matter how dimly, was understood by the founders of the Tabularium.

Postlude

Record-Keeping in the Parthian and Neo-Persian Empires

As has been pointed out, record-keeping practices of the Roman regime in Egypt carried over into the era of Byzantine and Arab control of that country and with the Arabs trickled into southern Europe. A similar continuity of practices becomes apparent if we focus our attention on Persia after the downfall of the Seleucid regime, about the middle of the third century B.C.

From ca. 250 B.C. to A.D. 642, Persia was ruled by native dynasties—the Arsacids until A.D. 226 and the Sassanians until the Arab conquest, A.D. 642. The two regimes, although both anchored in institutions of the Seleucid empire, differed in that the Parthian Arsacids, newcomers from outer and nomadic Iran, were eager to preserve existing institutions, so that Hellenistic influences increased rather than receded and the kingdom had a definite "Greek veneer."[1] "Whoever entered the realm of the Parthians from the west found a state with the unchanged physiognomy of the Seleucids, not only in its administration but also in the progressive Hellenization which at that time began to flourish with increased vigor at the princely court as well as in the nobility."[2] The Sassanians, on the other hand, consciously returned to pre-Hellenistic traditions and created a regime that was simultaneously centralistic-bureaucratic and feudalistic. It became for the Orient almost the model of a well-ordered state,[3] and so its basic features were retained by the Arab conquerors.

It might be considered futile to discuss the archives of the Arsacid and Sassanian dynasties, for the records of their governments have vanished and the scanty information we have stems

1. Ellis H. Minns, "Parchments of the Parthian Period from Avroman in Kurdistan," *Journal of Hellenic Studies*, XXXV (1915), 61.

2. Ernst Kornemann, *Weltgeschichte des Mittelmeerraumes von Philipp II. von Makedonien bis Muhammed*, ed. Hermann Bengtson (Munich, 1967), p. 331.

3. Theodor Nöldecke, *Geschichte der Perser und Araber zur Zeit der Sasaniden* (Leiden, 1879), p. 453.

from Byzantine and Arab literary sources. Yet we should not totally ignore a period of eight hundred years that saw the flowering of a great culture and in many respects left its mark on the regimes that followed it, those of the Arabs, the Mongols, and the Ottoman Turks.

Neither the Arsacids nor the Sassanians destroyed the framework of the Seleucid form of government they had taken over from the successors of Alexander. Under the last Seleucids, government institutions and procedures, especially those of the chancery and the financial administration, had been streamlined and improved by copying practices of the Egyptian Ptolemies, and it was in this form that the Partho-Sassanian ministry of finance, chancellery, poll tax, and cadastre, the originally Seleucid systems of division into *stratêgiai*, *eparchiai*, and *hyparchiai*, and even the court organization assumed an Iranian and feudal look.[4]

At the center of government was a well-organized system of communication and recording. A royal secretary drafted the king's orders in his presence, and another official registered the orders in a journal or daybook which was organized on a monthly basis. The fair copy of an order was prepared in the flourishing style of the Persian bureaucracy, submitted to the king by the secretary, compared with the entry in the journal, and—if the two versions agreed—sealed in the presence of the king or his most intimate confidant. The journal was closed at the end of each month, sealed by the king, and kept in the archives.[5]

The royal archives was situated in Ctesiphon, which had become the seat of the Sassanian government after Seleucia on the east side of the Tigris River had been conquered and sacked by the Romans in A.D. 197. From Ctesiphon the Grand Vizier

4. Fritz M. Heichelheim, "New Light on the Influence of Hellenistic Financial Administration in the Near East and India," *Economic History*, IV (1938), 1–2.

5. Nöldecke, *Geschichte der Perser und Araber*, p. 354, n. 2; Rudolf von Heckel, "Das päpstliche und sicilianische Registerwesen," *Archiv für Urkundenforschung*, I (1908), 418; Clément Huart and Louis Delaporte, *L'Iran antique: Elam et Perse et la civilisation iranienne* (Paris, 1952), p. 385.

and a number of secretaries directed the affairs of a far-flung empire through a well-organized postal system and with the help of official spies, the eyes and ears of the king. The secretaries, who headed the ministries called divans,[6] were "the true diplomats. They prepared all kinds of documents; kept the correspondence of the state; drafted and registered the royal decrees; compiled the tax rolls and the accounts of the state."[7]

We can be sure that the products of an elaborate and formalistic record-making process ended in the royal archives. That this is definitely true of the king's daybooks is borne out by their use in the writing of the *Five Books of History* of Agathias, Byzantine poet and historian (ca. A.D. 536–581). Through his interpreter Sergius, Agathias obtained, with the permission of the directors of the archives, material from the royal daybooks (*apomnêmoneumata*) that were kept in the Ctesiphon archives. Sergius translated into Greek his notes, which contained the names of the kings of Persia, their reigns, and their most important deeds, and forwarded them to Constantinople.[8] Whenever a new king ascended the throne, the documents in the archives were recopied in his name, although only the most indispensable changes were made. This information stems from Armenian sources and cannot be verified.[9]

In the feudal system of the Sassanians, in which the status of the nobility had to be safeguarded, records to that end were of the essence and had to be kept. This was done by registering the noble families of the realm "in the books and in the archives,"[10] that is, in a complete roll of the nobility.

For tax purposes land records were kept at the center of affairs in Ctesiphon and probably in the capitals of the satrapies.

6. On the history of the word and the institution, see *Encyclopaedia of Islam*, new ed., II (Leiden and London, 1965), 323–337.

7. Arthur Christensen, *L'Iran sous les Sassanides*, 2d ed. (Copenhagen, 1944), p. 134.

8. Nöldecke, *Geschichte der Perser und Araber*, p. 402; Rudolf Keydell, ed., *Agathiae Myrinaei Historiarum Libri Quinque* (Berlin, 1967), 30.3 (p. 162).

9. Christensen, *L'Iran sous les Sassanides*, p. 126, on the basis of M. K. Patkanian, "Essai d'une histoire de la dynastie des Sassanides, d'après les renseignements fournis par les historiens arméniens," *Journal Asiatique*, ser. 6, VII (1866), 113.

10. Christensen, *L'Iran sous les Sassanides*, p. 318.

This was certainly the case after the great Chusroe (A.D. 531–579) had completed the survey of the land begun by his father Kavadh, which was to form the basis of a more equitable tax system.[11] Even before this reform, land records must have been kept in continuation of Seleucid practices.

That land records of some kind did indeed exist before Chusroe's tax reform is suggested by the liquidation of the revolutionary movement called Mazdakism after its leader Mazdak (ca. A.D. 450–548).[12] As part of a program that did not lack its ethical impulses, Mazdak condemned individual property and preached a radical social system based on common ownership of property and women. First favored by Kavadh and temporarily in full control after Kavadh had been forced to flee, Mazdakism was cruelly suppressed after the king had returned to power. It then became necessary to remedy a confused situation in which "a man did not know his son any longer nor the son his father and in which nobody was able to enjoy his life."[13]

Since a *recherche de la paternité* was impossible because of the promiscuity that had prevailed, nothing could be done for offspring except to leave children with the families in which they happened to live. Regulations were adopted, however, to regularize the status of women who had been abducted, and, in the matter of socialized property, Chusroe ordered the return to the legal owners of the real estate and tangible property they had been deprived of.[14] Obviously, to establish such legal

11. Nöldecke, *Geschichte der Perser und Araber*, pp. 241–247; Ernst Stein, "Ein Kapitel vom persischen und byzantinischen Staate," *Byzantinisch-Neugriechische Jahrbücher*, I (1920), 64–67; Christensen, *L'Iran sous les Sassanides*, pp. 122, 366; Huart and Delaporte, *L'Iran antique*, p. 386; Franz Altheim and Ruth Stiehl, *Finanzgeschichte der Spätantike* (Frankfurt am Main, 1957), p. 7.

12. On the liquidation of Mazdakism, see Nöldecke, *Geschichte der Perser und Araber*, pp. 163, 455–467; Stein, "Ein Kapitel," p. 67; Arthur Christensen, *Le règne du roi Kawadh I et le communisme Mazdakite* (Copenhagen, 1925), pp. 122–123; Roman Ghirshman, *Iran from the Earliest Times to the Islamic Conquest*, trans. from French (Harmondsworth, Middlesex, 1954), pp. 302–304; and, in general, Otokar Klíma, *Mazdak: Geschichte einer sozialen Bewegung im sassanidischen Persien* (Prague, 1957).

13. Christensen, *Le règne du roi Kawadh I*, p. 35.

14. Nöldecke, *Geschichte der Perser und Araber*, p. 163; Christensen, *Le règne du roi Kawadh I*, pp. 122–123; Ghirshman, *Iran*, pp. 302–304.

ownership recourse had to be had to the land records. The value of land records demonstrated in this connection may have prompted Chusroe to deposit a set of his new tax rolls in the archives.[15]

Although the records of the Arsacid and Sassanian regimes have disappeared, a few scraps of private archival material have survived. About 1900, peasants discovered near Avromàn in Kurdistan a hermetically sealed stone jar with documents of the early Arsacid period, three of which are still extant.[16] Two of the documents are written in Greek and one is in Aramaic. All three were executed in duplicate with an inner and an outer text. Decayed millet seeds were found in the jar, possibly placed there to absorb humidity, since these seeds were thought to keep well.

In 1948, Soviet excavations in Parthian Nisaia produced an early Parthian archives, consisting of potsherds bearing Aramaic writing in black ink. Some of them have been published,[17] and M. E. Masson has furnished a photograph of the place in which the ostraca were found.[18]

Another ostraca archives was discovered in the former palace of the Roman *dux* in Dura-Europos, headquarters of the Sassanian commandant during the Persian occupation (A.D. 260–262). The archives contains receipts for wine taken from private stores and consumed by the staff of the Sassanian army.[19]

Except for these and other chance discoveries, our knowledge of the late Persian archives stems chiefly from the writings of Arab authors. That Seleucid institutions survived and were continued by successive regimes is not surprising. Nomadic peoples like the Parthians, the Arabs, the Mongols, and the Turks, who conquer a culturally advanced country and want to

15. Nöldecke, *Geschichte der Perser und Araber*, p. 247; Christensen, *L'Iran sous les Sassanides*, p. 367.

16. Minns, "Parchments," p. 22; Franz Altheim and Ruth Stiehl, *Ein asiatischer Staat: Feudalismus unter den Sasaniden und ihren Nachbarn* (Wiesbaden, 1954), pp. 229–241.

17. See the article by I. H. Diakonov, M. H. Diakonov, and W. A. Liwsic, *Vestnik drevneĭ istorii* (1953), no. 4, pp. 114–130.

18. *Ibid.* (1953), no. 1, p. 158.

19. Altheim and Stiehl, *Asiatischer Staat*, p. 237.

exploit its financial resources, depend on the instrumentalities of the preceding government. They must retain its tax system and, in the beginning at least, its experienced personnel and even its language. This the Arabs did when they conquered Persia, for until the beginning of the eighth century records were kept in Persian, and it was only then that Arabic became the administrative language of the land.[20]

The lasting impact of the Hellenicized financial institutions of Persia, and consequently of the requisite archival practices, has been admirably summed up by Walther Hinz:

> When, in the 11th century, the [Turkish] Seljuks organized their empire, which stretched from the Jaxartes to the Mediterranean, Persian administration penetrated as far as the Seljuk sword. The Ayyubids [1169–1250] continued this development. To what extent Persian methods of bookkeeping prevailed in the financial agencies of the Mameluke empire (1254–1517), will appear only when from this area also manuals of state financial administration have come to light. In the empires of the Mongolian Il-Khâns of the thirteenth and fourteenth century and in those of the Tatars and Turkomans of the fifteenth century, Persians controlled the entire civil administration. In the West this heritage was passed on to the Osmanlis through the Rum Seljuks; in the East, in the realm of the Great Moguls, it merged with the local tradition without losing its dominant role.
>
> Thus a surprisingly uniform system of fiscal accounting covers all of the Near East (*Vorderasien*) from the late Middle Ages to the eighteenth century.[21]

Hinz adds that later the Ottoman Turks, too, kept their official books in Persian down to recent times. Such continuation of fiscal practices is but one facet of a broader historical process, however. When about A.D. 750 the Abbasid dynasty came into power, Persians began to furnish most of the talent the new Arab government needed. They possessed administra-

20. Philip Khûri Hitti, *History of the Arabs from the Earliest Times to the Present*, 5th ed. (New York, 1951), p. 217, says in regard to the arabicization of the government: "The early conquerors, fresh from the desert and ignorant of book-keeping and finance," retained "the Greek-writing officials in Syria and the Persian-writing officials in al-ᶜIrāq and Persia."

21. Walther Hinz, "Das Rechnungswesen orientalischer Reichsfinanzämter im Mittelalter," *Islam*, XXIX (1949–1950), 4.

tive skills acquired under their Sassanian rulers, skills that through the preceding regimes of the Arsacids, Seleucids, and Achaemenids can be traced back to the days when scribes from Elam brought the art of writing to Iran. Under the Abbasids respect for the record as a document of literary excellence and for its preservation remained an important aspect of governmental administration, and when the Abbasid state disintegrated, the dynasties that succeeded it in the various regions, ruled them with the help of a highly literate elite that continued in the tradition of their Persian predecessors.

We do not have an adequate study of record-making and record-keeping practices in the Moslem world. There can be no doubt, however, that a sophisticated system of written communication produced, and depended on the use of, records of high quality and that their retention in archival institutions was considered essential. At a time when in Europe documents on parchment were still drafted and laboriously penned by ecclesiastics, the Moslem governments had well-organized chanceries and knew how to control the masses of records these chanceries produced with the help of archivists. This certainly was true of the Fatimid dynasty (A.D. 968–1171) in Egypt. A manual for the Fatimid state chancery of the early twelfth century not only provides for the position of an archivist but also prescribes in detail how he should keep his records and what finding aids he should prepare.[22]

The Fatimids took their advanced techniques of making, arranging, and preserving records into conquered Sicily. There the Normans, whose administrative ingenuity equaled that of the Persians, continued these techniques to good advantage. In that way record-keeping became an important administrative tool in the hands of the rulers of the Norman and later the Hohenstaufen kingdom, the first modern state of Western Europe.

[22] I have dealt with this subject in "Twelfth Century Job Descriptions for the Registrar and the Archivist of the Fatimid State Chancery," to be published in the *Festschrift für Hanns Leo Mikoletzky*, the 1972 issue of the *Mitteilungen des Österreichischen Staatsarchivs*.

Bibliography   Index

Bibliography

To facilitate the use of this bibliography, it has been organized in sections corresponding to the chapters of the text. In a few instances this has made it necessary to list the same work more than once. To avoid excessive duplication, however, works and articles of general scope have been placed at the beginning in a section headed General, and the literature on the archives of Republican and Imperial Rome has been combined in one section, because many of the basic works cited deal with the entire course of Roman institutional history. In addition to items referred to in the text, there have been included below some books and articles of special interest that, although not mentioned, have contributed to the general fabric of the text.

General

The earlier general works on archives administration by Eugenio Casanova and Adolf Brenneke pay relatively little attention to the ancient period. Karl Gross's article "Archiv" in *Reallexikon für Antike und Christentum*, I (1950), 614–631, though necessarily brief, is a most useful digest of information concerning ancient and early medieval archives. In the work *L'histoire et ses méthodes* (Paris, 1961), pp. 1120–1161, Robert-Henri Bautier devotes some well-considered pages to the early history of archives. Leopoldo Sandri's "La storia degli archivi," *Rassegna degli Archivi di Stato*, XVIII (1958), 109–134, deals thoughtfully with the uses and objectives of archival history.

Bautier, Robert-Henri. "Les archives." In *L'histoire et ses méthodes*, edited by Charles Samaran, pp. 1120–1166. Paris: Gallimard, 1961.

Bernhardt, Karl Heinz. *Die Umwelt des Alten Testaments*. I. *Die Quellen und ihre Erforschung*. Gütersloh: G. Mohn, 1967.

Brenneke, Adolf. *Archivkunde: Ein Beitrag zur Theorie und Geschichte des europäischen Archivwesens*. Edited by Wolfgang Leesch. Leipzig: Koehler and Amelang, 1953.

Casanova, Eugenio. *Archivistica*. 2d ed. Siena: Lazzeri, 1928.

———— and Bruno Katterbach. "Archivio e archivistica." In *Enciclopedia Italiana*, IV, 83–90. Rome: Istituto Giovanni Treccani, 1929.

Déléage, André. "Les cadastres antiques jusqu'à Dioclétien." *Etudes de Papyrologie*, II (1934), 73–225.

Diringer, David. *The Hand-Produced Book*. New York: Philosophical Library, 1953.

Erman, H. "Zum antiken Urkundenwesen." *Zeitschrift der Savigny-Stiftung für Rechtsgeschichte, Romanistische Abteilung*, XXVI (1905), 456–478.

Gross, Karl. "Archiv." In *Reallexikon für Antike und Christentum*, I (1950), 614–631. Stuttgart: Hiersemann, 1950.

Hunger, Herbert. "Antikes und mittelalterliches Buch-und Schriftwesen." In *Geschichte der Textüberlieferung der antiken und mittelalterlichen Literatur*, edited by Herbert Hunger and others, I, 25–147. Zürich: Atlantis, 1961.

Milkau, Fritz, ed. *Handbuch der Bibliothekswissenschaft*. Revised edition by Georg Leyh. 3 vols. Wiesbaden: O. Harrassowitz, 1952–1961.

Otto, Walter, ed. *Handbuch der Archäologie im Rahmen des Handbuchs der Altertumswissenschaft*, 3 vols. Munich: C. H. Beck, 1939.

———— "Die zukünftige Gestaltung der nichtliterarischen Papyrus-und Ostrakapublikationen." In *Actes du Ve Congrès International de Papyrologie, Oxford, 1939*, pp. 314–336. Brussels: Fondation Egyptologique Reine Elisabeth, 1938.

Robert, Louis. "Epigraphie." In *L'histoire et ses méthodes*, edited by Charles Samaran, pp. 453–497. Paris: Gallimard, 1961.

Sandri, Leopoldo. "La storia degli archivi." *Rassegna degli Archivi di Stato*, XVIII (1958), 109–134.

———— "La storia degli archivi." *Archivum*, XVIII (1968), 101–113.

Steinacker, Harold. *Die antiken Grundlagen der frühmittelalterlichen Privaturkunde*. Meisters Grundriss der Geschichtswissenschaft, supplement I. Leipzig and Berlin: B. G. Teubner, 1937.

Wendel, Carl. *Die griechisch-römische Buchbeschreibung verglichen mit der des vorderen Orients*. Halle a.d. Saale: M. Niemeyer, 1949.

Wilcken, Ulrich. "Über antike Urkundenlehre." In *Papyri und Altertumskunde*, edited by Walter Otto and Leopold Wenger, pp. 42–61. Münchener Beiträge zur Papyrusforschung und antiken Rechtsgeschichte, no. XIX. Munich: C. H. Beck, 1934.

[1] *The Clay Tablet Archives*

The development of archival thought with regard to the clay tablet discoveries has been placed in its professional perspective in Johannes Papritz, "Archive in Altmesopotamien: Theorie und Tatsachen," *Archivalische Zeitschrift*, LV (1959), 11–50. I am reluctant to offer any comments on the relative usefulness to the student of archives of the many general works on the clay tablet civilization. I have found A. Leo Oppenheim's *Ancient Mesopotamia* (Chicago, 1964) extraordinarily valuable and helpful. This great work includes discriminating bibliographical notes, a glossary of names and terms, and an "Appendix: Mesopotamian Chronology of the Historical Period."

Barnett, R. D. "Further Russian Excavations in Armenia (1949–1953)." *Iraq*, XXI (1959), 1–19.

——— and W. Watson. "Russian Excavations in Armenia." *Iraq*, XIV (1952), 132–147.

Bennett, Emmett L., Jr., ed. *The Pylos Tablets: Texts of the Inscriptions Found 1939–1954*. With a foreword by Carl W. Blegen. Princeton: Princeton University Press, 1955.

Bernhardt, Karl Heinz. *Die Umwelt des Alten Testaments*. I. *Die Quellen und ihre Erforschung*. Gütersloh: G. Mohn, 1967.

Birot, Maurice. "Les lettres de Iasîm-Sumû." *Syria*, XLI (1964), 25–65.

——— "Un recensement de femmes au Royaume de Mari." *Syria*, XXXV (1958), 9–26.

Bittel, Kurt. *Grundzüge der Vor-und Frühgeschichte Kleinasiens*. 2d ed. Tübingen: E. Wasmuth, 1950.

——— *Hattusha*. London: Oxford University Press, 1970.

——— "Untersuchungen auf Büyükkale." *Mitteilungen der Deutschen Orient-Gesellschaft*, XCI (1958), 57–72.

——— and others. *Boğazköy III. Funde aus den Grabungen 1952–1955*. Berlin: Gebrüder Mann, 1957.

——— "Vorläufiger Bericht über die Ausgrabungen in Boğazköy im Jahre 1957." *Mitteilungen der Deutschen Orient-Gesellschaft*, XCI (1958), 1–84.

——— and Rudolf Naumann. *Boğazköy-Hattusa*. Stuttgart: W. Kohlhammer, 1952.

Blegen, Carl W., and Marion Rawson. *A Guide to the Palace of Nestor*. Cincinnati: University of Cincinnati, 1962.

———— *The Palace of Nestor at Pylos in Western Messenia.* I. *The Buildings and Their Contents.* 2 vols. Princeton: Princeton University Press, 1966.

Bogaert, Raymond D. *Les origines de la banque de dépôt: Une mise au point accompagnée d'une esquisse des opérations de banque en Mésopotamie.* Leiden: A. W. Sijthoff, 1966.

Bossert, Helmuth T. "Sie schrieben auf Holz." In *Minoica: Festschrift zum 80. Geburtstag von Johannes Sundwall,* edited by Ernst Grumach, pp. 67–79. Berlin: Akademie-Verlag, 1958.

Boyer, G. "La place des textes d'Ugarit dans l'histoire de l'ancien droit oriental." In *Le palais royal d'Ugarit III,* edited by Claude F.-A. Schaeffer, pp. 281–308. Mission de Ras Shamra, vol. VI. Paris: Imprimerie Nationale, 1955.

Budge, Sir E. A. Wallis. *By Nile and Tigris.* 2 vols. London: J. Murray, 1920.

Cardascia, Guillaume. *Les archives des Muraŝû: Une famille d'hommes d'affaires babyloniens à l'époque perse (455–403 av. J.-C.).* Paris: Imprimerie Nationale, 1951.

Chiera, Edward. *They Wrote on Clay: The Babylonian Tablets Speak Today.* Edited by George G. Cameron. Chicago: University of Chicago Press, 1956.

Christian, Viktor. *Altertumskunde des Zweistromlandes.* 2 vols. Leipzig: K. W. Hiersemann, 1940.

Clay, Albert T., ed. *Documents from the Temple Archives of Nippur.* Babylonian Expedition of the University of Pennsylvania, ser. A. Philadelphia: Department of Archaeology, University of Pennsylvania, 1906.

Contenau, Georges. *Manuel d'archéologie orientale depuis les origines jusqu'à l'époque d'Alexandre.* 4 vols. Paris: A. Picard, 1927–1947.
———— *La vie quotidienne à Babylone et en Assyrie.* Paris: Hachette, 1950.

Deimel, Anton, S. J. *Sumerische Tempelwirtschaft zur Zeit Urukaginas und seiner Vorgänger.* Analecta Orientalia, no. II. Rome: Istituto Ponteficio Biblico, 1931.

Dentan, Robert Claude, ed. *The Idea of History in the Ancient Near East.* American Oriental Series, no. 38. New Haven: Yale University Press; London: Oxford University Press, 1955.

Diakonov, I. M. *Urartskie pis'ma i dokumenti* [Urartaean Letters and Documents]. Moscow and Leningrad: Academy of Sciences of the SSSR, 1963.

Dougherty, R. P. "Writing upon Parchment and Papyrus among the Babylonians and Assyrians." *Journal of the American Oriental Society*, XLII (1928), 109–135.

Driver, G. R. *Semitic Writing from Pictograph to Alphabet*. Rev. ed. London: Oxford University Press, 1954.

Evans, Sir Arthur. *Palace of Minos. A Comparative Account of the Successive Stages of the Early Cretan Civilisation as Illustrated by the Discoveries at Knossos*. 4 vols. in 6 and index. London: Macmillan and Co., 1922–1936.

Gadd, G. J. "Inscribed Barrel Cylinder of Marduk-apla-iddina II." *Iraq*, XV (1953), 123–134.

Garelli, Paul. *Les Assyriens en Cappadoce*. Bibliothèque Archéologique et Historique de l'Institut Français d'Archéologie d'Istanbul, vol. XIX. Paris: A. Maisonneuve, 1963.

Goetze, Albrecht. *Kleinasien*. Kulturgeschichte des alten Orients, sec. 3, pt. 1. 2d ed. Munich: C. H. Beck, 1957.

Goossens, Godefroy. "Asie Occidentale ancienne." In *Histoire Universelle*, edited by René Grousset and Emile Léonard, vol. I, 289–495. Paris: Gallimard, 1956.

———— "Classement des archives royales de Mari, I." *Revue d'Assyriologie*, XLVI (1952), 137–154.

———— "Introduction à l'archivéconomie de l'Asie Antérieure." *Revue d'Assyriologie*, XLVI (1952), 98–107.

Heuzey, Léon, ed. *Découvertes en Chaldée par Erneste de Sarzec*. 2 vols. Paris: E. Leroux, 1884–1912.

Hinz, Walther. *Das Reich Elam*. Stuttgart: W. Kohlhammer, 1964.

Hood, M. S. F. "The Tartaria Tablets." *Antiquity*, XLI (1967), 99–113.

Howard, Margaret. "Technical Description of the Ivory Writing-Boards from Nimrud." *Iraq*, XVII (1955), 14–20.

Hughes, T. M. McKenney. "On Some Waxed Tablets Said to Have Been Found at Cambridge." *Archaeologia*, LV (1897), 257–282.

Jones, Tom B. "Bookkeeping in Ancient Sumer." *Archaeology*, IX (1956), 16–21. Also in his *Paths to the Ancient Past*, pp. 136–147. New York: The Free Press; London: Collier-Macmillan Ltd., 1967.

Kampman, A. A. *Archieven en bibliotheken in het oude Nabije Oosten*. Schoten-Antwerpen: Lombaerts, 1942.

Korošec, V. "Keilschriftrecht." In *Handbuch der Orientalistik*, edited by Bertold Spuler, sec. 1, supplement III, pp. 49–219. Leiden and Cologne: E. J. Brill, 1964.

Kraeling, Carl H., and Robert M. Adams, eds. *City Invincible: A Symposium on Urbanization and Cultural Development in the Ancient Near East*. Chicago: University of Chicago Press, 1960.

Kramer, Samuel Noah. *History Begins at Sumer*. Garden City, N.Y.: Doubleday, 1959.

———— "Sumerian Historiography." *Israel Exploration Journal*, III (1953), 217–232.

———— *The Sumerians: Their History, Culture, and Character*. Chicago: University of Chicago Press, 1963.

———— "'Vox Populi' and the Sumerian Literary Documents," *Revue d'Assyriologie*, LVIII (1964), 149–156.

Kraus, F. R. "Nippur und Isin nach altbabylonischen Rechtsurkunden." *Journal of Cuneiform Studies*, III (1951), v–xiv, 1–209.

Labat, René. "Le rayonnement de la langue et de l'écriture akkadiennes au deuxième millénaire avant notre ère." *Syria*, XXXIX (1962), 1–27.

Læssøe, Jørgen. *People of Ancient Assyria: Their Inscriptions and Correspondence*. Translated from the Danish by F. S. Leigh-Browne. New York: Barnes and Noble, 1963.

Lambert, Maurice. "La naissance de la bureaucratie." *Revue Historique*, CCXXIV (1960), 1–26.

———— "Le premier triomphe de la bureaucratie." *Revue Historique*, CCXXV (1961), 21–46.

Lambert, W. G. "The Sultantepe Tablets: A Review Article." *Revue d'Assyriologie*, LIII (1959), 119–138.

Langdon, Stephen. *Ausgrabungen in Babylon seit 1918*. Leipzig: J. C. Hinrichs, 1928.

———— *Excavations at Kish*. Field Museum of Natural History, Chicago—Oxford University Joint Expedition to Mesopotamia. Vol. I. Paris: P. Geuthner, 1924.

Layard, Sir Austin Henry. *Discoveries Among the Ruins of Nineveh and Babylon*. New York: Harper's, 1856.

Lenzen, Heinrich. "Bericht über die XIV. and XV. Deutsche Warka-Campagne." *Mitteilungen der Deutschen Orient-Gesellschaft*, XC (1958), 3–21.

—— and others. *Vorläufiger Bericht über die . . . Ausgrabungen in Uruk-Warka, Winter 1953/54—Winter 1954/55.* Berlin: Gebrüder Mann, 1956.

Loud, Gordon, and Charles B. Altman. *Khorsabad.* II. *The Citadel and the Town.* The University of Chicago Oriental Institute Publications, vol. XL. Chicago: University of Chicago Press, 1938.

Mallowan, M. E. L. "The Excavations at Nimrud (Kalḫu), 1953," *Iraq,* XVI (1954), 39–114.

—— *Nimrud and Its Remains.* 3 vols. London: Collins; New York: Dodd, Mead, 1966.

—— *Twenty-five Years of Mesopotamian Discovery.* London: British School of Archaeology in Iraq, 1956.

McCown, Donald E., and Richard C. Haines, assisted by Donald P. Hanson. *Nippur.* I. *Temple of Enlil, Scribal Quarter, and Surroundings.* The University of Chicago Oriental Institute Publications, vol. LXXVIII. Chicago: University of Chicago Press, 1967.

McDonald, William A. *Progress into the Past: The Rediscovery of Mycenaean Civilization.* New York: Macmillan, 1969.

Meissner, Bruno. *Babylonien und Assyrien.* 2 vols. Heidelberg: C. Winter, 1920–1925.

Milkau, Fritz. *Geschichte der Bibliotheken im alten Orient.* Edited by Bruno Meissner. Leipzig: Harrassowitz, 1935.

Mylonas, George E. *Mycenae and the Mycenaean Age.* Princeton: Princeton University Press, 1966.

North, Robert. "Status of the Warka Excavation." *Orientalia,* XXVI (1957), 185–256.

Nougayrol, Jean. "Les archives internationales d'Ugarit (Ras Shamra—17e campagne)." In Académie des Inscriptions et Belles-Lettres, *Comptes rendus* (1954), pp. 30–41, 239–248.

Özgüç, Tahsin. "The Art and Architecture of Ancient Kanish," *Anatolia,* VIII (1964), 27–48.

Oppenheim, A. Leo. *Ancient Mesopotamia: Portrait of a Dead Civilization.* Chicago: University of Chicago Press, 1964.

—— *Letters from Mesopotamia.* Chicago and London: University of Chicago Press, 1967.

—— "A Note on the Scribes in Mesopotamia." In *Studies in Honor of Benno Landsberger . . .*, pp. 253–256. Chicago: University of Chicago Press, 1965.

———— "On an Operational Device in Mesopotamian Bureaucracy." *Journal of Near Eastern Studies*, XVIII (1959), 121–128.

———— "'Siege-documents' from Nippur." *Iraq*, XVII (1955), 69–89.

Organ, R. M. "The Conservation of Cuneiform Tablets." *British Museum Quarterly*, XXIII (1961), 52–58.

Otten, Heinrich. "Bibliotheken im alten Orient." *Das Altertum*, I (1955), 67–81.

———— "Inschriftliche Funde der Ausgrabung in Boğazköy 1953." *Mitteilungen der Deutschen Orient-Gesellschaft*, LXXXVII (1955), 13–25.

———— "Keilschrifttexte" [from Building K]. *Mitteilungen der Deutschen Orient-Gesellschaft*, XCI (1958), 73–84.

Papritz, Johannes. "Archive in Altmesopotamien: Theorie und Tatsachen." *Archivalische Zeitschrift*, LV (1959), 11–50.

Parker, Barbara. "Administrative Tablets from the North-West Palace, Nimrud." *Iraq*, XXIII (1961), 15–67.

———— "Nimrud Tablets, 1956—Economic and Legal Texts from the Nabu Temple." *Iraq*, XIX (1957), 125–138.

Parrot, André. *Archéologie Mésopotamienne*. 2 vols. Paris: A. Michel, 1946–53.

———— "Les fouilles de Mari: Quatorzième campagne." *Syria*, XLII (1965), 1–24.

———— "Les fouilles de Mari: Quinzième campagne." *Syria*, XLII (1965), 197–225.

———— "Les fouilles de Mari: Seizième campagne (Printemps 1966)" *Syria*, XLIV (1967), 1–26.

———— *Mari, une ville perdue . . . et retrouvée par l'archéologie française*. Paris: Edition "Je sers," 1936.

———— *Mission archéologique de Mari*. II. *Le palais*. Bibliothèque Archéologique et Historique de l'Institut d'Archéologie Français de Beyrouth, vols. LXVIII–LXX. 3 vols. Paris: P. Geuthner, 1958–1959.

————, ed. *Studia Mariana*. Leiden: E. J. Brill, 1950.

Pendlebury, John D. S. *The Archaeology of Crete*. London: Methuen and Co., 1939.

Piotrovskii, B. B. *Urartu: The Kingdom of Van and Its Art*. Translated from the Russian and edited by Peter S. Gelling. New York: Praeger, 1967.

Pohl, A. "Der Archivar und die Keilschriftforscher." *Orientalia*, XXIX (1960), 230–232.

———— "Bibliotheken und Archive im Alten Orient." *Orientalia*, XXV (1956), 105–109.

Rankin, J. M. "Diplomacy in Western Asia in the Early Second Millennium," *Iraq*, XVIII (1956), 68–110.

Ryckmans G. "Godefroy Goossens (15 avril 1912—22 février 1963)." *Syria*, XL (1963), 379–382.

Saggs, H. W. F. *Everyday Life in Babylonia and Assyria*. London: B. T. Bataford; New York: Putnam, 1965.

———— *The Greatness That Was Babylon: A Sketch of the Ancient Civilization of the Tigris-Euphrates Valley*. New York and Toronto: The New American Library, 1968.

San Nicolò, Marian. *Beiträge zur Rechtsgeschichte im Bereiche der keilschriftlichen Rechtsquellen*. Oslo: Instituttet for Sammenlignende Kulturforskning, 1931.

———— "Haben die Babylonier Wachstafeln als Schriftträger gekannt?" *Orientalia*, XVII (1948), 59–70.

Schachermeyer, F. *Die Minoische Kultur des alten Kreta*. Stuttgart: Kohlhammer, 1964.

Schaeffer, Claude F.-A. "Fouilles et découvertes des XVIIIe et XIXe campagnes, 1954–1955." In Schaeffer and others, *Ugaritica IV*, pp. 1–150. Mission de Ras Shamra, vol. XV. Paris: P. Geuthner, 1962.

————, ed. *Le palais royal d'Ugarit III*. Mission de Ras Shamra, vol. VI. Paris: Imprimerie Nationale, 1955.

———— "La première tablette." *Syria*, XXXIII (1956), 161–168.

Schawe, Joseph. "Der alte Vorderorient." In Milkau-Leyh, *Handbuch der Bibliothekswissenschaft*, vol. III. pt. 1, pp. 1–50. Wiesbaden: O. Harrassowitz, 1955.

Schmökel, Hartmut. *Geschichte des alten Vorderasien*. Handbuch der Orientalistik, edited by Bertold Spuler, vol. II, 3. Leiden: E. J. Brill, 1957.

———— *Ur, Assur und Babylon: Drei Jahrtausende im Zweistromland*. Stuttgart: Fretz and Wasmuth, 1955.

———— and others, *Kulturgeschichte des alten Orient: Mesopotamien, Hethiterreich, Syrien-Palästina, Urartu*. Stuttgart: A. Kröner, 1961.

Schneider, Nikolaus. "Die Lohnbücher der Mühle von Sagdana." *Archiv für Orientforschung*, III (1926), 121–122.

———— "Die Urkundenbehälter von Ur III und ihre archivalische Systematik." *Orientalia*, IX (1940), 1–16.

Semenovič, N. N. "Sposob izgotovleniia Vavilonskikh klinopisnykh tabletok" [The Making of the Babylonian Cuneiform Tablets]. *Vestnik Drevneĭ Istorii*, 1956, no. 1, pp. 134–142.

Starr, Richard F. S. *Nuzi.* 2 vols. Cambridge, Mass.: Harvard University Press, 1937–1939.

Thureau-Dangin, F. "Sur des etiquettes de paniers à tablettes provenant de Mari." In *Symbolae ad iura orientis antiqui pertinentes Paulo Koschaker dedicatae*, pp. 119–120. Leiden: E. J. Brill, 1939.

Unger, Eckhard. "Archiv." In *Reallexikon der Assyriologie*, edited by Erich Ebeling and Bruno Meissner, I, 142–143. Berlin and Leipzig: E. Weidner, 1932.

———— "Bibliothek." In *Reallexikon der Assyriologie*, edited by Erich Ebeling and Bruno Meissner, II, 24–25. Berlin and Leipzig: E. Weidner, 1938.

Weidner, Ernst. "Amts- und Privatarchive aus mittelassyrischer Zeit." In *Vorderasiatische Studien: Festschrift für Professor Viktor Christian . . . zum 70. Geburtstag*, edited by Kurt Schubert, pp. 111–118. Vienna, 1956.

Weitemeyer, Mogens. "Archive and Library Technique in Ancient Mesopotamia." *Libri*, VI (1956), 217–238.

———— *Babylonske og assyriske archiver og biblioteker.* Studier fra Sprog- og Oldtidsforsking udgivne af det Filologisk-Historisk Samfund," no. 227. Copenhagen: Branner and Korch, 1955.

Wiseman, D. J. *The Alalakh Tablets.* London: British Institute of Archaeology at Ancara, 1953.

———— "Assyrian Writing-Boards." *Iraq*, XVII (1955), 3–13.

———— "Books in the Ancient Near East and in the Old Testament." In *Cambridge History of the Bible*, I (1970), 30–48.

———— *The Expansion of Assyrian Studies.* London: School of Oriental and African Studies, University of London, 1962.

Wittfogel, Karl A. *Oriental Despotism: A Comparative Study of Total Power.* New Haven: Yale University Press, 1957.

Woolley, Sir Charles L. *Alalakh: An Account of the Excavations at Tell Atchana in the Hatay, 1937–1949.* Oxford: Oxford University Press for the Society of Antiquaries, 1955.

———— "Excavations at Atchana-Alalakh, 1938." *Antiquaries Journal*, XIX (1939), 1–37.

———— *Excavations at Ur: A Record of Twelve Years' Work*. London: E. Benn; New York: Crowell, 1954. 3d corrected impression, London, 1955.

[2] *Pharaonic Egypt*

There seems to be no treatise that deals with archives-keeping in Pharaonic Egypt. In the absence of such a specialized study, works on Egyptian government and administration have been helpful in preparing this chapter. Foremost among these are Jacques Pirenne, *Histoire des institutions et du droit privé de l'ancienne Egypte*, 3 vols. (Brussels, 1932–1935); his "L'administration civile et l'organisation judiciaire en Egypte sous la Ve dynastie," Institut de Philologie et d'Histoire Orientales, Université Libre de Bruxelles, *Annuaire*, III (1935), 363–386; and Wolfgang Helck, *Zur Verwaltung des Mittleren und Neuen Reichs* (Leiden and Cologne, 1958).

Of the general works on Egyptian history James H. Breasted, *A History of Egypt from the Earliest Times to the Persian Conquest*, 2d ed. (New York, 1912); Adolf Erman, *Ägypten und ägyptisches Leben*, rev. ed. by Hermann Ranke (Tübingen, 1923); and Hermann Kees, *Ägypten* (Munich, 1933), have furnished useful information. Georges Posener, *Dictionary of Egyptian Civilization*, translated from the French (New York, 1962), contains a number of pertinent articles.

For background reading Alexandre Moret, *The Nile and Egyptian Civilization* (New York, 1927), a translation of his *Le Nil et la civilisation égyptienne* (Paris, 1926); Walther Wolf, *Kulturgeschichte des alten Ägypten* (Stuttgart, 1962); Sir Alan Gardiner, *Egypt of the Pharaos* (Oxford, 1962); and Wolfgang Helck, *Geschichte des alten Ägypten* (Leiden and Cologne, 1968) might be consulted.

Borchardt, L. "Das Dienstgebäude des Auswärtigen Amts unter den Ramessiden." *Zeitschrift für ägyptische Sprache und Altertum*, XLIV (1907–1908), 59–61.

Breasted, James H., ed. and trans. *Ancient Records of Egypt: Historical Documents from the Earliest Times to the Persian Conquest.* 5 vols. Chicago: University of Chicago Press, 1906–1907.

———— *A History of Egypt from the Earliest Times to the Persian Conquest.* 2d ed. New York: Scribner's, 1912.

Buck, A. de. "The Judicial Papyrus of Turin." *Journal of Egyptian Archaeology*, XXIII (1937), 152–164.

Budge, Sir E. A. Wallis. *Osiris and the Egyptian Resurrection.* 2 vols. London: Warner; New York: Putnam, 1911.

Černý, V. Jaroslav. *Paper and Books in Ancient Egypt.* London: H. K. Lewis, 1952.

——— "The Will of Naunakte and the Related Documents," *Journal of Egyptian Archaeology,* XXXI (1945), 29–53.

Davies, Norman de Garis. *The Tomb of Rekh-mi-rēᶜ at Thebes.* 2 vols. New York: The Plantin Press, 1943.

Erman, Adolf. *Ägypten und ägyptisches Leben im Altertum.* Revised edition by Hermann Ranke. Tübingen: J. B. C. Mohr, 1923.

Farina, Giulio. "Le funzioni del visir faraonico sotto la XVIII dinastia secondo l'iscrizione nella tomba di Rechmirîe a Tebe." R. Accademia dei Lincei, Classe di Scienze Morali, Storiche e Filologiche, *Rendiconti,* 5th ser., vol. XXV (1916), 923–974.

Faulkner, R. O. "The Admonitions of an Egyptian Sage." *Journal of Egyptian Archaeology,* LI (1965), 53–62.

——— "The Installation of the Vizier." *Journal of Egyptian Archaeology,* XLI (1955), 18–29.

——— "Notes on 'The Admonitions of an Egyptian Sage.'" *Journal of Egyptian Archaeology,* L (1964), 24–36.

Gardiner, Sir Alan H. *Egypt of the Pharaohs.* Oxford: Clarendon Press, 1961.

——— *The Inscription of Mes: A Contribution to the Study of Egyptian Judicial Procedure.* Untersuchungen zur Geschichte und Altertumskunde Ägyptens, vol. IV, no. 3. Leipzig: J. C. Hinrichs, 1905.

Glanville, S. R. K., ed. *The Legacy of Egypt.* Oxford: Clarendon Press, 1942.

Goedicke, Hans. "Was Magic Used in the Harem Conspiracy against Ramesses III?" *Journal of Egyptian Archaeology,* XLIX (1963), 71–92.

Grenfell, Bernard P., and others. *The Tebtunis Papyri.* Vol. I. London and New York: Oxford University Press, 1902.

Helck, Wolfgang. *Geschichte des alten Ägypten.* In *Handbuch der Orientalistik,* edited by Bertold Spuler, sec. 1, vol. I, no. 3. Leiden and Cologne: E. J. Brill, 1968.

——— *Zur Verwaltung des Mittleren und Neuen Reichs.* Probleme der Ägyptologie, no. III. Leiden and Cologne: E. J. Brill, 1958.

Hepper, F. N., and T. Reynolds. "Papyrus and the Adhesive

Properties of Its Cell Sap in Relation to Paper-Making." *Journal of Egyptian Archaeology*, LIII (1967), 156–157.

Kees, Hermann. *Ägypten*. In Kulturgeschichte des Alten Orients, edited by A. Alt and others, sec. 1, pt. 1, vol. III, 1. Munich: C. H. Beck, 1933.

———— *Das Priestertum im ägyptischen Staat vom Neuen Reich bis zur Spätzeit*. Leiden: E. J. Brill, 1958.

———— *Totenglauben und Jenseitsvorstellungen der alten Ägypter*. 2d rev. ed. Berlin: Akademie-Verlag, 1956.

Knudtzon, Jørgen Alexander, ed. *Die El-Amarna-Tafeln*. 2 vols. Leipzig: J. C. Hinrichs, 1908–1915.

Moret, Alexandre. *Le Nil et la civilisation égyptienne*. Paris: La Renaissance du Livre, 1926.

Otto, Eberhard. "Ägyptisches Buch-und Bibliothekswesen." In Helmut Brunner and others, *Ägyptologie*, sec. 2, *Literatur*, pp. 220–226. *Handbuch der Orientalistik*, edited by Bertold Spuler, vol. I. Leiden and Cologne: E. J. Brill, 1952.

Pendlebury, John D. S., and others. *The City of Akhenaten*. Part III. *The Central City and the Official Quarters*. Vol. I. London and Boston: Egypt Exploration Society, 1951.

Pirenne, Jacques. "L'administration civile et l'organisation judiciaire en Egypte sous la Ve dynastie." Institut de Philologie et d'Histoire Orientales, Université Libre de Bruxelles, *Annuaire*, III (1935), 363–386.

———— *Histoire de l'Egypte ancienne*. 3 vols. Neuchâtel: A la Baconnière, 1961–1963.

———— *Histoire des institutions et du droit privé de l'ancienne Egypte*. 3 vols. Brussels: Fondation Egyptologique Reine Elisabeth, 1932–1935.

———— "Introduction bibliographique à l'histoire du droit égyptien jusqú'à l'époque d'Alexandre le Grand." *Archives d'Histoire du Droit Oriental*, III (1947–1948), 33–123.

Posener, Georges. With the assistance of Serge Sauneron and Jean Yoyotte. *Dictionary of Egyptian Civilization*. Translated from the French. New York: Tudor Publishing Co., 1962.

Preisendanz, Karl. *Papyrusfunde und Papyrusforschung*. Leipzig: A. Hiersemann, 1933.

Schott, Siegfried. "Schreiber und Schreibgerät im Jenseits," *Journal of Egyptian Archaeology*, LIV (1968), 45–50.

Seidl, Erwin. "Altägyptisches Recht." In *Orientalisches Recht*, pp. 1–48. *Handbuch der Orientalistik*, edited by Bertold Spuler, sec. 1, supplement III. Leiden and Cologne: E. J. Brill, 1964.

———— *Einführung in die ägyptische Rechtsgeschichte.* Ägyptologische Forschungen, no. 10. 2d ed. Glückstadt and New York: J. J. Augustin, 1951.

Sethe, Kurt, ed. *Urkunden des alten Reichs.* Vol. I. 2d ed. Leipzig: J. C. Hinrichs, 1932–1933.

Steindorff, George, ed. *Urkunden des ägyptischen Altertums.* Vol. IV. Leipzig: J. C. Hinrichs, 1909.

———— and Keith C. Seele. *When Egypt Ruled the East.* Chicago: University of Chicago Press, 1942.

Weil, Arthur. *Die Veziere des Pharaonenreiches.* Strassbourg: Schlesier & Schweikhardt, 1908.

Wente, Edward F. "A Letter of Complaint to the Vizier To." *Journal of Near Eastern Studies*, XX (1961), 252–257.

Winlock, Herbert E. *Models of Daily Life in Ancient Egypt from the Tomb of Meket-Rē͑ at Thebes.* Cambridge, Mass.: Harvard University Press, 1955.

Wittfogel, Karl A. *Oriental Despotism: A Comparative Study of Total Power.* New Haven: Yale University Press, 1957.

Wolf, Walther. *Kulturgeschichte des alten Ägypten.* Stuttgart: A. Kröner, 1962.

[3]   Greece

The best discussion of Greek archives administration, in general, is found in the following works: Adolf Wilhelm, *Beiträge zur griechischen Inschriftenkunde* (Vienna, 1909); Egon Weiss, *Griechisches Privatrecht auf rechtsvergleichender Grundlage* (Leipzig, 1923); and Harold Steinacker, *Die antiken Grundlagen der frühmittelalterlichen Privaturkunde* (Leipzig and Berlin, 1927). Some controversial points that had emerged in connection with these works have been cleared up in Günther Klaffenbach's "Bemerkungen zum griechischen Urkundenwesen," Deutsche Akademie der Wissenschaften zu Berlin, Klasse für Sprachen, Literatur und Kunst, *Sitzungsberichte*, no. 6 (1960). Earlier works on the Metroon, the archives of the Athenian *boulê*, are superseded by the American excavations on the Agora. The results of these excavations, insofar as they throw light on the Metroon, are discussed in Homer A. Thompson, "Buildings on the West Side of the Agora," *Hesperia*, VI (1937), 1–226, and in *The Athenian Agora: A Guide to the Excavation and Museum*, 2d ed. (Princeton, 1962). All literary and epigraphical evidence pertaining to the Metroon has been conveniently assembled in Richard E. Wycherley, *The Athenian Agora. III. Literary and Epigraphical Testimonia* (Princeton, 1957). A paper by Professor Alan L. Boegehold on "The Establishment of a Central Archives at Athens" has been accepted for publication by the *American Journal of Archaeology*.

The Athenian Agora: A Guide to the Excavation and Museum. 2d rev. ed. Princeton: American School of Classical Studies at Athens, 1962.

Barker, Sir Ernest, ed. and trans. *The Politics of Aristotle.* Oxford: Clarendon Press, 1952.

Beauchet, Ludovic. *Histoire du droit privé de la République Athénienne*, 4 vols. Paris: Chevalier-Marescq & Cie, 1897.

Bogaert, Raymond. *Banques et banquiers dans les cités grecques.* Leiden: A. W. Sijthoff, 1968.

Busolt, Georg. *Griechische Staatskunde.* 3d rev. ed. of *Griechische Staats- und Rechtsaltertümer.* 2 vols. Vol. II revised by H. Swoboda. Munich: C. H. Beck, 1920–1926.

Calhoun, George M. *The Business Life of Ancient Athens.* Chicago: University of Chicago Press, 1926.

Callmer, Christian. "Antike Bibliotheken." In Institutum Romanum Regni Sueciae, *Opuscula Archaelogica*, III (1944), 145–193.

Curtius, Carl. *Das Metroon in Athen als Staatsarchiv.* Berlin: Weidmann, 1868.

——— *De actorum publicorum cura apud Graecos.* Göttingen: Officina Academica Dieterichiana, 1865.

Dareste, R. "Le χρεωφυλάκιον dans les villes grecques," *Bulletin de Correspondence Hellénique*, VI (1882), 241–245.

Daux, Georges. "Chronique des fouilles 1961." *Bulletin de Correspondence Hellénique*, LXXXVI (1962), 794.

Dow, Sterling. *Prytaneis: A Study of the Inscriptions Honoring the Athenian Councillors. Hesperia*, supplement I. Athens: American School of Classical Studies at Athens, 1937.

Ehrenberg, Victor. *Der Staat der Griechen.* 2 vols. Leipzig: B. G. Teubner, 1957–1958.

Fine, John V. A. *Horoi: Studies in Mortgage, Real Security, and Land Tenure in Ancient Athens. Hesperia*, Supplement IX. Baltimore: American School of Classical Studies at Athens, 1951.

Gardthausen, Viktor Emil. *Griechische Paleographie*. 2d ed. 2 vols. Leipzig: Veit, 1911–1913.

Glotz, Gustave. *La cité grecque*. New edition by Paul Cloché. Paris: La Renaissance du Livre, 1953.

Harrison, A. R. W. "Law-Making at Athens at the End of the Fifth Century B.C." *Journal of Hellenic Studies*, LXXV (1955), 26–35.

Harrison, Jane E., and Margaret de G. Verrall, eds. *Mythology and Monuments of Ancient Athens*. London and New York: Macmillan, 1890.

Homolle, Théophile. *Les archives de l'intendance sacrée à Délos*. Bibliothèque des Ecoles Françaises d'Athènes et de Rome," no. 49. Paris: E. Thorin, 1887.

Hunger, Herbert. "Papyrusfund in Griechenland." *Chronique d'Egypte*, XXXVIII (1962), 415–416.

Jacoby, Felix. *Atthis: The Local Chronicles of Ancient Athens*. Oxford: Clarendon Press, 1949.

Judeich, Walther. *Topographie von Athen*. In *Handbuch der Altertums-wissenschaft*, edited by Walter Otto, sec. 3, pt. 2, vol. II. 2d ed. Munich: C. H. Beck, 1931.

Kahrstedt, Ulrich. "Das Athenische Staatsarchiv." *Klio*, XXXI (1938), 25–32.

Kapsomenos, S. G. "Ὁ ὀρφικὸς πάπυρος τῆς Θεσσαλονίκης" [The Orphic Papyrus of Thessalonica]. *Archaiologikon Deltion*, XIX (1964), 17–25.

Keil, Bruno, ed. *Anonymus Argentinensis: Fragmente zur Geschichte des Perikleischen Athen aus einem Strassburger Papyrus*. Strassbourg: K. J. Trübner, 1902.

Kenyon, Sir Frederic G. *Books and Readers in Ancient Greece and Rome*. 2d ed. Oxford: Clarendon Press, 1951.

Klaffenbach, Günther. "Bemerkungen zum griechischen Urkunden-wesen." In Deutsche Akademie der Wissenschaften zu Berlin, Klasse für Sprachen, Literatur und Kunst, *Sitzungsberichte*, no. 6 (1960), 5–42.

———— *Griechische Epigraphik*. 2d rev. ed. Göttingen: Vandenhoeck & Ruprecht, 1966.

Kornemann, Ernst. "Tabulae publicae." In Pauly-Wissowa, *Real-Encyclopädie*, ser. 2, vol. IV (1932), 1957–1962.

Kroll, Wilhelm. "Metroon." In Pauly-Wissowa, *Real-Encyclopädie*, vol. XV (1932), 1488–1490.

Parke, Herbert W., and D. E. W. Wormell. *The Delphic Oracle*. 2 vols. Oxford: Blackwell, 1956.

Pernice, Erich. "Die literarischen Zeugnisse." In *Handbuch der Archäologie*, edited by Walter Otto, vol. I, 239–328. Munich: C. H. Beck, 1939.

Rehm, Albert. "Die Inschriften." In *Handbuch der Archäologie*, edited by Walter Otto, vol. I, 182–238. Munich: C. H. Beck, 1939.

Robert, Louis. "Epigraphie." In *L'histoire et ses méthodes*, edited by Charles Samaran, pp. 453–497. Paris: Gallimard, 1961.

Roberts, C. H. "Books in the Graeco-Roman World and in the New Testament." In *Cambridge History of the Bible*, I (1970), 48–66.

Sachers, Erich. "Tabula." In Pauly-Wissowa, *Real-Encyclopädie*, ser. 2, vol. IV (1932), 1881–1886.

Schubart, Wilhelm. *Das Buch bei den Griechen und Römern*. 2d ed. Berlin: G. Reimer, 1907.

Schulthess, R. "Γραμματεῖς." In Pauly-Wissowa, *Real-Encyclopädie*, VII (1912), 1708–1780.

Shear, T. Leslie, Jr. "The Athenian Agora: Excavations of 1968," *Hesperia*, XXXVIII (1969), 382–417.

Sisson, M. A. "The Stoa of Hadrian at Athens." In *Papers of the British School at Rome*, XI (1921), 50–72.

Stecchini, Livio Catullo, ed. and trans. Ἀθηναίων Πολιτεία: *The Constitution of the Athenians*. Glencoe, Ill.: Free Press, 1950.

Thompson, Homer A. "Buildings on the West Side of the Agora." *Hesperia*, VI (1937), 1–226.

Turner, Eric G. *Greek Papyri: An Introduction*. Princeton, N.J.: Princeton University Press, 1968.

Wachsmuth, Kurt. *Die Stadt Athen im Altertum*. 2 vols. Leipzig: B. G. Teubner, 1874–1890.

Weiss, Egon. *Griechisches Privatrecht auf rechtsvergleichender Grundlage*, I. Leipzig: Meiner, 1923.

Westermann, William L. "Warehousing and Trapezite Banking in Antiquity." *Journal of Economic and Business History*, III (1931), 30–54.

Wilamowitz-Moellendorff, Ulrich von. "Der Markt von Kekrops bis Kleisthenes." In his *Aus Kydathen*, pp. 195–212. Philologische Untersuchungen, edited by A. Kiessling and U. von Wilamowitz-Moellendorff, vol. I. Berlin: Weidmann, 1880.

Wilhelm, Adolf. *Beiträge zur griechischen Inschriftenkunde.* Sonderschriften des Österreichischen Archäologischen Instituts, vol. VII. Vienna: A. Hölder, 1909.

Wycherley, Richard E. *The Athenian Agora.* III. *Literary and Epigraphical Testimonia.* Princeton, N.J.: American School of Classical Studies at Athens, 1957.

Ziebarth, Erich. *Kulturbilder aus griechischen Städten.* Leipzig: B. G. Teubner, 1907.

[4]   *Persia, Alexander the Great, and the Seleucid Empire*

So far archives-keeping in the Persian Empire has not been the subject of a specialized study. For the Achaemenid period the excavations at Persepolis so admirably discussed in Erich F. Schmidt's *Persepolis*, 2 vols. (Chicago, 1953–1957) have furnished much valuable information. The concern of Alexander the Great with utilizing the records he found in Persia and with keeping his own records is discussed in Helmut Berve's *Das Alexanderreich auf prosopographischer Grundlage*, 2 vols. (Munich, 1926). M. I. Rostovtzeff's *Seleucid Babylonia* (New Haven, 1930) throws some light on record-keeping under the Seleucids.

Altheim, Franz. *Alexander und Asien: Geschichte eines geistigen Erbes.* Tübingen: N. Niemeyer, 1953.

——— and Ruth Stiehl. *Die aramäische Sprache unter den Achaimeniden.* 3 vols. Frankfurt am Main: V. Klostermann, [1959]–1963.

Arberry, Arthur J., ed. *The Legacy of Persia.* Oxford: Clarendon Press, 1953.

Berve, Helmut. *Das Alexanderreich auf prosopographischer Grundlage.* 2 vols. Munich: C. H. Beck, 1926.

Bikerman, E. *Institutions des Séleucides.* Paris: P. Geuthner, 1938.

Cameron, George G. "Darius' Daughter and the Persepolis Inscriptions." *Journal of Near Eastern Studies*, I (1942), 214–218.

——— "New Tablets from the Persepolis Treasury." *Journal of Near Eastern Studies*, XXIV (1965), 167–192.

——— *Persepolis Treasury Tablets.* University of Chicago Oriental

Institute Publications, vol. LXV. Chicago: University of Chicago Press, 1948.

——— "Persepolis Treasury Tablets, Old and New." *Journal of Near Eastern Studies*, XVII (1958), 161–176.

Christensen, Arthur. "Die Iranier." In *Kulturgeschichte des alten Orients*, edited by A. Alt and others, sec. 3, pt. 1, pp. 201–300. Munich: C. H. Beck, 1933.

Dölger, Franz. *Beiträge zur byzantinischen Finanzverwaltung, besonders des 10. und 11. Jahrhunderts*. Leipzig: B. G. Teubner, 1927.

Driver, Godfrey R., ed. *Aramaic Documents of the Fifth Century B.C.* Oxford: Clarendon Press, 1954.

Frye, Richard N., ed. *The Heritage of Persia*. Cleveland and New York: The World Publishing Co., 1963.

Ghirshman, Roman. *Iran from the Earliest Times to the Islamic Conquest*. Harmondsworth, Middlesex: Penguin Books, 1954.

Goossens, Godefroy. "Artistes et artisans étrangers en Perse sous les Achéménides." *Nouvelle Clio*, I (1949), 32–44.

Hallock, Richard T. "Notes on Achaemenid Elamite." *Journal of Near Eastern Studies*, XVII (1958), 256–262.

——— *Persepolis Fortification Tablets*. University of Chicago Oriental Institute Publications, vol. XCII. Chicago: University of Chicago Press, 1969.

Henning, W. B. "Mitteliranisch." In *Iranistik*. I. *Linguistik*, edited by Karl Hoffmann and others, pp. 20–130. *Handbuch der Orientalistik*, sec. 1, vol. IV. Leiden and Cologne: E. J. Brill, 1958.

Hinz, Walther. "Zu den Persepolis-Täfelchen." *Zeitschrift der Deutschen Morgenländischen Gesellschaft*, CX (1960), 236–251.

——— "Zur achämenidischen Hofverwaltung nach den Funden im Schatzhaus in Persepolis." *Zeitschrift der Deutschen Morgenländischen Gesellschaft*, CVIII (1958), 126–132.

Huart, Clément, and Louis Delaporte. *L'Iran antique: Elam et Perse et la civilisation iranienne*. Paris: A. Michel, 1952.

Iliffe, J. H. "Persia and the Ancient World." In *The Legacy of Persia*, edited by Arthur J. Arberry, pp. 1–38. Oxford: Clarendon Press, 1953.

Kaerst, Julius. "Ephemerides." In Pauly-Wissowa, *Real-Encyclopädie*, V (1905), 2749–2753.

McDowell, Robert H. *Stamped and Inscribed Objects from Seleucia on the Tigris*. Ann Arbor: University of Michigan Press, 1935.

Meyer, Eduard. *Geschichte des Altertums*. 3d ed. Vol. IV. Stuttgart: J. C. Cotta, 1939.

—— *Der Papyrusfund von Elephantine: Dokumente einer jüdischen Gemeinde aus der Perserzeit.* . . . Leipzig: J. C. Hinrichs, 1912.

Olmstead, Albert T. E. *History of the Persian Empire, Achaemenid Period*. Chicago: University of Chicago Press, 1948

Porten, Bezalel. *Archives from Elephantine: The Life of an Ancient Jewish Community*. Berkeley: University of California Press, 1968.

Rostovtzeff, M. I. *Seleucid Babylonia: Bullae and Seals of Clay with Greek Inscriptions*. New Haven: Yale University Press, 1930, 1932.

—— *The Social and Economic History of the Hellenistic World*. 3 vols. Oxford: Clarendon Press, 1953.

Schmidt, Erich F. *Persepolis*. 2 vols. University of Chicago Oriental Institute Publications, vols. LXVIII and LXIX. Chicago: University of Chicago Press, 1953 and 1957.

Welles, C. Bradford. *Royal Correspondence in the Hellenistic Period: A Study in Greek Epigraphy*. New Haven: Yale University Press; London: Humphrey Milford, Oxford University Press; Prague: Kondakov Institute, 1934.

Westermann, William L. "Land Registers of Western Asia under the Seleucids." *Classical Philology*, XVI (1921), 12–19.

Wilcken, Ulrich. "Ὑπομνηματισμοί." *Philologus*, LIII (1894), 80–126.

[5]   *Ptolemaic and Roman Egypt*

The literature on the papyri of Greco-Roman Egypt is enormous. It includes scholarly editions of texts, a wealth of writings on the paleographic and diplomatic problems the papyri present, and detailed studies of their legal, economic, and social aspects. The fundamental treatise on the Greco-Roman papyri is still Ludwig Mitteis and Ulrich Wilcken, *Grundzüge und Chrestomatie der Papyruskunde*, Parts I and II in 4 vols. (Leipzig and Berlin, 1912). The historical part (I), by Wilcken, is divided into two volumes entitled *Grundzüge* and *Chrestomatie*. The juridical part (II), by Mitteis, is organized and entitled the same way. Recent works on the papyri of Greco-Roman Egypt include Martin David and B. A. van

Groningen, *Papyrological Primer*, 4th ed. (Leiden, 1965); and Eric G. Turner, *Greek Papyri: An Introduction* (Princeton, 1968).

For the student of the history of archives administration Sir Harold Idris Bell, "The Custody of Records in Roman Egypt," *Indian Archives*, IV (1950), 116–123, is an invaluable guide. He might also consult Erwin Seidl, *Ptolemäische Rechtsgeschichte*, 2d rev. ed. (Glückstadt, Hamburg, and New York, 1962). Those able to read Dutch will profit from D. Cohen, *Schets van het notariaat in het oude Egypte*, Ars Notariatus, vol. V (Amsterdam, 1955). For background reading Bell's *Egypt from Alexander the Great to the Arab Conquest: A Study in the Diffusion and Decay of Hellenism* (Oxford, 1948), is recommended.

Adler, E. N. "The Adler Papyri: The Archive of a Family at Pathyris, Being a Collection of Greek and Demotic Papyri between 134 and 88 B.C." In Vth International Papyrological Congress at Oxford, *Actes*, pp. 12–19. Brussels: Fondation Egyptologique Reine Elisabeth, 1938.

—— and others, eds. *The Adler Papyri*. London: H. Milford, Oxford University Press, 1939.

Alzinger, Wilhelm. *Die Stadt des siebenten Weltwunders: Die Wiederentdeckung von Ephesus*. Vienna: Wollzeilen-Verlag, 1962.

Bell, Sir Harold Idris. "The Custody of Records in Roman Egypt," *Indian Archives*, IV (1950), 116–123.

—— *Egypt from Alexander the Great to the Arab Conquest: A Study in the Diffusion and Decay of Hellenism*. Oxford: Clarendon Press, 1948.

——, ed. *Jews and Christians in Egypt: The Jewish Troubles in Alexandria and the Athanasian Controversy*. London: Trustees of the British Museum, 1924.

Bengtson, Hermann. *Die Strategie in der hellenistischen Zeit: Ein Beitrag zum antiken Staatsrecht*. 3 vols. Munich: C. H. Beck, 1937–1952.

Boak, Arthur E. R., ed. *Papyri from Tebtunis*. Michigan Papyri, vols. II and V. Ann Arbor: University of Michigan Press, 1933–1944.

—— and Herbert Chayyim Youtie, eds. *The Archive of Aurelius Isidorus in the Egyptian Museum, Cairo, and the University of Michigan*. Ann Arbor: University of Michigan Press, 1960.

Cohen, D. *Schets van het notariaat in het Oude Egypte in het hellenistisch tijdvak en de eerste drie eeuwen van de Romeinse Keizertijd.* Stichting tot Bevordering der Notariële Wetenshap, Ars Notariatus, no. V. Amsterdam: Willink & Zoon, 1955.

Collomp, Paul. *Recherches sur la chancellerie et la diplomatique des Lagides.* Paris: Societé d'édition Les Belles Lettres, 1926.

David, M., and B. A. van Groningen. *Papyrological Primer.* 4th ed. Leiden: E. J. Brill, 1965.

Edgar, Campbell C. "Records of a Village Club." In *Raccolta di scritti in onore di Giacomo Lumbroso, 1844–1925,* pp. 369–376. Milan: Aegyptus, 1925.

———— *Zenon Papyri in the University of Michigan Collection.* Ann Arbor: University of Michigan Press, 1931.

Eger, Otto. *Zum ägyptischen Grundbuchwesen in römischer Zeit.* Leipzig and Berlin: B. G. Teubner, 1909.

Flore, Giuseppe. "Sulla βιβλιοθήκη τῶν ἐγκτήσεων." *Aegyptus,* VIII (1927), 43–88.

Fuks, Alexander. "Notes on the Archive of Nikanor." *Journal of Juristic Papyrology,* V (1951), 207–216.

Gilliam, E. H. "The Archives of the Temple of Soknobraisis at Bacchias." *Yale Classical Studies,* X (1947), 181–281.

Grenfell, Bernard P., and Arthur S. Hunt, eds. *The Oxyrhynchus Papyri,* pt. 1. London: Egypt Exploration Fund, 1898.

Groningen, B. A. van. "Un conflit du IIe siècle de notre ère." *Chronique d'Egypte,* XXII (1947), 313–332.

————, ed. *A Family-Archive from Tebtunis.* Papyrologica Lugduno-Batava, vol. VI. Leiden: E. J. Brill, 1950.

Heichelheim, Fritz. "Bericht über ein Papyrusverzeichnis nach Gauen, Archiven und Jahrhunderten geordnet." *Chronique d'Egypte,* VII (1932), 137–150.

Hombert, Marcel, and Claire Préaux. *Recherches sur le recensement dans l'Egypte romaine.* Papyrologica Lugduno-Batava, vol. V. Leiden: E. J. Brill, 1952.

Hunt, A. S., and C. C. Edgar, eds. *Select Papyri.* 2 vols. London: W. Heinemann Ltd.; New York: Putnam, 1932–1934, and Cambridge, Mass.: Harvard University Press; London: W. Heinemann, Ltd.

Jörs, Paul. "Δημοσίωσις und ἐκμαρτύρησις." *Zeitschrift der Savigny-Stiftung für Rechtsgeschichte, Romanistische Abteilung,* XXXIV (1913), 107–158.

Jouguet, Pierre. *Macedonian Imperialism and the Hellenization of the East*. London: Paul, Trench, Trubner; New York: Knopf, 1928.

Koschaker, Paul. "Der Archidikastes: Beiträge zur Geschichte des Urkunden- und Archivwesens im römischen Ägypten." *Zeitschrift der Savigny-Stiftung für Rechtsgeschichte, Romanistische Abteilung*, XXVIII (1907), 254–305, and XXIX (1908), 1–47.

Leclercq, H. "Paphnuce." In *Dictionnaire d'archéologie chrétienne et de liturgie*, XIII (Paris, 1936), 1358–1361.

Lewald, Hans. *Beiträge zur Kenntnis des römisch-ägyptischen Grundbuchrechts*. Leipzig: Veit, 1909.

Lewis, N. "'Greco-Roman' Egypt: Fact or Fiction?" *Bulletin of the American Society of Papyrologists*, V (1968), 49.

———— *L'industrie du papyrus dans l'Egypte gréco-romaine*. Paris: Rodstein, 1934.

———— *Inventory of Compulsory Services in Ptolemaic and Roman Egypt*. American Studies in Papyrology, vol. III. New Haven and Toronto: American Society of Papyrologists, 1968.

Martin, Victor. "Les papyrus et l'histoire administrative de l'Egypte Gréco-Romaine." In *Papyri und Altertumswissenschaft*, pp. 102–165. Munich: C. H. Beck, 1934.

Meyer, Paul M. *Juristische Papyri*. Berlin: Weidmann, 1920.

———— "Zum Rechts- und Urkundenwesen im ptolemäisch-römischen Ägypten." *Klio*, VI (1906), 95–114.

Miltner, Franz. *Ephesos, Stadt der Artemis und des Johannes*. Vienna: Franz Deuticke, 1958.

Mitteis, Ludwig, and Ulrich Wilcken. *Grundzüge und Chrestomatie der Papyruskunde*. Parts I and II in 4 vols. Leipzig: B. G. Teubner, 1912.

Müller, Wolfgang, ed. "Griechishe Ostraka." *Archiv für Papyrusforschung*, XVI (1958), 190–213.

Oertel, Friedrich. *Die Liturgie: Studien zur ptolemäischen und kaiserlichen Verwaltung Ägyptens*. Leipzig: B. G. Teubner, 1917.

Peremans, Willy, and others. *Le clergé, le notariat et les tribunaux*. Prosopographia Ptolemaica, no. III. Louvain: E. Nauwelaerts; Leiden: E. J. Brill, 1953.

Pestman, P. W. "Les archives privées de Pathyris à l'époque ptolémaique: La famille de Pétéharsemtheus, fils de Panebkhdunis." In *Studia Papyrologica Varia*, pp. 47–105. Leiden: E. J. Brill, 1965.

———— "A Family of Egyptian Scribes." *Bulletin of the American Society of Papyrologists*, V (1968), 61.

Poland, Franz. *Geschichte des griechischen Vereinswesens*. Leipzig: B. G. Teubner, 1909.

Préaux, Claire. *L'économie royale des Lagides*. Brussels: Fondation Reine Elisabeth, 1939.

———— *Les grecs en Egypte d'après les archives de Zénon*. Brussels: Office de Publication, 1947.

Preisendanz, Karl. *Papyrusfunde und Papyrusforschung*. Leipzig: A. Hiersemann, 1933.

———— "Papyruskunde." In Milkau-Leyh, *Handbuch der Bibliothekswissenschaft*, I, 163–248. Wiesbaden: O. Harrassowitz, 1952.

Preisigke, Friedrich, ed. *Fachwörter des öffentlichen Verwaltungsdienstes in den griechischen Papyrusurkunden der ptolemäisch-römischen Zeit*. Göttingen: Vandenhoeck & Ruprecht, 1915.

———— *Girowesen im griechischen Ägypten, enthaltend Korngiro, Geldgiro, Girobanknotariat mit Einschluss des Archivwesens*. Strassbourg: Schlesier & Schweikhardt, 1910.

———— "Das Wesen der βιβλιοθήκη ἐγκτήσεων." *Klio*, XII (1912), 402–460.

———— *Wörterbuch der griechischen Papyrusurkunden*. Vol. I. Berlin: Selbstverlag der Erben, 1925.

Reinmuth, Oscar William. *The Prefect of Egypt from Augustus to Diocletian*. *Klio*, supplement XXXIV, new ser., fasc. 21. Leipzig: Dieterich, 1935.

Roberts, Colin H. "The Codex." *Proceedings of the British Academy*, XL [1955], 170–204.

———— "The Greek Papyri." In *The Legacy of Egypt*, edited by S. R. K. Glanville. Oxford: Clarendon Press, 1942.

Ross, A. G. "Apollonius, strateg van Heptakomia." *Tijdschrift voor Geschiedenis*, XXXVII (1922), 1–40, 129–146.

Rostovtzeff, M. I. *A Large Estate in Egypt in the Third Century B.C.: A Study in Economic History*. Madison: University of Wisconsin Studies, 1922.

———— "Roman Exploitation of Egypt in the First Century A.D." *Journal of Economic and Business History*, I (1929), 337–364.

———— *The Social and Economic History of the Hellenistic World*. 3 vols. London: Oxford University Press, 1941.

Schubart, Wilhelm. *Ägypten von Alexander dem Grossen bis auf Mohammed*. Berlin: Weidmann, 1922.

———— "Die Bibliophylakes und ihr Grammateus." *Archiv für Papyrusforschung*, VIII (1927), 14–24.

Schur, Werner. "Zur Vorgeschichte des Ptolemäerreiches." *Klio*, XX (1925–1926), 270–302.

Schwartz, Jacques. *Les archives de Serapion et de ses fils: Une exploitation agricole aux environs d'Hermoupolis Magna (de 90 à 133 P.C.)*. Cairo: Institut Français d'Archéologie Orientale, 1961.

Schwind, Fritz Freiherr von. *Zur Frage der Publikation im Römischen Recht: Mit Ausblicken in das altgriechische und ptolemäische Rechtsgebiet*. Münchener Beiträge zur Papyrusforschung und antiken Rechtsgeschichte, no. 31. Munich: C. H. Beck, 1940.

Segrè, Angelo. "Note sul documento greco-egizio del grapheion." *Aegyptus*, VII (1926), 97–107.

Seidl, Erwin. *Ptolemäische Rechtsgeschichte*. Ägyptologische Forschungen, no. 22. 2d rev. ed. Glückstadt, Hamburg, and New York: Augustin, 1962.

Stein, Arthur. *Untersuchungen zur Geschichte und Verwaltung Ägyptens unter römischer Herrschaft*. Stuttgart: J. B. Metzler, 1915.

Tait, John G., ed. *Greek Ostraka in the Bodleian Library at Oxford and Various Other Collections*. 2 vols. Vol. II was coedited by Claire Préaux. London: Egypt Exploration Society, 1930–1955.

Tarn, William W. *Hellenistic Civilization*. 3d ed., revised by the author and G. T. Griffith. London: E. Arnold and Co., 1952.

Taubenschlag, Raphael. *The Law of Greco-Roman Egypt in the Light of the Papyri, 332 B.C.–640 A.D.* 2d rev. ed. Warsaw: State Science Publications, 1955.

Turner, Eric G. *Greek Papyri: An Introduction*. Princeton, N.J.: Princeton University Press, 1968.

Wallace, Sherman LeRoy. *Taxation in Egypt from Augustus to Diocletian*. Princeton: Princeton University Press; London: H. Milford, Oxford University Press, 1938.

Welles, C. Bradford. "The Ptolemaic Administration in Egypt." *Journal of Juristic Papyrology*, III (1949), 21–47.

———— *Royal Correspondence in the Hellenistic Period: A Study in Greek Epigraphy*. New Haven: Yale University Press; London: Humphrey Milford, Oxford University Press; Prague: Kondakov Institute, 1934.

Westermann, William L. "The Greek Exploitation of Egypt." *Political Science Quarterly*, XL (1925), 517–539.

—— "The Ptolemies and the Welfare of Their Subjects." *American Historical Review*, XLIII (1938), 270–287.

—— "Warehousing and Trapezite Banking in Antiquity." *Journal of Economic and Business History*, III (1931), 30–54.

Wilcken, Ulrich. *Griechische Ostraka aus Ägypten und Nubien.* 2 vols. Leipzig and Berlin: Giesecke & Devrient, 1899.

—— "Ὑπομνηματισμοί." *Philologus*, LIII (1894), 80–126.

—— "Papyrus-Urkunden." *Archiv für Papyrusforschung*, VII (1924), 67–114.

——, ed. *Urkunden der Ptolemäerzeit (Ältere Funde).* Berlin and Leipzig: de Gruyter, 1927–1935.

Winter, John Garrett. *Life and Letters in the Papyri.* Ann Arbor: University of Michigan Press, 1933.

Woess, Friedrich von. *Untersuchungen über das Urkundenwesen und den Publizitätsschutz im römischen Ägypten.* Münchener Beiträge zur Papyrusforschung und antiken Rechtsgeschichte, no. 6. Munich: C. H. Beck, 1924.

Wolff, Hans Julius. *Das Justizwesen der Ptolemäer.* Münchener Beiträge zur Papyrusforschung und antiken Rechtsgeschichte, no. 44. Munich: C. H. Beck, 1962.

[6 and 7]   Republican and Imperial Rome

The archival institutions and practices of Republican Rome have been quite thoroughly investigated. They have been placed in their constitutional and legal framework in Theodor Mommsen's *Römisches Staatsrecht*, 3d ed. (Leipzig, 1887–1888), and in his *Römisches Strafrecht* (Leipzig, 1899). The great Pauly-Wissowa, *Real-encyclopädie der klassischen Altertumswissenschaften*, customarily abbreviated *RE*, has supplied much additional data, especially in the following articles: "Acta," by Wilhelm Kubitschek; "Archive," by C. Dziatzko; "Commentarii," by A. von Premerstein; "Senatus" and "Senatus consultum," by O'Brien Moore; "Signum," by Leopold Wenger; "Tabulae publicae," by Ernst Kornemann; "Tabula" and "Tabularium," by Erich Sachers. Interpreting the original sources and the then available literature from the archivist's point of view, Giorgio Cencetti has contributed his comprehensive and authoritative article "Gli archivi dell' antica Roma nell' età repubblicana," *Archivi*, ser. 2, VII (1940), 7–49. Further important items not available to Cencetti are: Michelangelo Puma, *La conservazione dei documenti giuridici nell'antica Roma* (Palermo, 1934); Leopold Wenger, *Die Quellen des römischen Rechts* (Vienna, 1953). John E. A. Crake, "Archival Material in Livy 218–167 B.C.," Ph.D. diss., Johns Hopkins University, 1939, contains a chapter on Roman archives during the republican era.

The older work by M. Memelsdorff, *De archivis imperatorum Romanorum qualia fuerint usque ad Diocletiani aetatem*, Ph.D. diss., University of Halle (Berlin, 1890), is largely superseded by Giorgio Cencetti, "Tabularium Principis," in A. Giuffrè, ed., *Studi in onore di Cesare Manaresi*, I (Milan, 1953).

On the administrative background against which archival developments come to life, Mommsen's *Staatsrecht* and Wenger's *Quellen des Römischen Rechts*, both referred to, and Harold Mattingly, *The Imperial Civil Service of Rome* (Cambridge, Eng., 1910), must be consulted. Still indispensable for the same purpose is Otto Hirschfeld, *Die kaiserlichen Verwaltungsbeamten bis auf Diokletian*, 2d ed. (Berlin, 1905). Pertinent general literature on the history of the Roman Empire includes vols. X–XII of the *Cambridge Ancient History*; Hermann Peter, *Die geschichtliche Litteratur über die römische Kaiserzeit bis Theodosius I. und ihre Quellen*, 2 vols. (Leipzig, 1897); Otto Seeck, *Geschichte des Untergangs der antiken Welt*, 12 vols. (Stuttgart, 1920–1921); Ernst Stein, *Geschichte des spätrömischen Reiches*, I (Vienna, 1928); and Ferdinand Lot, *The End of the Ancient World and the Beginnings of the Middle Ages* (New York, 1961). A. H. M. Jones, *History of the Later Roman Empire, 284–602*, 3 vols. (Oxford, 1964) is a monumental addition to the field of Roman historiography.

B. Faass, "Studien zur Überlieferungsgeschichte der römischen Kaiserurkunde," *Archiv für Urkundenforschung*, I (1908), 185–272, and Peter Classen, "Kaiserreskript und Königsurkunde . . .," *Archiv für Diplomatik*, I (1955), 1–87, contribute to the understanding of the diplomatics of the imperial documentation.

Abbott, Frank F., and Allan C. Johnson. *Municipal Administration in the Roman Empire*. Princeton: Princeton University Press, 1926.
The Abinnaeus Archive: Papers of a Roman Officer in the Reign of Constantius II. Collected and reedited by H. I. Bell and others. Oxford: Clarendon Press, 1962.

Berneker, E. "Defensor civitatis." In *Reallexikon für Antike und Christentum*, III (1957), 649–656. Stuttgart: A. Hiersemann, 1957.

Birt, Theodor. *Die Buchrolle in der Kunst*. Leipzig: B. G. Teubner, 1907.

Blake, Marion Elizabeth W. *Ancient Roman Construction in Italy from the Prehistoric Period to Augustus*. Washington: Carnegie Institution of Washington, 1947.

Boak, Arthur E. R. "The Master of the Offices in the Later Roman and Byzantine Empires." In Arthur E. R. Boak and James F. Dunlap, *Two Studies in Later Roman and Byzantine Administration*. New York and London: Macmillan, 1924.

Boüard, Alain de. *Manuel de diplomatique française et pontificale*. 2 vols. Paris: A. Picard, 1929–1952.

Bresslau, Harry. "Die Commentarii der römischen Kaiser und die Registerbücher der Päpste." *Zeitschrift der Savigny-Stiftung für Rechtsgeschichte, Romanistische Abteilung*, VI (1885), 242–260.

———— *Handbuch der Urkundenlehre für Deutschland und Italien*. 2d ed. 2 vols. Leipzig: Veit and Comp., 1912–1931.

Broughton, T. Robert S. *The Magistrates of the Roman Republic*. With the cooperation of Marcia L. Patterson. 2 vols. New York: American Philological Association, 1951–1952.

Carettoni, Gianfilippo. "The House of Augustus." *Illustrated London News*, September 20, 1969.

Cassiodorus, Flavius Magnus Aurelius. *The Letters of Cassiodorus, Being a Condensed Translation of the Variae Epistolae of Magnus Aurelius Cassiodorus Senator*. With an introduction by Thomas Hodgkin. London: H. Froude, 1886.

Cencetti, Giorgio. "Gli archivi dell' antica Roma nell' età repubblicana," *Archivi*, ser. 2, VII (1940), 7–47.

———— "Tabularium principis." In *Studi . . . in onore di Cesare Manaresi*, edited by A. Giuffrè, I, 136–166. Milan: A. Giuffrè, 1953.

Classen, Peter. "Kaiserreskript und Königsurkunde: Diplomatische Studien zum römisch-germanischen Kontinuitätsproblem." *Archiv für Diplomatik*, I (1955), 1–87, and II (1956), 1–115.

Collinet, Paul. *Histoire de l'Ecole de Droit de Beyrouth*. Paris: Recueil Sirey, 1925.

Crake, John E. A. "The Annals of the Pontifex Maximus." *Classical Philology*, XXXV (1940), 375–386.

———— "Archival Material in Livy 218–167 B.C." Ph.D. dissertation, Johns Hopkins University, 1939.

Crook, John A. *Consilium Principis: Imperial Councils and Counsellors from Augustus to Diocletian.* Cambridge, Eng.: Cambridge University Press, 1955.

Curtius, Ludwig. *Das antike Rom.* Edited by Ernest Nash. 3d ed. Vienna: A. Schroll, 1957.

Delbrück, Richard. *Hellenistische Bauten in Latium.* 2 vols. Strassbourg: K. J. Trübner, 1907–1912.

Dziatzko, C. "Archive." In Pauly-Wissowa, *Real-Encyclopädie*, II (1896), 553–564.

Elia, Olga. "Il portico dei triclini del Pagus Maritimus di Pompei." *Bolletino d'arte*, XLVI (1961), 200–211.

Faas, B. "Studien zur Überlieferungsgeschichte der römischen Kaiserurkunde (von der Zeit des Augustus bis auf Justinian)." *Archiv für Urkundenforschung*, I (1908), 185–272.

Foerster, Hans. *Abriss der lateinischen Paläographie.* 2d ed. Stuttgart: A. Hiersemann, 1963.

Frank, Tenney. *Roman Buildings of the Republic: An Attempt to Date Them from Their Materials.* American Academy in Rome, Papers and Monographs, vol. III. Rome: American Academy in Rome, 1924.

Frend, W. H. C. *Martyrdom and Persecution in the Early Church.* Oxford: Blackwell, 1965.

Friedländer, Ludwig. *Darstellungen aus der Sittengeschichte Roms in der Zeit von Augustus bis zum Ausgang der Antonine.* 10th ed. by Georg Wissowa. 3 vols. Leipzig: S. Hirzel, 1922–1923.

Gardthausen, Viktor Emil. *Griechische Paleographie.* 2d ed. Vol. I. Leipzig: Veit and Comp., 1901.

Gregorii I Papae Registrum Epistolarum, Pt. II, edited by Ludovicus M. Hartmann. Monumenta Germaniae Historica, Epistolae, vol. II. Berlin: Weidmann, 1899.

Günther, Otto. *Avellana-Studien.* Sitzungsberichte der Kaiserlichen Akademie der Wissenschaften in Wien, Philosophisch-Historische Classe, CXXXIV, no. V. Vienna: C. Gerold's Sohn, 1896.

Heckel, Rudolf von. "Das päpstliche und sicilianische Registerwesen in vergleichender Darstellung mit besonderer Berücksichtigung der Ursprünge." *Archiv für Urkundenforschung*, I (1908), 371–510.

Hirschfeld, Bruno. *Die Gesta Municipalia in römischer und frühger-manischer Zeit.* Ph.D. dissertation, University of Marburg, Hamburg, 1904.

Hirschfeld, Otto. *Die kaiserlichen Verwaltungsbeamten bis auf Dio-cletian.* 2d rev. ed. Berlin: Weidmann, 1905.

Jörs, Paul. *Römische Rechtswissenschaft zur Zeit der Republik.* I. *Bis auf die Zeit der Catonen.* Berlin: F. Vahlen, 1888.

Jolowicz, Herbert F. *Historical Introduction to the Study of Roman Law.* Cambridge, Eng.: Cambridge University Press, 1952.

Jones, A. H. M. *History of the Later Roman Empire, 284–602.* 3 vols. Oxford: Blackwell, 1964.

——— *Studies in Roman Government and Law.* Oxford: Blackwell, 1960.

Jones, H. Stuart. "Administration." In *The Legacy of Rome,* edited by Cyril Bailey, pp. 91–139. Oxford: Clarendon Press, 1923.

Kenyon, Sir Frederic G. *Books and Readers in Ancient Greece and Rome.* 2d ed. Oxford: Clarendon Press, 1951.

Kornemann, Ernst. "Tabulae publicae." In Pauly-Wissowa, *Real-Encyclopädie,* ser. 2, vol. iv (1932), 1957–1962.

Krüger, Paul. *Geschichte der Quellen und Litteratur des Römischen Rechts.* 2d ed. Munich and Leipzig: Duncker and Humblot, 1912.

Kubitschek, Wilhelm. "Acta." In Pauly-Wissowa, *Real-Encyclo-pädie,* I (1894), 285–301.

——— "Aerarium." In Pauly-Wissowa, *Real-Encyclopädie,* I (1894), 667–674.

——— "Ein Soldatendiplom des Kaisers Vespasian (Tafeln III und IV)." *Jahreshefte des Österreichischen Archäologischen Institutes in Wien,* XVII (1914), 148–193.

Künzle, Paul. "Del cosi-detto 'titulus archivorum' di papa Damaso." *Rivista di Storia della Chiesa in Italia,* VII (1953), 1–26.

Leclercq, Dom H. *Les martyrs.* 3d ed. 15 vols. Paris: Oudin, 1902–1924.

Liebenam, Wilhelm. *Städteverwaltung im römischen Kaiserreiche.* Leipzig: Duncker and Humblot, 1900.

Lorenz, Herbert. *Untersuchungen zum Praetorium: Katalog der Prä-torien und Entwicklungsgeschichte ihrer Typen.* Halle: A. John, 1936.

Lot, Ferdinand. *The End of the Ancient World and the Beginnings of the Middle Ages.* Translated from the French by Philip and Mariette Leon. New York: Harper and Brothers, 1961.

Marini, Abate Gaetano, ed. *I papiri diplomatici* . . . Rome: Stamperia della Sacra Congregazione de Propaganda Fide, 1805.

Marquardt, Joachim. *Römische Staatsverwaltung.* 3d ed. 3 vols. Darmstadt: H. Gentner, 1957.

Mattingly, Harold. *The Imperial Civil Service of Rome.* Cambridge, Eng.: Cambridge University Press, 1910.

———— *Roman Imperial Civilisation.* Garden City, N.Y.: Doubleday and Co:, 1959.

Memelsdorff, M. *De archivis imperatorum romanorum qualia fuerint usque ad Diocletiani aetatem.* Ph.D. dissertation, University of Halle. Berlin, 1890.

Mitteis, Ludwig. *Reichsrecht und Volksrecht in den östlichen Provinzen des römischen Kaiserreichs: Mit Beiträgen zur Kenntnis des griechischen Rechts und der spätrömischen Rechtsentwicklung.* Leipzig: B. G. Teubner, 1891.

Mommsen, Theodor. "Constitutiones corporis munimenta." *Zeitschrift der Savigny-Stiftung für Rechtsgeschichte, Romanistische Abteilung,* XI (1890), 146–149.

———— "Decret des Proconsuls von Sardinien L. Helvetius Agrippa J. 68 n. Chr." In his *Gesammelte Schriften,* vol. V, 325–351. Berlin: Weidmann, 1908.

———— "Sui modi usati da' Romani nel conservare e pubblicare le leggi ed i senatus consulti." In his *Gesammelte Schriften,* vol. III, 290–313. Berlin: Weidmann, 1907.

———— "Die pompeianischen Quittungstafeln des L. Caecilius Jucundus." *Hermes,* XII (1877), 88–141.

———— "Der Rechtsstreit zwischen Oropus und den römischen Steuerpächtern." In his *Gesammelte Schriften,* vol. V, 495–513. Berlin: Weidmann, 1908.

———— *Römisches Staatsrecht.* Handbuch der römischen Altertümer, edited by Joachim Marquardt and Theodor Mommsen. 3d ed. 3 vols. Leipzig: Duncker and Humblot, 1887–1888.

———— *Römisches Strafrecht.* Systematisches Handbuch der deutschen Rechtswissenschaft, edited by Karl Binding, I, 4. Leipzig: Duncker and Humblot, 1899.

———— "Das theodosische Gesetzbuch." *Zeitschrift der Savigny-Stiftung für Rechtsgeschichte, Romanistische Abteilung*, XXI (1900), 149–190.

Moore, O'Brien. "Senatus." In Pauly-Wissowa, *Real-Encyclopädie*, supplement VI (1935), 660–800.

———— "Senatus consultum." In Pauly-Wissowa, *Real-Encyclopädie*, supplement VI (1935), 800–812.

Nash, Ernest. *Bildlexikon zur Topographie des antiken Rom*. 2 vols. Tübingen: E. Wasmuth, 1961–1962. Also in English translation under the title *Pictorial Dictionary of Ancient Rome*. 2 vols. New York: Praeger, 1961–1962.

Niedermeyer, Hans. *Über antike Protokoll-Literatur*. Göttingen: W. F. Kaestner, 1918.

Noailles, Pierre. *Les collections de Novelles de l'Empereur Justinien*. 2 vols. Paris: Recueil Sirey, 1912–1914.

Notitia dignitatum: Accedunt notitia urbis Constantinopolitanae et laterculi provinciarum. Edited by Otto Seeck. Berlin: Weidmann, 1876.

Notitia dignitatum Imperii Romani. Reproduced by the Bibliothèque Nationale, Département des Manuscripts from MS. Lat. 9661. Paris: Berthaud, n.d.

Pallotino, Massimo. *The Etruscans*. Translated from the Italian by J. Cremona. Harmondsworth, Middlesex: Penguin Books Ltd., 1955.

Peter, Hermann. *Die geschichtliche Litteratur über die römische Kaiserzeit bis auf Theodosius I. und ihre Quellen*. 2 vols. Leipzig: B. G. Teubner, 1897.

Platner, Samuel Ball. *A Topographical Dictionary of Ancient Rome*. Completed and revised by Thomas Ashby. London: Oxford University Press, 1929.

Polaschek, E. "Notitia dignitatum." In Pauly-Wissowa, *Real-Encyclopädie*, XVII (1937), 1077–1116.

Preisigke, Friedrich. *Die Inschrift von Skaptoparene in ihrer Beziehung zur kaiserlichen Kanzlei in Rom*. Strassbourg: K. J. Trübner, 1917.

Premerstein, A. von. "Commentarii." In Pauly-Wissowa, *Real-Encyclopädie*, IV (1901), 726–759.

———— "A commentariis." In Pauly-Wissowa, *Real-Encyclopädie*, IV (1901), 759–768.

———— "Libellus." In Pauly-Wissowa, *Real-Encyclopädie*, XIII (1927), 26–61.

Puma, Michelangelo. *La conservazione dei documenti giuridici nell' antica Roma.* Palermo: La Tradizione, 1934.

Roberts, Lucy G. "The Gallic Fire and Roman Archives." *Memoirs of the American Academy in Rome,* II (1918), 55–65.

Rostovtzeff, M. I., ed. *The Excavations at Dura-Europos. . . . Preliminary Report of the Fifth Season of Work, October 1931–March 1932.* New Haven: Yale University Press, 1934.

———— "Das Militärarchiv von Dura." In Walter Otto and Leopold Wenger, eds., *Papyri und Altertumswissenschaft* (Munich, 1934), pp. 351–378.

———— *The Social and Economic History of the Roman Empire.* 2d ed. revised by P. M. Fraser. 2 vols. Oxford: Clarendon Press, 1957.

———— and others, eds. *The Excavations at Dura-Europos . . . Preliminary Report of the Ninth Season of Work, 1935–1936.* Pt. 1. New Haven: Yale University Press, 1944.

Roussel, Pierre, and Fernand de Visscher. "Les inscriptions du Temple de Dmeir." *Syria,* XXIII (1942–1943), 173–200.

Sachers, Erich. "Tabula." In Pauly-Wissowa, *Real-Encyclopädie,* ser. 2, vol. IV (1932), 1881–1886.

———— "Tabularium." In Pauly-Wissowa, *Real-Encyclopädie,* ser. 2, vol. IV (1932), 1962–1969.

Santifaller, Leo. *Beiträge zur Geschichte der Beschreibstoffe im Mittelalter.* I. *Untersuchungen.* Mitteilungen des Instituts für Österreichische Geschichtsforschung, supplement XVI, no. 1. Graz and Cologne: H. Böhlaus Nachfolger, 1953.

———— "Über späte Papyrusrollen und frühe Pergamentrollen." In *Speculum Historiale* (Festschrift Johannes Spörl dargebracht), edited by Clemens Bauer and others. Munich: K. Alber, 1965.

Schwind, Fritz Freiherr von. *Zur Frage der Publikation im römischen Recht.* Munich: C. H. Beck, 1940.

Scott, Samuel Parsons, ed. *The Civil Law . . .* 17 vols. in 7. Cincinnati: Central Trust Co., 1932.

Scullard, H. H. *The Etruscan Cities and Rome.* London: Thames and Hudson; Ithaca: Cornell University Press, 1967.

Seeck, Otto. "Scrinium." In Pauly-Wissowa, *Real-Encyclopädie,* ser. 2, vol. II (1923), 893–904.

Siber, Heinrich. *Römisches Verfassungsrecht in geschichtlicher Entwicklung.* Lahr: W. Schauenburg, 1952.

Stein, Ernst. "Beiträge zur ältesten römischen Geschichte." *Wiener Studien*, XXXVII (1915), 353–366.

—— *Geschichte des spätrömischen Reiches*. I. *Vom römischen zum byzantinischen Staate (284–476)*. Vienna: L. W. Seidel, 1928. Also in a French edition by Jean-Rémy Palanque. Paris: Desclée, de Brouwer, 1959.

Steinacker, Harold. "Zum Zusammenhang zwischen antikem und frümittelalterlichem Registerwesen," *Wiener Studien*, XXIV (1902), 301–306.

Steinwenter, Artur. *Beiträge zum öffentlichen Urkundenwesen der Römer*. Graz: Moser (J. Meyerhoff), 1915.

Stemplinger, E. "Qu. Horatius Flaccus." In Pauly-Wissowa, *Real-Encyclopädie*, VIII (1913), 2336–2399.

Tablettes Albertini: Actes privés de l'époque vandale, fin du Ve siècle. Edited by Christian Courtois and others. 2 vols. Paris: Arts et Métiers Graphiques, 1952.

The Theodosian Code and Novels and the Sirmondian Constitutions. Translated by Clyde Pharr. Princeton: Princeton University Press, 1952.

Tjäder, Jan-Olof. *Die nichtliterarischen Papyri Italiens aus der Zeit 445–700*. Vol. I. Skrifter utgivna av Svenska Institutet i Roma, no. XIX, 1 and 3. Lund: C. W. K. Gleerup, 1955.

Volkmann, H. "Valerii Poplicolae." In Pauly-Wissowa, *Real-Encyclopädie*, ser. 2, vol. VIII (1955), 180–188.

Welles, C. Bradford. "Die zivilen Archive in Dura." In Walter Otto and Leopold Wenger, eds., *Papyri und Altertumswissenschaft*, (Munich, 1934), pp. 379–399.

Welles, C. Bradford, and others. *The Parchments and Papyri*. The Excavations at Dura-Europos . . . Final Report V, pt. I, edited by Ann Perkins for the Department of Classics of Yale University. New Haven: Yale University Press, 1959.

Wenger, Leopold. *Die Quellen des römischen Rechts*. Österreichische Akademie der Wissenschaften, Denkschriften der Gesamtakademie, vol. II. Vienna: A. Holzhausen, 1953.

—— "Signum." In Pauly-Wissowa, *Real-Encyclopädie*, ser. 2, vol. II (1923), 2361–2448.

Wieacker, Franz. *Textstufen klassischer Juristen*. Göttingen: Vandenhoeck and Ruprecht, 1960.

[*Postlude*]   *Record-Keeping in the Parthian
            and Neo-Persian Empires*

Arthur Christensen's *L'Iran sous les Sassanides*, 2d ed. (Copenhagen, 1944) is particularly useful for understanding the governmental and social conditions that explain the role of records in the Neo-Persian Empire. For the lasting impact of that Empire's administrative and record-keeping arrangements on the succeeding regimes of the Arabs, Mongols, and Turks, one must consult Walther Hinz, "Das Rechnungswesen orientalischer Reichsfinanzämter im Mittelalter," *Islam*, XXIX (1949–1950), 1–29, 113–141.

Agathias, Myrinaeus. *Historiarum libri quinque.* Edited by Rudolf Keydell. Berlin: W. de Gruyter, 1967.

Altheim, Franz, and Ruth Stiehl. *Ein asiatischer Staat: Feudalismus unter den Sasaniden und ihren Nachbarn.* Wiesbaden: Limes-Verlag, 1954.

——— *Finanzgeschichte der Spätantike.* Frankfurt am Main: V. Klostermann, 1957.

Christensen, Arthur. *L'Iran sous les Sassanides.* 2d ed. Copenhagen: E. Munksgaard, 1944.

——— *Le règne du roi Kawadh I et le communisme Mazdakite.* Det Kgl. Danske Videnskabernes Selskab, Historisk-Filologisk Meddelelser, IX, no. 6. Copenhagen: Høst and Son, 1925.

Diakonov, I. M., and others. "Parfianskiĭ arkhiv iz Drevneĭ Nisy" [On an economic archives on ostraca from Nisaia in Parthia]. *Vestnik Drevneĭ Istorii*, 1953, no. 4, 114–130.

Duri, A. A., and others. "Dīwān." In *Encyclopaedia of Islam*, new ed., vol. II, 323–337. Leiden: E. J. Brill; London: Luzac and Co., 1965.

Heichelheim, Fritz M. "New Light on the Influence of Hellenistic Financial Administration in the Near East and India." *Economic History*, IV (1938), 1–12.

Hinz, Walther, "Das Rechnungswesen orientalischer Reichsfinanzämter im Mittelalter." *Islam*, XXIX (1949–1950), 1–29, 113–141.

Hitti, Philip Kûri. *History of the Arabs from the Earliest Times to the Present.* 5th ed. New York: Macmillan, 1951.

Klíma, Otakar. *Mazdak: Geschichte einer sozialen Bewegung im sassanidischen Persien.* Prague: Czecho-Slovakian Academy, 1957.

Kornemann, Ernst. *Weltgeschichte des Mittelmeerraumes von Philipp II. von Makedonien bis Muhammed*. Edited by Hermann Bengtson. Munich: C. H. Beck, 1967.

Lewis, B. "Daftar." In *Encyclopaedia of Islam*, new ed., vol. II, 77–81. Leiden: E. J. Brill; London: Luzac and Co., 1965.

Minns, Ellis H. "Parchments of the Parthian Period from Avroman in Kurdistan." *Journal of Hellenic Studies*, XXXV (1915), 22–65.

Moravcsik, Gyula. *Byzantinoturcica*. I. *Die byzantinischen Quellen der Geschichte der Türkvölker*. 2d rev. ed. Berlin: Akademie-Verlag, 1958.

Nöldecke, Theodor. *Geschichte der Perser und Araber zur Zeit der Sasaniden, aus der arabischen Chronik des Tabari* . . . Leiden: E. J. Brill, 1879.

Patkanian, M. K. "Essai d'une histoire de la dynastie des Sassanides, d'après les renseignements fournis par les historiens arméniens." *Journal Asiatique*, ser. 6, VII (1866), 101–238.

Spuler, Bertold. *Iran in früh-islamischer Zeit: Politik, Kultur, Verwaltung und öffentliches Leben zwischen der arabischen und der seldschukischen Eroberung 633–1055*. Wiesbaden: F. Steiner, 1952.

Stein, Ernst. "Ein Kapitel vom persischen und byzantinischen Staate." *Byzantinisch-Neugriechische Jahrbücher*, I (1920), 50–89.

Index